UK Family Trends
1994-2004

Helen Barrett

National
Family &
Parenting
Institute

The National Family and Parenting Institute is an independent charity set up to enhance the quality of family life, by encouraging families and parents to ask for help when they need it, by ensuring they can find the right information and advice and by influencing public policy to make society more family friendly.

Visit our website at www.nfpi.org for information about our publications and research.

The NFPI would like to thank the Families Division at the DfES.

Helen Barrett has researched on and worked with children, their families and their carers in a wide range of family and community settings. Formerly a senior lecturer in developmental psychology, she joined the National Family and Parenting Institute as Research Fellow in July 2002. She is particularly interested in the influence of non-traditional care settings and separation experiences on children's and parents' emotional development and relationships.

Series Editor: Clem Henricson, Head of Research & Policy at the National family and Parenting Institute. She was formerly a social policy consultant with a variety of family policy organisations and has published widely in the field of family research.

Published by
National Family and Parenting Institute
430 Highgate Studios
53–79 Highgate Road
London NW5 1TL

Tel: 020 7424 3460
Fax: 020 7485 3590
Email: info@nfpi.org
www.nfpi.org

Design and print by Intertype
ISBN 1 903615 34 8
Registered charity no. 1077444

Contents

Acknowledgements

I would like to thank all those who gave their help and support. Special thanks to Carena Rogers for her help with chapter two, to Luzia de Almeida and Rebecca Goldman for help with locating information, to Clem Henricson for her advice and encouragement, to the rest of the research team for their sympathetic support, and to Ruth Lawrence for getting the work into print.

The National Family and Parenting Institute would also like to thank the Department of Education and Skills for their financial support for this project. The views expressed in this report are not necessarily those of the DfES nor of any other Government department.

Preface

In this report, we draw a picture of UK families, and of attitudes to families and family life in the UK, during the decade which spans the first International Year of the Family in 1994 to its tenth anniversary in 2004. Ten years is a relatively short time to observe change. Typically, unless changes are very dramatic, differences between time points tend to be rather small, so to understand what the importance of small differences might be, we have also looked at a longer time period to check whether or not changes are consistent with longer term trends.

Our report focuses on four key aspects of family life in the UK: first, its diversity, that is, the range of family forms and cultures that it encompasses; second, fathers' and mothers' negotiation of the 'private/public' divide, i.e. their behaviours and attitudes towards the demands of work and family including the question of whether parents' roles as providers and carers may have changed; third, we examine the nature of relationships between parents and children and, with a particular emphasis upon the management of roles, rights and power dynamics, we investigate the balance between parents' and children's needs; finally, we consider the effects of increased geographical mobility and population ageing on kinship networks and the extent to which families appear able to draw upon internal resources to meet the emotional and material needs of individual members. In our consideration of these key areas, we will try to determine whether attitudes toward family life and issues confronting families have been changing during this period and what, if anything, might contribute to a sense of change.

We are aware that sociologists and social historians commentating upon family life in the twentieth century have tended to fall into one of several camps: those who view family life as having remained, in essence, much the same or, at least, less different than is popularly believed (e.g. Laslett, 1972; Hareven, 1994; Crow, 2002), those who point to shortcomings in demographic record-keeping and the impossibility of being sure about the exact nature of family life over time, especially in respect of intimate relationships and sexual behaviour (e.g. Gillies, 2003), and those who identify changes but who view these changes either as predominantly functional and adaptive (e.g. Parsons, 1965; Anderson, 1971; Skolnick, 1992; Weeks et al.,

2001) or, conversely, as indicative of a decline in the capacity of the family to act as society's chief teacher and guardian of moral values (e.g. Goode, 1963; Murray, 1990; Popenoe, 1993, 1996).

Certain demographic trends widely regarded as having characterised families in the late twentieth century have been central to these understandings. Those most frequently cited include a rise in the proportion of couples who cohabit before marriage, older age at first marriage, an increasing proportion of children born outside marriage, higher divorce rates, more lone parents and step-families, increased incidence of dual-earner households, and earlier return to work after childbirth. In addition, a tendency for women to defer childbirth and to have smaller families has been noted although, somewhat contradictorily, there has also been concern about relatively high levels of teenage pregnancy in the UK (in comparison with European rather than US statistics) and about earlier awareness of and engagement in sexual activity.

The influence of technological developments on the nature and quality of family life and relationships has also been apparent, for example, leading to greater mobility in response to global markets, increased accessibility to internet information and communication, wider availability of DNA testing, and qualitative differences in distribution of health care resources across classes and cultures. Some commentators have suggested that such changes may have transformed kinship networks, transformed the role of grandparents in family life and presented a challenge to continued inter-generational transmission of values and cultural traditions.

Throughout the last decade, therefore, questions have arisen concerning the extent to which a process of 'de-traditionalisation' is occurring, whether family group allegiances are being replaced by more individualistic self-focused interests and, in short, what meaning might be attributed to changing social contexts (e.g. Jamieson, 1998; Gillies, 2003).

New Labour made its position clear in relation to these issues in its policy document entitled *Supporting Families: A consultation document*. In this, families were described as being "at the heart of our society... because... they provide love, support and care. They educate us, and they teach right from wrong" (Straw and the Ministerial Group on the Family, 1998, p.4). The Government went on to express the view that families are the essential catalyst for the wellbeing of children and so for the future of society. It also acknowledged that families were under stress due to rising divorce rates, subsequently increased numbers of single parent and step-families and associated problems of poverty, crime and drug abuse. In response to this conceptualisation of the difficulties of UK families in the Nineties, New Labour set out to offer better financial support and services with the aim of strengthening marriages, enabling parents to better balance work and home lives, and to assist those with more serious problems.

A number of strategies was introduced in order to effect this support-giving. These included setting up a National Family and Parenting Institute as a centre of expertise to advise on family issues, to map and disseminate information and good practice, to help develop parenting support programmes, to promote and guide research on the family and parenting, and to work with other organisations in order to raise public awareness about good practice. Schemes were also introduced to help parents who were socially disadvantaged or who might be experiencing difficulties of various sorts, including changes in access to and type of benefit, widening the remit of the ParentLine helpline, introducing Sure Start, providing more proactive, preventive services to parents through enhanced health visiting schemes, promotion of family-friendly employment practices and provision of more, higher quality and more affordable childcare. To strengthen marriages, support parents in difficulty, improve children's educational opportunities and to address problems such youth offending and teenage pregnancy, a wide range of educational and judiciary measures has also been instigated.

At around the same time, in the BBC Reith Lectures, Professor Anthony Giddens echoed the Government's concern about the state of the family: "We continue to talk of the nation, the family, work, tradition, nature, as if they were all the same as in the past. They are not. The outer shell remains, but inside all is different – and this is happening not only in the US, Britain, or France, but almost everywhere. They are what I call shell institutions... they are institutions that have become inadequate to the tasks they are called upon to perform" (Giddens, 1999a, Lecture 1). Giddens urged that change wreaked by globalisation is not "a global order driven by collective human will. Instead, it is emerging in an anarchic, haphazard fashion," as a "runaway world" which can only be controlled if the old "shell institutions" are either reconstructed or replaced by new ones. His solution was not to turn back to traditional family life which anyway, he claimed, emerged only in the 1950s. Rather, he suggested that families could be re-conceptualised as essentially consisting of a "pure relationship" between a couple who negotiate their social identities as equals within a "democracy of emotions" depending upon emotional communication, self-disclosure, civility and acceptance of obligations to other family members. In this environment, he argued, children would no longer be seen and not heard, but should have in-principle equality in a democratic relationship with parents who have authority due to their ownership of experience and property. Parents, in his view, should be legally obliged to provide for their children until adulthood regardless of their living arrangements and marriage should be seen no longer as an economic institution, but "as a ritual commitment" that "can help stabilise otherwise fragile relationships" (Giddens, 1999b, Lecture 4).

Positions as different as these give rise to important questions about the nature of family life in the UK during this decade and how its role might best be understood. In this report, we will draw upon information from major surveys, longitudinal studies, literature reviews and population census data to elicit evidence for beliefs about changing trends and to explore perceptions of family life. In our first chapter, we consider the nature of demographic changes in the UK population, focusing on the nature of population growth and change, the impact of immigration and changes in access to global information networks. In the next four chapters, we turn our attention to the way in which the nature of family life may, or may not, have changed within this wider context. In chapter two, we look at the role of mothers and consider how work-life balance issues may have affected their relationships with their children, with other family members and with themselves. In chapter three, we consider the role of fathers and the extent to which the quality of fathers' involvement in family life may have been influenced by evolving family formations as well as by tendencies towards democratisation of relationships. In chapter four, we examine parent-child relationships and ask whether qualitative changes may be observed in these or in attitudes toward socialisation, parental care and supervision. In chapter five, we think about the wider social context and ask whether family networks and support needs might have changed throughout the diverse communities that constitute UK society in 2004. In conclusion, we sum up our view of major trends and consider what implications they might have for future research and policy.

References

Anderson, M. (1971) Family, household and the industrial revolution. In M. Anderson (Ed.), *Sociology of the family*. Harmondsworth: Penguin.

Crow, G. (2002) *Social solidarities: Theories, identities and social change*. Buckingham: Open University Press.

Giddens, A. (1999a) *BBC Reith Lecture 1: Globalisation*. Available on the LSE website by courtesy of the BBC.

Giddens, A. (1999b) *BBC Reith Lecture 4: Family*. Available on the LSE website by courtesy of the BBC.

Gillies, V. (2003) *Families and intimate relationships: A review of the sociological research*. London: Families and Social Capital ESRC Research Group.

Goode, W. (1963) *World revolution and family patterns*. New York: Free Press.

Hareven, T. (1994) Recent research on the history of the family. In M. Drake (Ed.), *Time, family and community: Perspectives on family and community history*. Buckingham: Open University Press.

Jamieson, L. (1998) *Intimacy: Personal relationships in modern societies*. Cambridge: Polity Press.

Laslett, P. (1972) *Household and family in past time*. Cambridge: Cambridge University Press.

Murray, C. (1990) *The emerging British underclass*. London: IEA Health and Welfare Unit.

Parsons, T. (1965) *Family, socialisation and interaction process*. London: Routledge and Kegan Paul.

Popenoe, D. (1993) American family decline (1960-1990): A review and appraisal. *Journal of Marriage and the Family,* **55(3)**, 527-542.

Popenoe, D. (1996) *Life without father: Compelling new evidence that fatherhood and marriage are indispensable for the good of children and society*. New York: Free Press.

Skolnick, A. (1992) *The intimate environment: Exploring marriage and the family*. New York: Harper and Collins.

Weeks, J., Donovan, C. and Heaphy, B. (2001) *Same sex intimacies: Families of choice and other life experiments*. London: Routledge.

1 | Major demographic trends

"There are three kinds of lies: lies, damned lies and statistics."
(attributed to Disraeli)

A guide to the nature of demographic changes in the UK population between 1994 and 2004 can be obtained from 1991 and 2001 census data and from estimates based on these (although it is not always easy to make direct comparison between time points, as will be seen, due to variations in data-gathering practices between times). We have also drawn upon major population surveys e.g. General Housing Surveys, Labour Force Surveys, British Household Panel Surveys, etc.) as well as upon reports on national birth cohort studies (e.g. National Child Development Study, British Birth Cohort Studies, 1946, 1958, 1970) in our attempt to obtain a picture of UK family life during the last decade. Finally, we use findings from British Social Attitude surveys to give an indication of popular feeling about life in the UK. Where possible, we relate this information to its wider context in the sense of trends which have been identified across the twentieth century. Where relevant information is available, we also present comparisons with other European countries.

In this chapter, we wanted to find out exactly how and in which ways family shapes and sizes may have changed in recent years. We were particularly interested to discover which kinds of families are most common, how families are formed, how they might be evolving and how these patterns differ from previous patterns. Specifically, we sought information about the overall make-up of the British population, rates of marriage, cohabitation and family breakdown, patterns of childbirth and evidence of changing attitudes towards these phenomena among residents in different communities throughout the UK. In addition, we were eager to explore the extent to which these facts might support a view that families in the UK are more fragile and are coping less well than in the past, a view which is often emphasised by the media.

Media reports often leave the impression that the state of families in the UK is precarious. For example, the media watch web page of One Plus One noted, in August 2003, the following reports: the number of marriages ending in divorce has reached a seven-year high (*Guardian,* August 29), the UK's fertility rate is the lowest on record (*Guardian,* August 13), the divorce rate has left 150,000 children in broken homes and a quarter of these children are under the age of five (*Daily Mail,* August 29), according to an American study, couples cohabiting before marriage are less likely to have happy marriages and more likely to divorce (*Daily Telegraph,* August 8). In the same month, reports were carried about the birth of a third son through surrogacy to a gay couple (*Daily Mail,* August 19) and of the conception of the first baby in Britain from sperm purchased by the internet (*Daily Mail,* August 20).

To say that media reports tend toward sensationalism is perhaps to state the obvious. But the search for newsworthy stories can leave a very skewed impression of what is actually happening, not only due to the emphasis given to the unusual, but also due to the tendency to weight negative events more highly than routine or more positive events (e.g. the birth of a baby, avoidance of accidents, illness, no change, nothing to worry about). Processes such as over-simplification, taking conclusions out of context and over-generalisation are also at work. As can be seen in the examples above, newspapers readily frame events in superlative terms. These tactics feed, play on and pander to public fears and prejudices. But how accurate are they?

In this chapter, we examine several aspects of UK life and, as in later chapters, focus our discussion around seven questions. Here, we ask the following questions, all of which can be linked to common fears, beliefs or prejudices:

1.1   How are fertility rates and family size changing?
1.2   How is the make-up of the UK population changing?
1.3   How many children are born outside marriage?
1.4   How have attitudes to marriage and cohabitation changed?
1.5   How many families are headed by heterosexual couples?
1.6   How common is divorce and how long do marriages last?
1.7   Which families are the least well off?

1.1   How are fertility rates and family size changing?

General population: actual numbers

The population of the UK, well over 85 per cent of which is located in England, has continued to increase steadily throughout the twentieth century. Throughout the nineties, the growth rate was slightly less than 0.3 per cent per year and this growth is expected to continue (table 1.1). These figures have more recently been revised upward on the basis of projections by the Government Actuary's Department which estimated the population of the UK in the middle of 2002 as 59,231,900 (GAD, 2004). The UK currently is one of the most densely populated countries in Europe.

Table 1.1: Population[1] of the United Kingdom, 1991-2002, with estimates until 2021
Source: Office for National Statistics; Government Actuary's Department; General Register Office for Scotland; Northern Ireland Statistics and Research Agency

(millions)	1991	2001	2002	2011	2021
England	47.9	49.4	49.6	50.9	52.7
Wales	2.9	2.9	2.9	2.9	3.0
Scotland	5.1	5.1	5.1	5.0	4.9
Northern Ireland	1.6	1.7	1.7	1.7	1.8
United Kingdom	55.9	56.4	57.4	59.1	59.2

1 Mid-year estimates for 1991 to 2002; 2001-based projections for 2011 to 2021. Population estimates for 2001 and 2002 include provisional results from the Manchester matching exercise.

Birth rates

The contribution to population growth from child birth is estimated at around 1.4-1.73 per mother during the time period of interest to this report though there is some variation between communities in different parts of the UK (for example, the population rose by 10 per cent in Ireland between 1981 and 2002 but dropped by 2.4 per cent in Scotland, while families tend to be larger in some minority ethnic communities). Within a context of increasing numbers of childless couples and women (this will be further discussed in chapter five), rates of childbirth in the UK are currently lower than the population replacement rate. However, other factors, such as immigration, improvements in health and associated greater longevity and population ageing (Government Actuary Department predict an increase in mean age from 39.3 in 2002 to 43.6 in 2031) all contribute to continued overall growth.

Different rates of ageing in general and particular populations within the UK

Age trends in the general population indicate a gradual increase in the proportion of individuals aged over 65 and projections estimate that this proportion will continue to increase in the future. Taking account of the change in the women's retirement age, the number of people over pensionable age is projected to increase from 11.2 million in 2006 to 11.9 million in 2011 (2000-based National Statistics, Crown Copyright 2002, table 3.2: Actual and projected population by age, UK, 2000-2025).

In addition, the number of people living alone increased steadily over the latter half of the twentieth century and is projected to continue increasing. By contrast, family sizes have been decreasing.

These trends, which are described as 'population ageing' have clear implications for family life and for social policy. Table 1.2 provides details of the age distribution of the UK population as a whole and shows that at the time of the 2001 census, there had been increases in numbers of males and females aged 45 and above (38 and 42 per cent respectively in comparison with 35 and 39 per cent in 1991). These increases correspond with underlying longer term trends.

Table 1.2: Population: by age and sex (United Kingdom), 1991-2001
Source: Office for National Statistics; General Register Office for Scotland; Government Actuary's Department; Northern Ireland Statistics and Research Agency

(Percentages)	<16	16-24	25-34	35-44	45-54	55-64	65-74	75+
Males								
1991[1]	21	14	16	14	12	10	8	5
2001	21	11	14	15	13	11	8	6
Females								
1991[1]	19	12	15	13	11	10	9	9
2001	19	11	14	15	13	11	9	9

1 Data for 1991 are interim population estimates revised following the 2001 Census and are subject to further revision.

Table 1.3 further shows how, while the proportion of children younger than 16 has been gradually shrinking, at the other end of the lifespan, the proportion of people older than 64 has been growing. On the assumption that these patterns will continue in the future, the table also presents projections from data within the 2001 census which indicate that, during the next decade, the proportion of people over 64 can be expected to outweigh that of children under 16.

Table 1.3: Dependent population:[1] by age (United Kingdom), 1994-2001, with projections until 2021
Source: Office for National Statistics; Government Actuary's Department; General Register Office for Scotland; Northern Ireland Statistics and Research Agency

(Millions)	Under 16	65 and over
1994	12.003	9.173
1995	12.027	9.210
1996	12.012	9.234
1997	12.013	9.250
1998	12.007	9.267
1999	12.001	9.267
2000	11.936	9.302
2001	11.851	9.362
2002[2]	11.759	9.430
2003[2]	11.691	9.480
2004[2]	11.597	9.540
2016[2]	11.020	11.404
2017[2]	11.063	11.556
2018[2]	11.110	11.710
2019[2]	11.143	11.868
2020[2]	11.177	12.016
2021[2]	11.210	12.177

1 Population estimates for 2001 and 2002 include provisional results from the Manchester matching exercise.
2 2001-based projections.

Although there is some indication that the health of over fifties in the UK has generally been improving throughout the twentieth century, this improvement is by no means evenly distributed across classes and cultures (Maxwell and Harding, 1998; Nazroo, 1997; Raleigh, 1996; Wadsworth et al., 2003). Also, while the phenomenon of population ageing is well established across the UK population generally, the same cannot be said for every section of society. Table 1.4 illustrates the distribution of individuals within different age groups by ethnic identity.

Table 1.4: Population (United Kingdom): by ethnic group and age, 2001-02[1]
Source: Annual Local Area Labour Force Survey, Office for National Statistics

(Percentages)	Under 16	16-34	35-64	65+
White	19	25	40	16
Mixed	55	27	16	2
Asian or Asian British				
Indian	22	33	38	6
Pakistani	35	36	25	4
Bangladeshi	38	38	20	3
Other Asian	22	36	38	4
Black or Black British				
Black Caribbean	25	25	42	9
Black African	33	35	30	2
Other Black[2]	35	34	26	—
Chinese	18	40	38	5
Other	20	37	39	4
All ethnic groups[3]	20	26	39	15

1 Population living in private households 2001-02.
2 Sample size was too small for a reliable estimate of the 65 and over age group.
3 Includes those who did not state their ethnic group.

From table 1.4, it can be seen that, particularly among more recent immigrant populations, age distributions differ considerably. Whereas, overall, around 20 per cent of the population was aged under 16 at the time of each census, the proportion of under sixteens was more than a third in Pakistani, Bangladeshi and Black African samples and over half in people identified as of mixed ethnicity. At the other end of the lifespan, a considerably smaller proportion of minority ethnic people were aged 65 or over at the time of the 2001 census (between two to nine per cent as opposed to fifteen or sixteen per cent of the rest of the population). Such differences may provide a partial explanation of differences in fertility between some minority ethnic and white populations since, within age ranges where women might be most expected to give birth (i.e. between the 16-34 age range), there were approximately 10 per cent more minority ethnic than white residents at the time of the 2001 census. From other sources, though, there are indications that differences between some white and minority ethnic communities in preferences for ideal family size may contribute towards differential rates of childbirth (Penn and Lambert, 2002).

Later in this report, we will examine this evidence more closely in an attempt to understand more about support needs of families in different social communities where patterns of population growth and ageing differ. For the present, it seems pertinent to comment that these data do appear to indicate that the support needs of certain minority ethnic people will also be different, both from those of other minority ethnic people and from the general population (which, given economic and class differences, is also far from homogeneous). This situation would have obtained throughout the period of interest to this report.

Family size

Although changes in family size can be guaged approximately by changes in household size, it is not safe to assume that the two are synonymous. Older children may have left the home, divorce or other events may have resulted in some degree of family dispersal, households can contain members who are not related, and so on. This point raises the larger question of how 'family' is defined or identified, a question about which there is far less agreeement than is popularly supposed (e.g. Pullinger and Summerfield, 1997). For ease and to simplify our account, we have chosen to frame this discussion around information about households but we recognise the limitations of this approach. Table 1.5 shows that, within the general population, household size remained fairly constant over the decade between censuses.

Table 1.5: Households:[1] by size (Great Britain)

Source: Census, Labour Force Survey, Office for National Statistics

	1991	2002[2]
One person	27	29
Two people	34	35
Three people	16	16
Four people	16	14
Five people	5	5
Six or more people	2	2
Total (%)	(100)	(101)
All households (millions)	22.4	24.4
Average household size (number of people)	2.5	2.4

1 These estimates for 2002 are not seasonally adjusted and have not been adjusted to take account of the 2001 Census results.
2 At spring 2002.

A slightly different impression emerges when household type is taken into account (Table 1.6). Although, overall, just under 30 per cent of households consisted of a single person, around 60 per cent were couples and about 10 per cent were lone parent households at both time points, there would appear to have been a distinct rise in the proportion of multi-occupied households containing two or more unrelated adults. These differences across the space of a decade are small and it is not possible to state with any certainty whether they arise from chance variability, from between-census changes in data-classification methods, or from other sources. From the information given, it is not certain either whether the percentage of households containing co-resident adults reflects increases in childless cohabiting partnerships or in co-resident single people.

Table 1.6: Households: by type of household and family (Great Britain), 1991-2003

Source: Census, Labour Force Survey, Office for National Statistics

(Percentages)	1991	2001[1]	2003[1]
One person			
Under state pension age	11	14	15
Over state pension age	16	15	14
Two or more unrelated adults	3	8	8
One family households			
Couple[2]			
No children	28	28	28
1-2 dependent children[3]	20	19	18
3 or more dependent children[3]	5	4	4
Non-dependent children only	8	6	6
Lone parent[2]			
Dependent children[3]	6	5	5
Non-dependent children only	4	3	3
Multi-family households	1	1	1

1 At spring. Estimates are not seasonally adjusted and have not been adjusted to take account of Census 2001 results.
2 Other individuals who were not family members may also be included.
3 May also include non-dependent children.

Figure 1.1 illustrates differences in household size by ethnic group and indicates that Asian households tend to be larger than those in other ethnic groups while Black Caribbean and Other Black households are similar in size to White households, with 2.3 people.

Evidence from a study by Penn and Lambert (2002) also indicates that patterns of family formation, and particularly preferences and practices in relation to family size, vary considerably across different ethnic communities, with higher fertility among South Asian and some African groups (e.g. Moroccans) and large differences between these peoples and Western Europeans in preferences related to ideal family size. Within Britain, Penn and Lambert found that 56 per cent of Indians and 64 per cent of Pakistanis preferred to have more than two children, compared with only a third of other British respondents (33 per cent).

Figure 1.1: Household size by ethnic group
Source: Labour Force Survey, Spring 2002

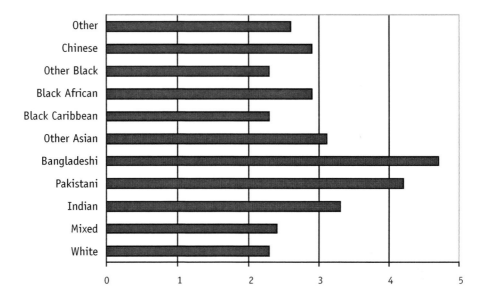

In conclusion, the UK population certainly does not appear to be in danger of extinction. Even though fertility rates may be lower than in the early part of the twentieth century, the population has continued to grow.

1.2   How is the make-up of the UK population changing?

Impact of immigration

Particularly among right-wing journalists and campaign groups concerned to limit population growth, much has been made of the disproportionate contribution of immigrant communities to population increase. O'Brien (2004) notes that estimates have sometimes attributed as much as 70 per cent of population growth over the last decade to immigration. Concerns, too, have frequently been voiced about the number of refugees being granted asylum under the current government (Travis,

2003; Guardian Refugees website), about the process of assessing asylum applications (Stewart, 2004), about policies on housing asylum seekers (Boswell, 2003), about the effectiveness of legislation against discrimination and about the effects of foreign immigration on the availability of employment for the resident population.

In reality, studies have been fairly consistent in showing a generally benign influence on the economy of immigrant populations (Dobson and McLaughlan, 2001; Dustman et al., 2003) and, although the rate of immigration may have increased throughout the decade, the UK population continues to be predominantly white, particularly in rural areas and in countries outside England. Census records indicate that more than 90 per cent of the UK population identify as white (around 94 and 92 per cent respectively at the times of the 1991 and 2001 censuses). Further, it is evident that very considerable diversity exists among the minority of UK residents who identify themselves as belonging to a minority ethnic group (Table 1.7).

Table 1.7: Population by ethnic group, 1991 and 2001
Source of 1991 data: ONS Census division 1991 Census Monitor;
Source of 2001 data: Census, April 2001, Office for National Statistics

(Percentages)	1991				2001, April	
	GB	England	Scotland	Wales	Number	%
White	94.5	93.8	98.7	98.5	54,153,898	92.1
Black or Black British						
Black Caribbean	0.9	1.1	0	0.1	565,876	1.0
Black African	0.4	0.4	0.1	0.1	485,277	0.8
Black Other	0.3	0.4	0.1	0.1	97,585	0.2
Asian or Asian British						
Indian	1.5	1.8	0.2	0.2	1,053,411	1.8
Pakistani	0.9	1	0.4	0.2	747,285	1.3
Bangladeshi	0.3	0.3	0	0.1	283,063	0.5
Other Asian groups	0.4	0.4	0.1	0.1	247,664	0.4
Chinese	0.3	0.3	0.2	0.2	247,403	0.4
Other	0.5	0.6	0.2	0.3	230,615	0.4
Mixed	No info	No info	No info	No info	677,117	1.2
All minority ethnic	5.5	6.2	1.3	1.5	4,635,296	7.9
All population	100	100	100	100	58,789,194	100

A number of difficulties make it hard to obtain a very clear picture, on the basis of the broad groupings adopted here, of the precise extent to which the cultural make-up of the UK population may, or may not, have changed over the last decade. Chief among these is lack of a co-ordinated strategy on how and which information to collect. For example, as can be seen in table 1.7, at each of the recent censuses, classification of ethnic groups differed slightly. It is conceivable that, had the 1991 figures included a 'mixed' category, the overall percentage of minority ethnic residents may have been around eight per cent of the UK population at both time points. Doubts may also be raised about the reliability or validity of distinctions between 'White' and 'Other' categories taking into account the existence of people of 'non-visible' ethnic extraction.

It also seems evident that a full picture of the extent of racial and cultural diversity within the UK population and a deep understanding of ways in which the population may be changing cannot emerge until a far more complex classificatory system is developed. This point seems particularly relevant to an understanding of the nature of ways in which families may, or may not, be changing throughout different parts of the UK.

In theory, it is conceivable that there are families, for example, based in rural East Anglia in which all members derive from pure Viking stock. It may also be conceivable that such 'all-white single-ethnicity' families may exist in other parts of the UK with very different ancestry. Nevertheless, it is well established that patterns of re-location and marriage over many generations have typically produced very hybrid family units throughout the UK and that it is not at all uncommon for families to contain, either within immediate, extended or blended family circles, members of different race, culture, ethnicity and country of origin. Within current systems of data gathering, collation and analysis, because these finer distinctions are indiscernible, the full complexity of family life in the UK is hidden. Even if there had been major changes between 1994 and 2004, we would have no way of knowing!

Growing tolerance of racial difference?

Perhaps the most important conclusion to be drawn from the information presented so far is the possibility that family life among particular minority ethnic communities is almost inevitably mis-described if general population statistics are considered. Both in terms of access to resources and life stage, there are likely to be differences between first and later generation immigrants as well as between different minority communities. Indeed, it may be the case that one of the few commonalities among minority ethnic communities is their minority group status. This shared experience of being in an unequal relationship with the 'majority' culture may put all minority ethnic individuals more in danger of racist aggression. Even this, though, is not a given, particularly for less 'visible' minority ethnic group members.

Summarising results from British Social Attitudes (BSA) survey data between 1994 and 2002, Rothon and Heath (2003) reported responses to the question, "How would you describe yourself... as very prejudiced against people of other races, a little prejudiced, or not prejudiced at all?" Arguing that self reports of being prejudiced are a good predictor of behaviour, they presented information which appeared to indicate that a consistently small minority (two per cent) of people are very prejudiced, around a third (from 34 per cent in 1994 to 29 per cent in 2002) were a little prejudiced and the other two-thirds (63 per cent in 1994 to 67 per cent in 2002) were not prejudiced at all. Rothon and Heath suggested that this was a indication of a growing racial tolerance. However, in the 2002 BSA survey, respondents were asked to give opinions on whether immigration, by people of the same or a different race or ethnic group as themselves, should be allowed. Outcomes are shown in Table 1.8.

Table 1.8: Proportion of respondents agreeing that immigrants should be allowed

Source: British Social Attitudes Survey, 2002 (Rothon and Heath, 2003)

(Percentages)	None	A few	Some	Many
Of same race or ethnic group	8	27	52	11
Of different race or ethnic group	15	34	42	8

It is not clear from this report whether those people who were against same race immigrants were consistent in their opposition to immigrants of a different background, i.e. whether closer examination of responses might reveal higher levels overall of opposition. What does seem to be clearly indicated, though, is the presence of high levels of prejudice. This would seem to bring into question the view that Britain is becoming more tolerant.

In conclusion, the highly diverse population of families from minority ethnic backgrounds continues to represent a relatively small proportion of the overall population of the UK. Fears that they might out-number white UK residents are clearly unfounded. Of greater concern is the fact that the needs of these families may differ in ways that are not sufficiently understood and that, as a result, they will be disadvantaged. We return to this question in chapter five.

1.3   How many children are born outside marriage?

Several changes in parenting practices have taken place in relation to childbirth. As we mentioned earlier, women are generally tending to have fewer children. They are also tending to have children rather later in their lives (Table 1.9).

Table 1.9: Average age of mother at childbirth (England & Wales)
Source: Office for National Statistics

	Mean age (years)	
	1991	**2000**
All births		
All live births	27.7	29.1
All first births	25.7	27.1
Births inside marriage		
All births inside marriage	28.9	30.8
First births inside marriage	27.5	29.6
Births outside marriage		
All births outside marriage	24.8	26.5

During the nineties, the proportion of babies born outside marriage increased by ten per cent and there is no reason to believe that in recent years this trend has abated (table 1.10). Findings from the Millennium Cohort Study of 18,553 families into which children were born in 2001/2 suggest that conception outside marriage, for first-born children, is now almost as common as conception within marriage (Kiernan, 2004). Only just over half of first-born children (52 per cent) were born within marriage, 18 per cent to women living alone and 30 per cent to women in a cohabiting relationship.

Table 1.10: Births outside marriage as a percentage of all live births (United Kingdom)
Source: Office for National Statistics; General Register Office for Scotland;
Northern Ireland Statistics and Research Agency

Percentages	Jointly registered	Solely registered	All births outside marriage
1991	22.0	7.8	29.8
1992	23.3	7.5	30.8
1993	24.3	7.5	31.8
1994	24.6	7.4	32.0
1995	26.2	7.4	33.6
1996	27.6	7.9	35.5
1997	28.9	7.9	36.8
1998	29.7	7.9	37.6
1999	31.0	7.8	38.8
2000	31.9	7.6	39.5
2001	32.7	7.4	40.1
2002	—	—	40.6
2003	—	—	41.4

— = not available

However, interestingly, throughout the 1990s, a steady proportion of births outside marriage was registered only by one parent. By contrast the more common practice, and one that showed signs of becoming more common over the decade, was that birth registration involved recording the names of two parents (figure 1.2). This raises the possibility that it is attitudes toward the marital status of relationships that may have changed rather than beliefs about the need for children to be raised by two parents. Some support for this view may be deduced from consideration of the wider context of similar changes in other European countries.

Figure 1.2: Patterns of birth registration for births outside marriage, UK, 1988-2001
Source: Office for National Statistics

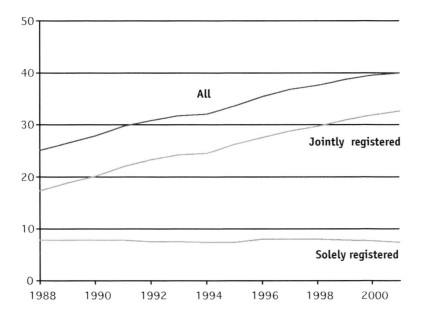

Table 1.11 shows that the UK's record on births outside marriage in recent years more closely resembles North European countries (with the exception of Germany) which tend to have offered more parent-friendly employment and day care arrangements (an issue that we discuss further in chapter two) throughout the late twentieth century. Patterns in the UK, nevertheless, are still quite different from those in Sweden which has a far larger proportion of births outside marriage than any other European country. By contrast, in countries characterised by Catholicism, considerably fewer births outside marriage were recorded in this period. It is possible that the practice of combining figures from East and West Germany may have obscured more deeply rooted within-country differences and produced a slightly misleading picture of how Germany compares with its European counterparts in this aspect of family life.

Table 1.11: Births outside marriage: EU comparison, 1990-2002
Source: Eurostat

(Percentages)	1990	2000	2002[1]
Sweden	47	55	56
Denmark	46	45	45
France	30	43	44
United Kingdom	28	40	41
Finland	25	39	40
Austria	24	31	34
Ireland	15	32	31
Netherlands	11	25	29
Belgium	12	26	28
Portugal	15	22	26
Germany	15	23	25
Luxembourg	13	22	23
Spain	10	18	19
Italy	7	10	10
Greece	2	4	4
EU average	20	29	29

[1] Data for Belgium, Spain, Italy, and EU average are for 2001.

There do appear to be marked differences between minority ethnic communities in relation to the incidence of conception outside marriage. Whereas it is rare for Bangladeshi or Pakistani women to register a birth outside marriage, single parenthood is rather more common among African-Caribbean mothers.

To sum up this section, whilst the incidence of birth outside marriage has been rising, it would appear that the majority of children do continue to have two named, i.e. legal, guardians. This serves perhaps to underscore the complexity of the term 'illegitimacy'.

1.4 How have attitudes to marriage and cohabitation changed?

Tables 1.12 and 1.13 indicate how patterns of marriage have altered between 1991 and 2001: lower age at first marriage, higher age at divorce and a drop in the proportion of married couples. These data agree with more distinct changes that have taken place across the latter half of the twentieth century in the nature of relationship formation and dissolution.

Table 1.12: Average age (in years) at marriage and divorce (England & Wales), 1991-2001
Source: Office for National Statistics

	First marriage		Divorce	
	1991	**2001**	**1991**	**2001**
Males	27.5	30.6	38.6	41.5
Females	25.5	28.4	36.0	39.1

Table 1.13: Adults aged 16 and over: by marital status and sex (Great Britain), 1991-2000
Source: Office for National Statistics; General Register Office for Scotland

(Percentages)	1991	2000
Males		
Single	31	34
Married	60	54
Widowed	4	4
Divorced	6	8
All males	100	100
Females		
Single	23	26
Married	56	52
Widowed	14	13
Divorced	7	9
All females	100	100

As intimated in the previous section, the last two decades have seen a rapid rise in cohabitation in the UK, particularly among white UK residents. Haskey (1999a), reporting on 1994/5 Omnibus Survey data on patterns of cohabitation among adults (aged 16-69) in the UK, noted in excess of 13 different patterns of relationship history: overall, more than three quarters of all adults surveyed had been married at least once (76.6 per cent) and the majority (63 per cent) had married only once and had not cohabited. Almost 15 per cent (14.8 per cent) had cohabited and, of these, seven per cent had only had one cohabiting relationship while five per cent had also married; the remainder had a range of other relationships.

Haskey (1999b) further reported that, by the late 1980s, only about 40 per cent of marriages had not been preceded by premarital cohabitation, the same proportion (40 per cent) of marriages had been preceded by premarital cohabitation, and co-habitations which had not led to marriage had become more common (20 per cent of all unions). He described cohabiting relationships as generally less stable than marriages (with or without premarital cohabitation), irrespective of age on entering a partnership. However, the earlier a cohabiting relationship began, the shorter it was likely to be and early co-residence, too, was found to be positively associated with shorter lasting later marriages.

By 1996, Haskey (2001) reported that the proportion of first marriages preceded by cohabitation had risen again, to around three quarters (77 per cent); almost all second marriages were preceded by cohabitation. While, in 1986, one in thirty families with children contained cohabiting parents, by 1998, one in twelve did. Haskey (2001) predicted that, by 2021, on the basis of data available at 1996, if trends in cohabitation continue at the same rate, it can be expected that more than one in five partnerships will consist of cohabiting couples. He further predicted that it would become increasingly common for children to be born to never-marrying cohabiting couples.

Kiernan (1999a), though, observed that first marriages which were preceded by cohabitation were no more likely to end in divorce than those not preceded by co-habitation. Looking at patterns throughout Europe, she found that, in most of West and Northern Europe, cohabitation was more common than marriage in first formed partnerships, suggesting that it might simply have replaced some marriages. Kiernan also remarked though that Britain was exceptional in having a growing population of lone parents: in other countries where cohabitation had increased, she saw little evidence that the propensity to become a couple had declined (Kiernan, 1999b).

More recently, Kiernan (2004) has reported that the childrearing environment provided by cohabiting mothers may not match up to that provided within mar-riage: data from the Millennium Cohort Study indicates that mothers in cohabiting relationships tend to be more likely to have had an unplanned pregnancy, live in a disadvantaged neighbourhood, attend fewer ante-natal classes, are less likely to breast feed, smoke more and have lower incomes than married mothers. However, their male partners were as involved in caring for the baby as husbands of married mothers. Both cohabiting and married mothers scored higher on all health and social indices than mothers who lived alone. Kiernan therefore concluded that cohabitation might be viewed as a poorer person's marriage. However, it is perhaps still too early to regard these findings as conclusive.

Kiernan and Smith (2003), again using data from the Millennium Cohort Study, found considerable diversity among different ethnic groups: Asian women were most likely to be married, Black women were most likely to be without partners, and White women were most likely to cohabit. Perhaps not surprisingly, cohabiting couples were less well-off than married couples but better off than non-partnered women. Fathers were as likely to be seeing children regularly in some cohabiting relationships as they were in other types of relationship. Kiernan and Smith (2003, p.33) conclude that these findings "highlight the complexity and fuzziness of parental relationships that exist at the beginning of the 21st century and suggest that simple dichotomies of married versus unmarried or even comparisons such as married versus cohabiting versus non-partnered can disguise a good deal of the variation that exists in the connections between parents, particularly fathers, and their children."

Attitudes to marriage and cohabitation

Information from British Social Attitudes surveys carried out from 1984 to 2000 (Barlow et al., 2001/2002) appeared to confirm the notion that cohabitation was being seen as more acceptable, both as a prelude to marriage and as an alternative to it, and that childbearing within cohabiting relationships was also becoming more acceptable. Around two thirds of respondents at each of the time points when questions on cohabitation were asked agreed that, "It is all right for a couple to live together without intending to get married" (1994, 64 per cent; 1998, 62 per cent; 2000, 67 per cent) while over half agreed that "It is a good idea for a couple who intend to get married to live together first (1994, 58 per cent; 1998, 61 per cent; 2000, 56 per cent).

More detailed questions about marriage and cohabitation, though, did not begin to be asked until the 2000 British Social Attitudes survey. This indicated that more than half of respondents (59 per cent) agreed with the statement that "Even though it might not work out for some people, marriage is still the best kind of relation-ship" while just under half (48 per cent) agreed that "Marriage gives couples more financial security than living together". Almost three quarters of respondents (73 per cent) disagreed with the statement, "There is no point in getting married – it's only a piece of paper" and just over two thirds (69 per cent) agreed that "Too many people just drift into marriage without really thinking about it". Given the fact that so many marriages by this time were preceded by cohabitation, the level of agreement with the last statement seems perhaps rather surprising. Little support, however, was found for the view that "Married couples make better parents than unmarried ones": 27 per cent of respondents agreed, 43 per cent disagreed and 28 per cent neither agreed nor disagreed. The sample was not large enough to permit examination of differences in attitudes among members of minority ethnic groups though, as we discuss later in this chapter, there is reason to believe that very different attitudes might exist in some communities.

The statement, "People who want children ought to get married" was included in surveys carried out in 1989 and 2000, and Barlow et al. reported an overall change, from 70 per cent agreement in 1989 to 54 per cent in 2000. Analysing these same data by age of respondent, they found that younger people were considerably less likely to agree with the statement than older people (Table 1.14).

Table 1.14: "People who want children ought to get married", by age, 1989 and 2000

Source: Barlow et el., 2001/2002, British Social Attitudes surveys

	1989		2000	
	%	*Base*	**%**	*Base*
18-24	**41**	*167*	**33**	*225*
25-34	**51**	*254*	**38**	*541*
35-44	**65**	*248*	**36**	*632*
45-54	**80**	*207*	**50**	*470*
55-64	**90**	*180*	**76**	*452*
65+	**93**	*248*	**85**	*656*

As can be seen from Table 1.14, though, the numbers of respondents involved in these surveys was not large and so the results must only be seen to be suggestive rather than as reliable reflections of attitudes among British people more widely.

Summarising this section, then, it seems fair to say that, although cohabitation has become much more common, it does not appear to have replaced marriage. Rather, the role of marriage within relationships appears to have changed. In addition, attitudes towards marriage and cohabitation seem to vary considerably throughout communities within the UK. New findings are still up-dating understandings of this situation.

1.5 How many families are headed by heterosexual couples?

As Table 1.6 indicated, throughout the nineties, the majority of single family households with dependent children were headed by couples (just over 80 per cent) and, of these couples, around nine out of ten were married (Family Policy Studies Centre, 1999) Further support for this view comes from the General Household Survey (table 1.15) which illustrates that, despite the fact that divorce has become a more common feature in UK society and that it is popularly, though possibly erroneously, believed that only about two-thirds or even as few as half of all marriages last long enough for children to be raised within them, the most common living arrangement for children throughout the 1990s was in households headed by a couple (84 per cent in 1992, 80 per cent in 2001, 78 per cent in 2003). Where children were living with one parent, the majority lived with mothers (13 per cent in 1992, 26 per cent in 2001, 20 per cent in 2003) and a minority with fathers (two per cent in 1992, two per cent in 2001, three per cent in 2003).

Table 1.15: Percentage of dependent children living in different family types (Great Britain), 1991-2003

Source: General Household Survey, Census, Labour Force Survey, Office for National Statistics

(Percentages)	1992[1]	2001[1]	2003[1]
Couple families			
1 child	18	17	17
2 children	39	38	37
3 or more children	27	25	24
Lone mother families			
1 child	4	6	6
2 children	5	7	8
3 or more children	4	5	6
Lone father families			
1 child	1	1	2
2 or more children	1	1	1
All children[2]	100	100	100

1 At spring. These estimates are not seasonally adjusted and have not been adjusted to take account of the Census 2001 results.
2 Excludes cases where the dependent child is a family unit, for example, a foster child.

Records suggest that most couples are heterosexual and estimates indicate that fewer than one per cent of couples with dependent children are gay, lesbian or bisexual. However, to our knowledge, no survey to date has elicited sufficiently detailed or accurate information about householders' sexual preferences and activity to permit confident conclusions to be drawn on this matter. What does seem true is that few children would have had direct experience of living with a gay, lesbian or bisexual couple while fewer still are likely to be aware of the sexual orientation of their parents or guardians.

Fears that alternative family forms are taking over, therefore, appear to have very little foundation in reality. Having said this, a growing proportion of children living in households headed by couples, at some point in their lives, will live with an adult who is not biologically related to them.

1.6 How common is divorce and how long do marriages last?

Figure 1.3 illustrates trends since 1950 and shows that, during 1991-2001, numbers of marriages continued to fall while the increase in actual numbers of divorces appeared to drop off slightly. However, taking into account the fall in actual numbers of marriages, the ratio of divorces to marriages appears to have continued to rise throughout this decade, from around 50 per cent in 1991 to just over 54 per cent in 2001. The 'crude divorce rate' (number of divorces per thousand marriages) for England and Wales was 13.7 in 1994 and 13.3 in 2002 (ranging between 12.7 and 13.8 over the 1994-2002 period: ONS website, 2004) with the highest rates occurring among couples under 40 (among married couples in their sixties, rates of divorce were between 1.1 and 1.3 per thousand). The median length of marriages ending in divorce in 1994 was 9.8 years and in 2002, it was 11.1 years.

Figure 1.3: Marriages, re-marriages and divorces[1] (United Kingdom), 1991-2001
Source: Office for National Statistics, General Register Office for Scotland; Northern Ireland Statistics and Research Agency

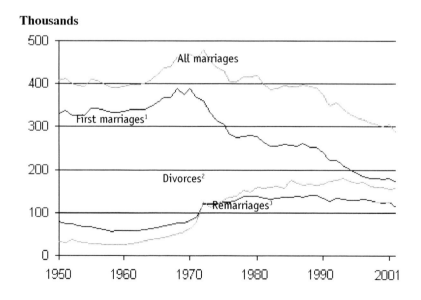

1 For both partners.
2 Includes annulments. Data for 1950 to 1970 are for Great Britain only.
3 For one or both partners.

Much has been made of the fact that, by the nineties, Britain had the highest divorce rate in Europe and the fastest growing population of unmarried mothers. As has already been intimated earlier in this report, it has been argued by many that it was increasing divorce rates alongside the growth in the number of children born outside marriage that forced the issue of fathers onto policy-makers' agendas in the UK (Lewis, 2002). Yet, in 1992, evidence from the British Household Panel Study showed that nine out of ten children were born to married fathers, five out of six fathers were still living with all of their biological children, and more than seven in ten fathers still lived in households formed from their first child-bearing relationship.

Table 1.15 also showed that, in spite the fact that divorce has become a more common feature in UK society and that it is popularly, though possibly erroneously, believed that only about two-thirds or even as few as half of all marriages last long enough for children to be raised within them, the most common living arrangement for children throughout the 1990s was in households headed by a couple (84 per cent in 1992, 80 per cent in 2001, 78 per cent in 2003). Where children were living with one parent, the majority lived with mothers (13 per cent in 1992, 26 per cent in 2001, 20 per cent in 2003) and a minority with fathers (two per cent in 1992, two per cent in 2001, three per cent in 2003).

At the current time in UK society, the lowest rates of divorce and separation are associated with those communities with the highest rates of population growth and the most recent immigration history, that is, Pakistani and Bangladeshi communities where family relationships might perhaps be most likely to continue to be characterised by patriarchal traditions.[1] These differences are also apparent in relation to attitudes towards marriage and divorce.

Despite the divorce statistics outlined above, the notion that one in three marriages end in divorce and that marriages do not last long – eleven years is sometimes quoted – seems to have become quite widely accepted. We wondered what the basis might be for these beliefs. How, for instance, it might be possible to arrive at the conclusion that one in three marriages end in divorce? There are at least three potential sources of information: official records, longitudinal and cross-sectional studies.

Relevant official records are kept on marriages, divorces, births and deaths. On inspection of annual records of numbers of marriages (including re-marriages) and divorces throughout the nineties and the turn of the century, as mentioned earlier in this section, it is possible to calculate that the incidence of divorce is approximately half as high as marriage. Basing predictions on this data, therefore, we could arrive at the conclusion that one in two, not one in three, marriages will end in

---

1   Similar observations were made in a study of Moroccan Islamic families in the Netherlands (Pels, 2000) of a tendency to increased effort to maintain traditional patriarchal roles and practices when migrant families are placed under acute stress.

divorce. However, this conclusion would only be accurate if it was possible to assume that both sets of information were drawn from the same or at least comparable populations. It is not safe to make this assumption for several important reasons. First, in most cases, divorce and marriage statistics relate to people at different life stages which means that no assumptions are warranted in respect of continuity (for example, marriages end not only in divorce but also in death and married couples might, for example, leave the country or not appear in the census for other reasons); also, since both sets of statistics include re-marriages and re-divorces, it is likely that the smaller proportion of people who experience multiple marriages and divorces will be over-represented so will produce a biased and over-inflated estimate of divorce rates; finally, divorce statistics usually include annulments, i.e. marriages ended through natural causes. Calculations like these, based on records kept over longer time period (1960 onwards), have been used to generate a 'crude divorce rate' of two in five marriages (Clarke and Berrington, 1999). However this method has the same limitations.

Problems due to lack of continuity can be overcome with longitudinal studies, particularly if these involve large, nationally representative samples and if people can be consistently followed up. Several birth cohort studies have been conducted in the UK, starting, for example, in 1958, 1970 and 2001. However, one of the most striking findings from these studies is that, as might be expected given the rise in divorce rates starting in the seventies, earlier birth cohorts experienced far lower rates of divorce than later cohorts while the most recent cohorts are still too young for their experiences either to have occurred or to have been recorded. Only by assuming that conditions similar to those responsible for the rise that has been seen (e.g. legislative changes) could recur could we be confident of basing predictions on these patterns of data.

The same problem arises in relation to the third potential source of information, cross-sectional studies and a further constraint on these is that they would need to be based on very large sample sizes to be capable of producing a valid estimate. For all these reasons, it seems that assertions about the exact proportion of marriages that can be predicted to end in divorce must be treated with great caution. They may turn out to be little more than myth.

Calculating length of marriage is equally problematic. Statistics are available concerning the length of marital unions before divorce and these have indicated that the median length of marriage before divorce in the last decade has been around eleven years. However, this is likely to be considerably shorter than the length of marriages which do not end in divorce, many of which will continue until one or other of the couple dies. It is also important to understand that median length of marriages is reported as opposed to average length because lengths of marriage ending in divorce are not evenly distributed so it does not make mathematical sense to compute an average length.

Figure 1.4 illustrates this distribution and shows that, although the median length may have been around 11 years, the modal length was closer to three, four and five years, that is, it was relatively common for marriages ending in divorce to have ended within the first six years of marriage. In other words, as perhaps might be expected, the longer the marriage lasted, the less likely it was to end in divorce. Whether this is due to the changing historical context or to other factors within the marriage is unclear.

Another interesting feature of this diagram is the apparent tendency for marital breakdowns to have occurred earlier on in relationships in 1991 than in 2001. This raises the question of whether pre-marital cohabitation might protect against more obvious relationship difficulties. This possibility has been explored by a number of researchers but has still not been conclusively answered. In some samples (e.g. the 1958 birth cohort), it would appear that pre-marital cohabitation was linked with initial reservations about commitment to a relationship and that these reservations may have persisted throughout some later marriages. It is not clear that the same findings arise in data from later cohorts.

Figure 1.4: Distribution of length of marriages ending in divorce

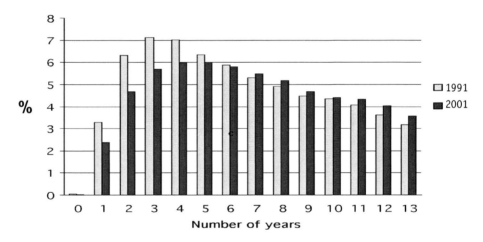

To sum up, from the evidence explored in this section, it would appear that divorce is still not 'the norm'. More marriages survive than end in divorce and, although cohabitation has increased, most children still grow up in households headed by married parents. Many assertions concerning the short-lasting nature of marriages and the frequency of divorce are misleading. The actual situation is far more diverse and complex.

Families after divorce

The census data shown in Table 1.16 provides a little more information about the nature of post-divorce family life. It indicates that the majority of children under 16 who were living in stepfamilies during the decade under review had been born within their mother's previous relationship. It appeared to be relatively uncommon for children to live either with their parent's new partner's children or with their biological father.

Table 1.16: Stepfamilies[1] with dependent children[2] (Great Britain), 1991/2-2001/2

Source: General Household Survey, Office for National Statistics

(Percentages)	1991/92	1996/97	2000/01	2001/02
Child(ren) from the woman's previous marriage/cohabitation	86	84	88	83
Child(ren) from the man's previous marriage/cohabitation	6	12	9	9
Child(ren) from the both partners' previous marriage/cohabitation	6	4	3	8
Lone parent with child(ren) from a former partner's previous marriage	1	—	—	—
All	100	100	100	100

1 Family head aged 16-59.

2 Dependent children are persons under 16, or aged 16-18 and in full-time education, in the family unit, and living in the household.

It is not clear what implications, if any, these statistics might have in terms of parental attitudes toward relationships or whether parents post-divorce employ deliberate strategies to buffer the impact upon their children's lives of their own relationship difficulties. Is it possible that parents in this decade consider their need for relationship satisfaction to be greater than their children's need for a stable environment or that, for some reason, they are increasingly finding relationships more difficult to sustain? Or is it the case that parents no longer believe that children need to live with their biological parents or, perhaps, that the experience of divorce is an inevitable transition en route to more beneficial living arrangements for all? These data do not give any indication either of the average length of time parents spend between relationships, how children experience and cope with these transitional periods, the amount of choice children feel they have over their living arrangements or the capacity of children to adapt to evolved family forms which often contain complex relationships between biological parents, their new partners and other new family members.

1.7 Which families are the least well off?

Families in poverty

At the end of the twentieth century, it would appear that it most certainly is not the case that material wellbeing is spread equally across all ethnic communities within the UK (Figure 1.5). The reasons for these inequalities is unclear. While some of the disparity might be associated with being at an early point in adaptation to the demands of a new social environment, discriminatory employment practices have also been implicated (Lindley, 2002). More recently, the TUC has expressed concern about the situation of minority ethnic workers and has acknowledged the possibility of discrimination, particularly, against Muslim men and women (TUC conference, 2004).

In both 1995-96 and 2000-01, a larger percentage of people from minority ethnic groups than from the white population lived in low-income households, whether income was calculated before or after housing costs. Low income is defined as having less than 60 per cent of the median equivalised disposable income (i.e. income from wages and salaries, self-employment, and social security benefits minus deductions for income tax, local taxes, and pension and National Insurance contributions, adjusted to take account of family size and composition).

Pakistanis and Bangladeshis were living on the lowest incomes: almost 60 per cent were living in low-income households before housing costs were deducted; 68 per cent after deduction of housing costs. Relatively few white people lived in low-income households: 16 per cent before and 21 per cent after housing costs were deducted.

Figure 1.5 : Households on low-income: by ethnic group of head of household, 2001-02
Source: Households Below Average Income (HBAI), Department for Work and Pensions.

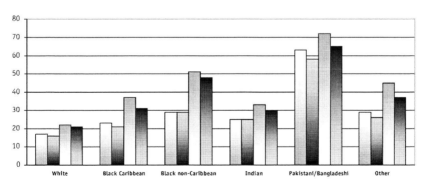

☐ 1995/6 Before housing costs ▨ 2000/1 Before housing costs ☐ 1995/6 After housing costs ▨ 2000/1 After housing costs

Looking at the after housing costs data, figure 1.4 illustrates that, although inequalities remained high, the percentage of people living in poverty appeared to have dropped slightly over this period for all ethnic groups. With regard to relatively high levels of poverty among Pakistani and Bangladeshi people, the relative recency of immigration for many families, the larger percentage of younger people, and the possibility that family members in middle and older age groups may not have been able to contribute to pension schemes across their life span (HMSO, 2003) may all have contributed. These families, Black non-Caribbean families and people from smaller groups ('other') of minority ethnic people in the UK appear especially disadvantaged. This indicates a clear need for more efforts to be made to address these inequalities.

The question of whether the poor must always be with us obviously depends on how we define 'poor'. If poverty is defined in relative terms, then on statistical grounds alone, it will always exist. But this does not mean that who it affects is unchangeable. The unequal distribution of wealth between ethnic communities in the UK must be a matter for concern.

References for chapter 1

Barlow, A., Duncan, S., James, G. and Park, A. (2001/2002) Just a piece of paper? Marriage and cohabitation. In A. Park, J. Curtice, K. Thomson, L. Jarvis and C. Bromley (Eds.), *British Social Attitudes. Public policy, social ties* (27-57). London: Sage.

Boswell, C. (2003) Burden-sharing in the European Union: Lessons from the German and UK experience. *Journal of Refugee Studies,* **16(3),** 316-335.

Clarke, L. and Berrington, A. (1999) *Socioeconomic and demographic predictors of marital dissolution: A review.* Lord chancellor's Dept. Research Paper 2/99.

Dobson, J. and McLaughlan, G. (2001) International migration to and from the United Kingdom, 1975-1999: consistency, change and implications for the labour market. *Population Trends,* **106,** 29-38.

Dustman, C., Fabbri, F., Preston, I. and Wadsworth, J. (2003) *The local labour market effects of immigration in the UK.* Home Office Report 06/03. Available online at: http://www.homeoffice.gov.uk/rds/onlinepubs1.html

Family Policy Studies Centre (1999) *Family change: Guide to the issues.* Family Briefing Paper No. 12. London: Family Policy Studies Centre.

GAD (2004) Information online at: http://www.gad.gov.uk/Publications/Demography_and_Statistics.htm

Guardian Refugees website: http://www.guardian.co.uk/Refugees_in_Britain/0,2759,180745,00.html

HMSO (2003) *Aspects of the economics of an ageing population. Select committee on economic affairs. 4th report, 2002-2003.* House of Lords, London: HMSO.

Haskey, J. (1999a) Cohabitational and marital histories of adults in Great Britain. *Population Trends,* **96,** 13-24.

Haskey, J. (1999b) Having a birth outside marriage: the proportions of lone mothers and cohabiting mothers who subsequently marry. *Population Trends,* **97,** 6-18.

Haskey, J. (2001) Cohabitation in Great Britain: past, present and future trends – and attitudes. *Population Trends,* **103,** 4-25.

Kiernan, K. (1999a) Cohabitation in Western Europe. *Population Trends,* **96,** 25-32.

Kiernan, K. (1999b) Childbearing outside marriage in Western Europe. *Population Trends,* **98,** 11-20.

Kiernan, K. and Smith, K. (2003) Unmarried parenthood: new insights from the Millennium Cohort Study. *Population Trends,* **114,** 26-33.

Kiernan, K. (2004) *Redrawing the boundaries of marriage: The rise of cohabitation and unmarried parenthood.* Paper presented at the Parent and Child 2004, Family Futures, conference, London, 18 June.

Lewis, J. (2002) The problem of fathers: policy and behaviour in Britain. In B. Hobson (Ed.), *Making men into fathers: Men, masculinities and the social position of fatherhood* (125-149). Cambridge: Cambridge University Press.

Lindley, J. (2002) Race or religion? The impact of religion on the employment and earnings of Britain's ethnic communities. *Journal of Ethnic and Migration Studies,* **28(3),** 427-442.

Maxwell, R. and Harding, S. (1998) Mortality of migrants from outside England and Wales by marital status. *Population Trends,* **91,** 15-22

Nazroo, J.Y. (1997) *The health of Britain's ethnic minorities: findings from a national survey.* London: Policy Studies Institute.

O'Brien, M. (2004) Social science and public policy perspectives on fatherhood in the European Union. In M.E. Lamb (Ed.), *The role of the father in child development* (121-145). 4th edition. Mahwah, NJ: Lawrence Erlbaum Associates.

Pels, T. (2000) Muslim families from Morocco in the Netherlands: Gender dynamics and fathers' roles in a context of change. *Current Sociology,* **48(4),** 75-93.

Penn, R. and Lambert, P. (2002) Attitudes towards ideal family size of different ethnic/nationality groups in Great Britain, France and Germany. *Population Trends,* **108,** 49-58.

Pullinger, J. and Summerfield, C. (1997) *Social focus on families.* London: The Stationery Office.

Raleigh, V.S. (1996) Suicide patterns and trends in people of Indian subcontinent and Caribbean origin in England and Wales. *Ethnicity and Health,* **1(1),** 55-63.

Rothon, C. and Heath, A. (2003) Trends in racial prejudice. In A. Park, J. Curtice, K. Thomson, L. Jarvis and C. Bromley (Eds.), *Continuity and change over two decades* (189-214). British Social Attitudes, 20th Report. London: Sage.

Schoon, I. and Parsons, S. (2003) Lifestyle and health-related behaviour. In E. Ferri, J. Bynner and M. Wadsworth (Eds.), *Changing Britain, changing lives. Three Generations at the turn of the century* (237-260). London: Institute of Education.

Stewart, E. (2004) Deficiencies in UK asylum data: Practical and theoretical challenges. *Journal of Refugee Studies,* **17(1),** 29-49.

Travis, A. (8 May 2003) Increase in asylum seekers 'threatens unrest'. *The Guardian.* Online at: http://www.obv.org.uk/reports/2003/rpt20030508a.html

Wadsworth, M., Butterworth, S., Montgomery, S., Ehlin, A. and Bartley, M. (2003) Health. In E. Ferri, J. Bynner and M. Wadsworth (Eds.), *Changing Britain, changing lives. Three Generations at the turn of the century* (207-236). London: Institute of Education.

Walker, A., O'Brien, M., Traynor, J., Fox, K., Goddard, E. and Foster, K. (2002) *Living in Britain. Results of the 2001 General Household Survey.* London: HMSO.

2 | Mothers, childcare, work and life

By the latter end of the twentieth century, changes set in motion by the introduction of birth control had become well established. Both within and outside marriage, the majority of women had gained more control over their fertility so that, if they chose to do so, they could delay child-rearing and limit the numbers of children they conceived. Changes, too, occurred in the workplace, in the kinds of work available, in conditions of employment and in the proportion of the workforce made up of women.

For some commentators, greater involvement of mothers in the workplace has been equated with lower investment in care of the family and potential erosion of essential social capital (e.g. Murray, 1990; Dennis and Erdos, 1992; Popenoe, 1993). Others, rather more cautiously, stress the need for more research on this matter and point to the possibility that mothers' involvement in the workplace may also have the capacity to confer benefits on children, by increasing the mothers' ability to access information and resources to which she and her offspring may otherwise be barred (e.g. Furstenberg and Kaplan, 2004).

At a recent seminar hosted by the Department of Transport and Industry[2] (DTI, February 2004), mainly on the basis of data from Labour Force Surveys, it was suggested that the UK economy over the past eight years could be characterised as follows: there has been strong job growth and unemployment has been steadily falling so that employment rates by 2003 are relatively high (just below 75 per cent); the UK labour market compares very favourably with other countries in terms of flexibility and is experiencing the lowest rate of industrial disputes on record. Work conditions have also improved: between 1993 and 2003, the percentage of full-time employees with fewer than 20 days' annual leave (including bank holidays) halved, and big rises for low paid employees have particularly benefited low-paid women (reducing

2   These seminars are hosted by the DTI but the views expressed are not necessarily those of the DTI or any other Government department; they also adhere to the Chatham House rule which states that participants are free to use the information received but neither the identity nor the affiliation of speakers or participants may be revealed.

the percentage from around nine per cent in 1993 to one per cent in 2003); these changes were also thought to be accompanied by solid gains in real wages.

There were a number of less positive aspects: the UK was still lagging behind the US in productivity growth; unemployment rates in some parts of the UK country were still relatively high (above the UK average in Yorkshire and the North East, the West Midlands, Scotland, Northern Ireland and London); although the percentage of economically inactive females had been dropping, that of males had been rising, as had numbers of men and women registered as disabled; in addition there was a culture of long working hours for males, although it was claimed that most men were content with this situation; most seriously, the gap between employment rates among minority ethnic and white people had wavered between approximately 17 to 21 per cent, and the gender earnings gap, though closing slightly, was also still evident, particularly in respect of part-time work (calculated as women's mean part-time hourly earnings as a percentage of men's full time average hourly earnings) which had fluctuated in between 51 and 59 per cent (a percentage which was considerably less than the 87 per cent observed by Harkness, 1996).

The report concluded that, while there was progress in many areas, certain aspects still need to be addressed more effectively, for example, working parents were thought to need more support, especially in balancing work and home life.

In this chapter, we examine the work experiences of mothers in the UK: the kinds of work they undertake, their reasons for working, their feelings about their conditions of work, and whether or how they manage to balance their work and their family lives.

Specifically, we address the following seven questions:

2.1 Which mothers work and what do they do?

2.2 What hours do mothers work?

2.3 At what point in the lives of their children do mothers take up or return to paid employment?

2.4 What incentives are there for mothers to work and how do they feel about it?

2.5 Is there any evidence that employment conditions for working mothers have improved?

2.6 How satisfactory is day care and nursery provision for children of working parents?

2.7 What do mothers feel about their ability to balance work and home life?

2.1   Which mothers work and what do they do?

As observed by the DTI (2004), among women generally, small upward employment trends (from 63.7 per cent in 1979 to 68.5 per cent in 1997) have been mirrored by downward trends for men (from 88.1 per cent in 1978 to 75 per cent in 1997). These trends have continued so that, by the late 1990s, the 'gender employment gap' appeared almost to have closed (Myck and Paull, 2001). By 2003, 50 per cent of the workforce was made up of women (ONS, 2004).

According to Labour Force Surveys, data from which are available on the website of the Office of National Statistics, the proportion of mothers in the workforce also slowly rose from 1990 through 2000 to 2003: 57.4 per cent of mothers were employed in spring 1990 compared with 65 per cent by the spring of 2000[3] and this figure had risen to 68 per cent by spring 2003.

Fewer lone mothers were in paid work outside the home than mothers who were cohabiting or married (58 per cent compared with 72 per cent). Also, fewer mothers with children under five were working (55 per cent of all mothers and 38 per of lone mothers) than mothers of older children. Among mothers with children aged 5-10, almost three quarters were working though less than two-thirds of lone mothers (73 per cent of all mothers versus 60 per cent of lone mothers; four-fifths of mothers with children aged 11-15 were working (80 per cent). However, by the time their children were over 16, almost as many lone mothers were in paid employment as partnered mothers with children of this age.

Increased numbers of women in the workforce need not imply either that jobs are more evenly distributed or that conditions of work for women have improved. It may be, for example, that women nowadays are more prepared to take over what have traditionally been 'jobs for men' for less pay, or that both men and women are under more strain, or that mothers are just earning 'pin money'.

It is not always easy to obtain information about the exact nature of work undertaken by mothers as data is often collected and presented on the basis of sex rather than parental status. Therefore, while information is available about the kind of work undertaken by women as compared with men (table 2.1), more precise details about what kinds of jobs parents take on as compared to non-parents are not currently available.

Looking at patterns among men and women more generally, there seem to be clear indications that qualitative differences still exist: a far higher percentage of women than men are employed in occupations involving social care while men still form the bulk of the workforce in manufacturing and construction industries. Reduced participation in manufacturing industries appears to have affected women at least

---

3   In spring 2000, the 4.9 million mothers then in employment represented almost one fifth of all workers (18 per cent).

as much, if not more, than men, and men's participation in some service industries appears to have increased although women's has remained steady over these two decades. Only in transport and communication services do male and female participation patterns appear to be in opposite directions and the changes here are so small that they may be accounted for by normal variability. So it seems likely that these differences apply to mothers as well as to other women, although more research is needed to examine this issue.

Table 2.1: Employee jobs[1]: by sex and industry (UK, percentages)

Source: Short-term Turnover and Employment Survey, Office for National Statistics

	Males			Females		
	1983	1993	2003	1983	1993	2003
Distribution, hotels, catering and repairs	17	20	22	26	26	26
Manufacturing	29	24	20	16	11	7
Financial and business services	12	17	20	14	17	19
Transport and communication	10	10	8	2	2	4
Construction	8	7	8	2	1	1
Agriculture	2	2	1	1	1	—
Energy and water supply	4	2	1	1	1	—
Other services[2]	17	19	20	39	41	42
All employee jobs (100 per cent) (millions)	12.4	11.3	13.0	9.9	11.5	12.8

1 Data are at June each year and are not seasonally adjusted.
2 Public administration, education, health and other community, social and personal service activities.

Different patterns of job distribution also occur among minority ethnic and white mothers, according to a report by the Equal Opportunities Commission (Hurrell, 2003; ONS, 2004, online). Analyses of the Labour Force Survey for spring 2002 indicate that around ten per cent of Black African women and White Irish women were working as nurses in 2001-02 in comparison with three per cent of White British women. In addition, five times more Indian than White British women were working as sewing machinists and packers, bottlers, canners and fillers. More information about these kinds of differences between mothers from different ethnic communities would be valuable, especially in view of the potential impact of mothers' access to career opportunities and lifestyle changes on families' ethos and aspirations.

Information from Eurostat's Labour Force Survey indicates that, throughout Europe, the distribution of high status jobs is still very much weighted towards men (table 2.2).[4]

Table 2.2: Women and men in managerial positions in European countries.
Source: Eurostat Labour Force Survey, 24.03.04

Country	Women (%)	Men (%)
Liechtenstein	48	52
Latvia	39	61
Estonia	37	63
France	36	64
Hungary	35	65
Spain	32	68
Slovakia	32	68
UK	32	68
Belgium	31	69
Iceland	31	69
Sweden	31	69
Portugal	30	70
Average	30	70
Austria	29	71
Slovenia	29	71
Finland	28	72
Ireland	28	72
Germany	27	73
Greece	26	74
The Netherlands	26	74
Luxembourg	22	78
Denmark	21	79
Italy	20	80
Cyprus	19	81

From the available data, it would appear that the UK is comparable with other countries in having fewer than a third of managerial positions[5] filled by women. The only country where these positions seem to be evenly distributed is Liechtenstein.

4   No data were available in the cases of Bulgaria, Norway and Romania at this time.

5   Managerial positions are defined as directors, chief executives, production and operating managers, and other specialist managers and managers of small enterprises using the International Standard Classification of Occupations: categories 12 and 13.

Overall, these figures strongly suggest that sex discrimination is still the norm across the European community at this highly influential level. Regardless of what may be happening at other levels, this seems to imply that the workplace is still heavily dominated by men. It is impossible to tell whether this situation might be sustained by consensus, through persisting discriminatory practices, or by other mechanisms. Evidence from a number of sources points to the fact that mothers find it particularly difficult to attain and retain top level posts (we discuss this issue further later in this chapter).

2.2   What hours do mothers work?

Information from a variety of sources indicates that more mothers than fathers work part-time and that fewer mothers than fathers are in paid employment outside the home (e.g. O'Brien and Shemilt, 2003; Dex, 2003). This pattern does appear to been changing slightly, as mothers have been taking on longer hours of work. Table 2.3 shows that, between 1992 and 2001, the proportion of mothers who worked fewer than 16 hours per week decreased (from 15 to 11 per cent) while the proportion of mothers who worked between 16 and 40 hours increased (from 35 per cent to 46 per cent). Almost one in ten mothers was in paid employment outside the home for more than 40 hours per week.

As suggested by Dex's (2003) concept of the 'typical' 1.5 earner household, therefore, for many mothers, the preferred employment option is part-time working. According to the Labour Force Survey 2002 (EOC, 2003), reasons most frequently given by women for working part-time relate to their family or domestic situation. In total, 54 per cent of female part-time employees said that they either wanted to spend more time with their family, had domestic commitments which prevented them working full-time, or felt there were insufficient childcare facilities available. By contrast, only five per cent of male part-time employees stated that their reason for working part-time related to their family or domestic situation. Instead, the most common response, accounting for 44 per cent of male part-time employees, was that they worked part-time because they were a 'student or at school'. Although more than four-fifths (82 per cent) of part-time employees were women, almost all (98 per cent) of those citing family or domestic reasons were women.

Table 2.3: Changing patterns of work among mothers and fathers (1992-2001)
Source: O'Brien and Shemilt, 2003

(Percentages)	1992		1995		1998		2001	
Full-time	Mothers	Fathers	Mothers	Fathers	Mothers	Fathers	Mothers	Fathers
41+ hours	8	58	9	60	10	60	10	59
31-40 hours	15	26	16	24	20	26	22	27
All full-time	23	84	25	84	30	86	32	86
Part-time	Mothers	Fathers	Mothers	Fathers	Mothers	Fathers	Mothers	Fathers
16-30 hours	20	2	22	2	22	2	24	2
<16 hours	15	0	13	1	13	1	11	0
All part-time	35	2	35	3	35	3	35	2

It seems unlikely that these patterns of work are the same across mothers from all ethnic groups. Lindley, Dale and Dex (2004) pooled Quarterly Labour Force Surveys over seven spring quarters to form an early time cohort (1992-1995) and a later time cohort (2000-2002). They found major differences between ethnic groups, as well as significant changes over life stage. These variations are illustrated in figures 2.1-2.5 and appear to indicate that fewer Bangladeshi and Pakistani women are in paid work outside the home than women in other ethnic communities, with the exception of younger women without partners or children. Since the Bangladeshi and Pakistani communities tend to be among the most recent immigrants, Lindley et al. (2004) suggest that, as this community evolves, these patterns may be expected to change.

Examining Labour Force Survey data for Spring 2003, Clegg (2003) reported similar ethnic group differences among mothers with children under five. In relation to part-time work, 69 per cent of White mothers, 56 per cent of Indian mothers (55 per cent of Asian or Asian British mothers), 48 per cent of Caribbean mothers and 40 per cent of Black British mothers worked.[6] The same patterns obtained over all work (full- and part-time): 57 per cent of White mothers, 52 per cent of Indian mothers (but only 32 per cent of Asian or Asian British mothers), 52 per cent of Caribbean mothers, 44 per cent of Black British mothers, 35 per cent of African mothers but only 17 per cent of Pakistani and Bangladeshi mothers were working. Clegg (2003) further observed that, among all women (not only mothers), Pakistani and Bangladeshi women had the highest economic inactivity rates (74 per cent) and Caribbean women the lowest (26 per cent). It would appear that levels of economic activity amongst Pakistani and Bangladeshi women fall substantially once they have a partner

---

6   The populations of Bangladeshi, Pakistani, Chinese, African and Mixed race mothers with children under five and in part-time employment were too small to calculate percentages.

and again when they have children (Dale et al., 2004) and that Bangladeshi and Pakistani women may stop working when they marry as they believe it is culturally unacceptable for them to work (Burniston and Rodger, 2003).

Figure 2.1: Work patterns among women, by ethnic group and life stage
Figure 2.1.1

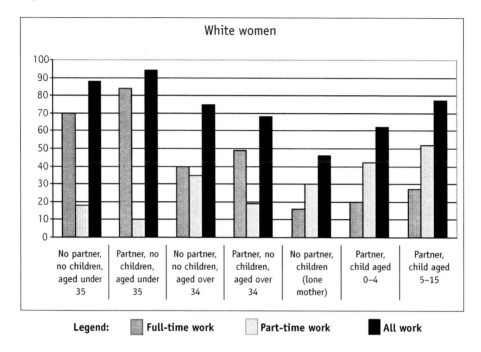

Figure 2.1.2

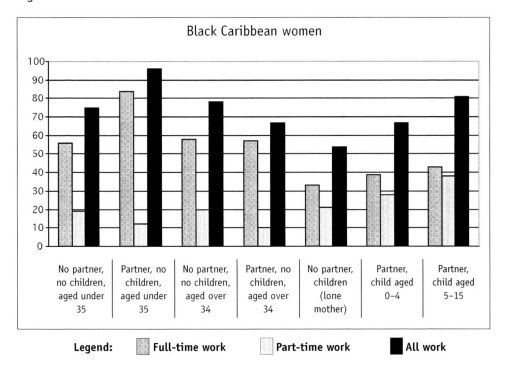

Figure 2.1.3

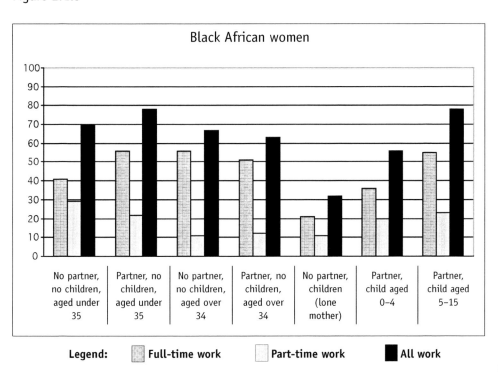

Figure 2.1.4

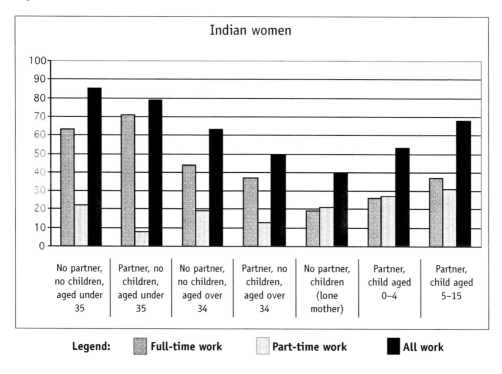

Figure 2.1.5

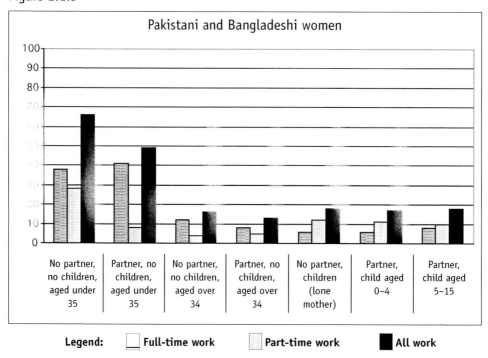

These variations suggest distinctly different patterns among mothers from specific minority ethnic groups and it not yet fully understood what the underlying processes might be, that is, whether they are due to differences in attitudes and practices in relation to childbirth or childcare, to cultural variations in expectations of women's roles, to the kinds of jobs that women from different ethnic groups undertake, to differences in skill level, or discriminatory influences in the workplace, etc. Given that Bangladeshi and Pakistani families are the most likely to experience poverty (as already mentioned), it seems important that these matters should be investigated further so that the support needs of families in these communities can be better understood and met.

Also as already suggested, patterns of employment among lone parents differ considerably from those of dual-earner families. Both mothers and fathers with partners are more likely than lone mothers or fathers to be in paid employment outside the home (table 2.4). Kasparova et al. (2003), examining 2000/2001 data on British families' work patterns and childcare usage, observed that three quarters of all non-working families were headed by lone parents and, confirming other findings, noted that substantially fewer lone than partnered mothers worked for 16 hours or more each week: whereas in nearly all working couples, one person was working at least 30 hours a week, this was the case for only 24 per cent of lone parents.

Commenting on patterns of work among lone parents in the decade before 1995, One Parent Families (One Parent Families, 1998) suggested that lone parents, like their married or cohabiting counterparts, prefer to work part-time but may be deterred due to the difficulty of finding suitable, affordable childcare as well as having to meet housing costs. They supported their argument by demonstrating that housing costs increased very steeply in relation to lone parents' income because their housing benefit tapered off so sharply as income increased. At the time of the 1998 report, lone parents with mortgages received no financial assistance towards housing costs and were therefore likely either to remain in receipt of benefits or to opt to work full-time.

Table 2.4: 2001 Patterns of employment for men and women,[1] by parenthood and relationship status

Source: O'Brien and Shemilt, 2003; based on Labour Force Surveys, Spring 1998, Spring 2001, ONS

	Full-time		Part-time		Unemployed		Econ. inactive	
	1998	2001	1998	2001	1998	2001	1998	2001
All fathers	85	86	3	3	4	3	8	8
Couple fathers	86	87	3	3	4	3	7	7
Lone fathers	53	55	7	7	10	9	30	29
Other men	70	71	5	5	5	4	20	20
All mothers	28	31	35	36	4	3	32	30
Couple mothers	30	32	38	38	3	2	28	27
Lone mothers	21	25	24	25	9	7	46	44
Other women	53	55	20	19	35	2	23	28

[1] Relates to men and women of working age (16-64 for men; 16-59 for women); figures are weighted estimates for the whole population

Table 2.5 shows in more detail the relationship between responsibility for children and rates of employment among lone mothers between 1992 and 2002 and suggests that the earlier downward trend may have reversed. Over this period, the number of lone mothers working increased by five per cent for women working full-time and by eight per cent for those working part-time, i.e. there was a thirteen per cent increase across all this group of working mothers. These increases appear to have been distributed fairly evenly across both full-time and part-time work and do not appear to relate to the age of mothers' youngest children. Again, as was shown in Figure 2.1, rates of work among lone parents with children varied among different minority groups: according to Lindley et al. (2003), just over half of Black Caribbean lone mothers were in paid employment outside the home, just under half of White mothers, but considerably smaller proportions of mothers from other ethnic groups.

Table 2.5: Economic activity status of female lone parents:[1] by age of youngest dependent child, 1992 and 2002 (Percentages) (United Kingdom)
Source: Labour Force Survey, Office for National Statistics

	Age of youngest dependent child				
	Under 5	5-10	11-15	16-18	All
1992					
Working full-time	8	18	35	39	18
Working part-time	13	26	26	24	20
All working	21	44	61	63	38
Unemployed	8	12	6	..	9
Economically active	29	55	67	72	48
Looking after family/ home	65	35	19	..	43
Other inactive	6	10	14	17	9
2002					
Working full-time	12	23	33	45	23
Working part-time	22	32	31	29	28
All working	34	56	64	74	51
Unemployed	5	8	7	..	6
Economically active	39	62	70	80	57
Looking after family/home	52	25	15	..	31
Other inactive	9	13	15	16	12

1 Females aged 16-59. At spring each year. These estimates are not seasonally adjusted and have not been adjusted to take account of the Census 2001 results.

There is evidence that a substantial number of parents are working antisocial hours, that is, they regularly work nights, early evenings, early mornings or at week-ends. La Valle et al. (2002) found that just over a half of working mothers (53 per cent of all working mothers and 54 per cent of lone mothers) and more than three quarters of working fathers (79 per cent) were working atypical hours. Further, combining atypical work times for working couples, it emerged that, in 43 per cent of couples, both parents were working atypical hours. These data suggest that a substantial proportion of working parents need to work at times that might interfere quite considerably with family life.

La Valle et al. (2002) explored why parents were engaging in antisocial hours of work. They found that three quarters of mothers working atypical hours did so because it was a requirement of their employment rather than an active choice. The majority of mothers stated that they would prefer to work different hours. Just over a quarter of mothers with partners (29 per cent) cited 'shift parenting' and the availability of a partner to look after the children while they worked as a factor in working atypical hours and just under a quarter (24 per cent) stated that childcare arrangements were more easily facilitated. A much smaller minority of lone mothers (eight per cent) working atypical hours explained that their hours of work mapped onto times that non-resident fathers were available to care for children.

Table 2.6 shows the break-down of atypical hours among mothers and fathers and indicates that the most common patterns appear to affect the amount of time that fathers are able to spend with young children. Because the experience of working outside 'traditional' nine-to-five office working hours is so common, Dex (Dex, 2003) poses the question of whether, in the current British working culture, it is really still appropriate to use the term 'normal working hours' at all.

Table 2.6: Atypical hours worked by mothers and fathers (as percentage of all hours worked)
Source: La Valle et al. (2002)

Atypical hours	Mothers	Fathers
Nights (8.30 pm – 6 am)	14	17
6-8.30 am/5.30-8.30 pm several times a week	21	41
Every week-end	4	6

To conclude this section, the evidence suggests that the hours that parents typically work do not, in general, appear to fit very well with family life. This seems to indicate that there may be some need to examine the way that work is organised in UK society, and to consider whether more congenial arrangements might be possible.

2.3　At what point in the lives of their children do mothers take up or return to paid employment?

Throughout much of the latter half of the twentieth century, the question of whether British mothers should leave their children and go out to work has given rise to disquiet. Whether this was the case earlier in the century seems unclear but, in the forties and fifties, child psychiatrists like John Bowlby (Bowlby, 1951, 1953) began to draw attention to potential links between maternal separation and later poor outcomes for children. Specifically, Bowlby posited a link between juvenile delinquency and severe separation experiences. In a World Health Organisation monograph (Bowlby, 1951) which had been commissioned to chart the effects of separation on young children and which later became a widely-known book on childcare (Bowlby,

1953), Bowlby asserted the opinion that mothers of young children should not be encouraged to work since they could contribute little to the workforce and were more valuable to the long-term economy if they stayed at home to look after the children. According to Bowlby, it would be more beneficial to society if lone mothers were paid to stay at home, although he recommended that lone fathers should be supplied with childcare assistance so that they could work to support the family. Bowlby was not alone in expressing views of this kind. They were shared by many childcare professionals, informed policies on provision of nurseries and day care, and also, to varying degrees, permeated British attitudes to childcare more widely.

Chief among beliefs held at this time was the notion that children younger than three would find it difficult to cope with any kind of separation from mother as, having limited powers of mental representation, they need mother to be physically available in order to retain a sense of her psychological availability and, consequently, of their own value. These dogma reinforced a commonly-held view that 'woman's place is in the home', at least while her children are young and especially when they are not yet old enough for school.

Yet, since at least the 1970s, patterns of employment among mothers have been changing and this is particularly true for women with pre-school age children. Between 1990 and 2000, the number of mothers with pre-school children in employment rose considerably (Bower, 2001): while fewer than half the population of mothers with children under five were employed in 1990 (41 per cent), more than half were employed by 2000 (55 per cent). In addition, the time at which women return to work or take up work has been changing. According to Callender et al. (1997), in 1996, two thirds of mothers were taking up or returning to work within a year of their child's birth compared with only a quarter in 1979.

Statham and Mooney (2003) found that a common perception among both parents and society in general was that, outside standard working hours, children are better off at home with a parent or family and friends. Childcare at atypical times was regarded with ambivalence and sometimes outright hostility by many childcare providers. However, noting that there was little research to demonstrate whether children are adversely affected by being in formal childcare at atypical times, Statham and Mooney call for a broader debate about children's place in society and about ways of achieving a balance between children's and parents' needs in relation to the requirements of work.

While previously mothers' entry to work may have coincided with the age at which the youngest child started school, more recently, it appears to have been more closely related to the point at which maternity benefit for the youngest child has run out (Paull et al., 2002). Dex (2003) also suggests that the rise in employment of mothers may be due to a combination of factors, such as legislation on equality of pay and employment opportunities (first introduced in the 1970s and enhanced through subsequent directives designed to encourage flexible working and work-life balance) and women's greater success in gaining higher educational qualifications.

Such factors, Dex argues, have agglomerated to create a climate in which women's earning potential is much higher than in the past (Dex, 2003).

Nevertheless, the pattern of work for mothers can still be seen to be influenced both by their responsibility for child rearing and the ages of dependent children, since mothers' hours of work tend to increase steadily up to the end of the age of dependence. Responsibility for children still has a strong bearing on mothers' participation in paid employment, hours of work, pay and type of occupation. Even so, the nature of mothers' involvement in the workplace does appear to have changed and this fact raises a number of questions, for example, about what the processes might be that support these changes and whether they have been accompanied by corresponding changes in attitudes towards mothers' employment.

2.4   Why do mothers work and how do they feel about it?

As Dex (2003) acknowledges, the second half of the twentieth century has seen enormous changes in the labour market. Many of these changes have altered the position of women, both in the workplace and at home. In the workplace, the continued decline of agricultural and manufacturing jobs traditionally held by men has weakened men's position while the growth of service jobs more compatible with women's desire to work part-time has strengthened that of women. For Dex (2003), women's increased participation in the labour force is viewed very much as a consequence of the decline in men's wages and the growing insecurity of men's earnings throughout the 1990s, which has affected not just traditional male sector occupations such as manufacturing but also professional and managerial positions. As mentioned earlier in this chapter, women and mothers do continue to work in more traditional paid employment (e.g. secretarial, administrative and retail posts) but they now also work in a wider range of occupations, associated with childcare, social services and health care. In many of these occupations, they are now paid to offer services that previously they may have been providing in an unpaid capacity at home.

To some extent, some of the conditions which might have provided a disincentive for women to work may have begun to be eroded with the passing of equal opportunities legislation in the 1970s: the Equal Pay Act (1970) stipulated that women and men should receive equal wages for equal work and the Sex Discrimination Act (1975) outlawed discrimination in the workplace on the grounds of sex or marital status. The passing of such Acts perhaps paved the way for changes to take place though, as will be seen in the next section, their impact has by no means been dramatic or immediate.

Further incentives to work have been provided by more recent policy initiatives aiming to tackle poverty and social exclusion (Appendix 2.2). For families with young children, work has been seen as the way out of poverty and this has resulted in localised initiatives, alongside the introduction of the right to more flexible working arrangements. Although there has continued to be some talk of work-life balance, especially in relation to women returning to work in the early years after birth and to support for fathers, the greater emphasis so far has been on the further development of in-work incentives such as tax credits and the introduction of better maternity and paternity leave. It is not clear that these inducements to work have been seen by mothers as positive, or as placing them under more strain as they find themselves increasingly expected to work outside the home at the same time as running a home.

At the beginning of the decade which is the subject of this report, Burns and Scott (1994) described relationships between men and women as characterised by a growing decomplementarity as each responded differently to financial pressures. They took the view that it was the combination of women's increasing financial independence and men's declining capacity to support families that underlay the rise in mother-headed (lone parent) families. In other words, women might be increasingly successful in obtaining paid employment outside the home, but they may be less likely to be able to sustain a relationship than in the past. Does this mean that women's involvement in work might have been altering traditional gender role relationships in a way that is more congenial to women than to men?

It is difficult to test this hypothesis but information from a longitudinal study carried out by Houston and Marks (2000) to investigate women's feelings about returning to full- or part-time work after the birth of a first child suggest little support for this view. Houston and Marks asked 400 women to complete questionnaires before their babies' birth, then again six and twelve months after the birth. Before the birth, mothers were asked about their intention to return to work, their feelings about working, their partners' and friends' attitudes to work, and their expectations of support. Houston and Marks found that women who intended to return to work full-time tended to earn more than women either intending to return to work part-time or to stay at home, had a strong positive attitude to work, believed that their friends and family thought they should work full-time, and also expected that their partner would support and help them when the baby arrived. Women who intended to work part-time appeared less committed to working but agreed to it because they felt this was what important people in their lives would want them to do; they also anticipated that their partners would help them. On the other hand, women who intended to stay at home tended to have a negative attitude towards work and thought that it would not be the 'right' thing to do; having a partner's help did not seem to play a part in their decision to stay at home. When babies were six months old, around a quarter of the women who had stated that they would return to work had stayed at home and the only thing which appeared to discriminate between those who returned to work and those who did not was the existence of a clear plan in relation to returning to work.

When babies were 12 months old, women who had stayed at home seemed even more sure that this was the best choice for their child. Women who were working, whether full- or part-time, seem less sure and rated their children's happiness, security and contentment lower than non-working mothers. Nevertheless, full-time working mothers felt that the choice to work was the best thing for them personally, though part-time working mothers were not so sure about this. Mothers who stayed at home, like part-time working mothers, were not too sure that being at home was the best thing for them. In addition, both full- and part-time working mothers reported that they felt stressed. All mothers, whether at home or working, reported that work commitments had prevented their partners from spending time with children (84 per cent of non-working mothers and 63 per cent of working mothers).

This study, then, appears to suggest that many women who put into effect their decision to return to work feel uncomfortable about the impact of their decision on their children. It also points to the existence of a substantial number of women who prefer to stay at home with their children but are somewhat uncomfortable about the impact of their decision on themselves. In other words, neither group of women appears to have avoided some degree of role strain. The sample size in this study is, however, quite small and more research might be valuable if more is to be learned about the generality of these experiences and the way that they might affect relationships between parents.

British Social Attitudes (BSA) surveys, which have been carried out by the National Centre for Social Research since the early 1980s, can provide some information about changing attitudes to work. However, some limitations do exist within this data as question formats are not always consistent across surveys, detailed information about standardisation, validity and reliability of questions is not usually presented and cell sizes are not always very large: while the total population of respondents may be as many as a thousand or more, subsets are rarely much larger than two or three hundred. In addition, unlike many of the large datasets on the ONS website, BSA data is less easily accessed and it is necessary to rely on reports in which often only selected details are presented (i.e. the outcomes considered important by the reporters). Nevertheless, bearing these reservations in mind, it is possible to glean some information about women's attitudes to work from this source.

In a report prepared for the Cabinet Office Women's Unit, Jarvis et al. (2000) revealed that in 1997 just over half of all women surveyed (51 per cent) agreed with the statement: "I would enjoy having a paid job even if I did not need the money." Around the same proportion of women surveyed in 1989 (53 per cent) agreed with the statement and, though cell sizes were rather small in these subsets, there was some indication that particular groups of women held these opinions more strongly: 58 per cent of women with children under 12, 64 per cent of women with A-levels or equivalent and 70 per cent of women with higher educational qualifications agreed with the statement.

Attitudes toward the gendered division of labour also appear to have changed. Inspecting BSA surveys from 1989, 1994 and 2002, Crompton et al. (2002) noted that only a minority of men and women stated that they agreed with the statement that "A man's job is to earn money; a woman's job is to look after the home and family" (28, 24 and 17 per cent in 1989, 1994 and 2002 respectively). Also, consistently fewer women than men agreed with the statement (26, 21 and 15 per cent compared with 32, 26 and 20 per cent). Unfortunately, this statement is probably an example of a rather weak BSA survey item: as it contains more than one idea, it is difficult to ascertain which elements respondents may have disagreed with.

Jarvis et al. (2000) gathered information about attitudes towards work from a slightly larger sample of women during the period 1983-1998. They found that a third of older women (over 54) agreed with the statement that "women shouldn't try to combine a career and children" while only nine per cent of 18-34 year-olds did. The size of the samples here mitigates against over-confidence in the generality of these findings but the data do seem to suggest that attitudes may fluctuate across different samples. Along similar lines, Crompton et al. (2002), inspecting BSA survey responses between 1989 and 2002, reported a trend towards greater confidence in the compatibility of childcare and work for women (table 2.7). Again, men tended to lag behind women in espousing this attitude.

Table 2.7: Percentage of men and women agreeing that "A working woman can establish just as warm and secure a relationship with her children as a mother who does not work."

	1989	1994	2002
Women	63	69	69
Men	51	57	58
All	58	63	64

In a separate report on data collected from British Social Attitudes surveys, carried out in 1994 and 1998, Hinds and Jarvis (2000) suggest that men's and women's attitudes towards women's work may be rather different, particularly in respect of single mothers, and that these attitudes appear to have changed over the two survey times. More men than women tended to agree with the statement that "a single mother with a pre-school child has a special duty to stay at home and look after her child" (26 versus 17 per cent in 1994; 29 versus 20 per cent in 1998). More women than men agreed with the statement that "a single mother with a pre-school child should do as she chooses, like everyone else" (67 versus 52 per cent in 1994 and 58 versus 42 per cent in 1998). Very few men or women agreed with the statement that "a single mother with a pre-school child has a special duty to go out to work to support her child" although, by 1998, more people (especially men) tended to endorse this opinion: in 1994, only eight per cent of women and nine per cent of men were in agreement while, in 1998, 20 per cent of men and 14 per cent of women agreed with it.

This change in attitudes was also reported by Crompton et al. (2003) who inspected responses from BSA surveys carried out in 1989, 1994 and 2002: over this period, the number of men and women who endorsed the view that a women should stay at home when her child is under school age fell considerably (see table 2.8).

Table 2.8: Percentage of men and women agreeing that "A woman should stay at home when her child is under school age"

	1989	1994	2002
Women	61	51	46
Men	67	60	51
All	64	55	48

With regard to mothers with school-aged children, similar patterns of differences emerged from men and women though, again, more 1998 than 1994 respondents were in favour of mothers going out to work (a view espoused more strongly by men than by women). The majority of women at both times considered that a single mother of school-aged children should "do as she chooses, like everyone else" (67 per cent in 1994 and 51 per cent in 1998) though a substantial minority thought that she has a special duty to go out to work to support her child (25 per cent in 1994 and 39 per cent in 1998).

By 1998, men's opinions appeared to have undergone a major change: in 1994 more than half (53 per cent) had endorsed the view that "a single mother should be free to choose whether or not to work" while only 31 per cent thought she has a special duty to go out to work. By 1998, this situation had reversed: more than half the men (51 per cent) surveyed thought women had a special duty to go out to work while 38 per cent thought she should do as she chooses. Very few respondents thought that single mothers of school-aged children should stay at home (four per cent of women and five per cent of men in 1998).

Contrary to a once-popular notion that women work primarily for 'pin' money (i.e. money for non-essential luxury items), Kasparova et al. (2003) found that 28 per of working mothers (15 per cent of all British mothers) were the family's sole breadwinner.[7] A corresponding report based on inspection of data collected during British Social Attitudes surveys (Crompton et al. 2003) indicated that by 2002, only 17 per cent of men were the sole breadwinner (compared with 31 per cent in 1989).

According to a British Social Attitudes survey carried out in 1999, though, men and women do appear to have rather different motivations to work: although the majority give the main reason for working as needing money to buy basic essentials (food, rent, mortgage, etc.), this reason was given by substantially more men than women (67 versus 44 per cent). Women were more likely to say that their main reason for working related to social or personal preference (e.g. to earn money of my own, to earn money to buy extras, for the company of other people, for a change from my children or housework). Almost a third of women (30 per cent) gave these kinds of

---

7   This finding would appear to agree with findings from the 1980 Women and Employment Survey which revealed that 30 per cent of employed married women at that time worked to buy necessities (Martin and Roberts, 1984).

reasons as their main reason for working as opposed to only eight per cent of men (Hinds and Jarvis, 2000). These differences appear to have been quite stable over the 1996 and 1998 surveys too, though this is perhaps a rather too short time frame and the sample size too small to expect major differences to show.

It seems that different motivations to work might obtain among some sections of minority ethnic communities: a study carried out by One Parent Families (One Parent Families, 2003) suggested that black lone mothers emphasise the importance of providing good, strong maternal role models for their children and in particular see employment as the best way to provide for their children.

Another study examined the diversity in employment profiles of British South Asian women and found evidence that challenged the simplified contrast often drawn between 'educated' and 'uneducated' South Asian women in Britain. In this study, Ahmad et al. (2003) reported that cultures which until recently might have been portrayed as opposed to the education and employment of women now seem to be producing growing numbers of highly motivated young women, more confident in expressing their identities through gender, ethnicity and religion. This study also highlighted the increasing numbers of young Muslim women with relatively high levels of education who are finding new ways of engaging with the labour market.

Earlier research had shown that women from India and East Africa had higher rates of participation in employment and higher education than Pakistani and Bangladeshi women (who are predominantly Muslim). However this report suggested that religious differences between South Asian and other women in terms of employment participation and career advancement may gradually be being reduced. Parental support was found to be particularly significant in the decision to pursue higher education and/or career, with older women being keen to encourage their daughters to succeed academically and professionally, although fathers also played a positive role. Younger women in professional employment were found to be taking alternative approaches to marriage, which resulted in re-negotiation rather than a rejection of 'traditional values'.

2.5   Is there any evidence that employment conditions for working mothers have improved?

Between 1994 and 2004, a number of developments have taken place which have been designed to improve employment conditions for men and women in the UK. These include changes in conditions of pay, in length of working hours and in availability of parental and maternity leave entitlements. Appendix 2.1 shows the number and nature of these changes, many of which have been of particular benefit to working mothers. In addition, as mentioned earlier, certain equal opportunities initiatives appear to have begun to pave the way for attitudes and practices more generally to change. These changes are also documented in Appendix 2.2.

Evaluation of the effects of these changes is difficult at this stage but it seems worth looking in more detail at how conditions for working mothers in Britain now appear to compare with those elsewhere in Europe. In the next section, we look first at how maternity leave arrangements in Britain compare with other countries (i.e. time and pay allowed to mothers around the time of childbirth). We then consider how Britain compares with other countries in respect of parental leave, that is, time allowed off work to attend to the needs of young children. Table 2.9 documents maternity leave entitlement within those countries from which information is available.

Table 2.9: Maternity Leave Entitlement

Sources of information: O'Brien, 2004, based on Deven and Moss, 2002; Clearinghouse on International Developments in Child, Youth and Family Policies at Columbia University

	MATERNITY LEAVE ENTITLEMENT		
	Length	Timing restrictions	Rate of payment
Austria	16 weeks	8 weeks before and after birth	100%
Belgium	15 weeks*	7 before, 8 after birth	75-80%
Czech Republic	28 weeks	37 weeks for multiple births	69%
Denmark	18 weeks	4 weeks before birth	90%
Finland	18 weeks		65%
France	16 weeks*	6 before, 10 after birth	100%
Germany	14 weeks	6 weeks before birth	100%
Greece	17 weeks		50%
Hungary	24 weeks		70%
Ireland	18 weeks	4 weeks before birth	70%
Italy	5 months	1 month before birth	80%
Luxembourg	16 weeks		100%
Netherlands	16 weeks		100%
Norway	52/42 weeks	Included in parental leave	80/100%
Poland	16/18/26 weeks*		100%
Portugal	6 weeks	Mandatory after birth	100%
Spain	16 weeks	May transfer 10 to father	100%
Sweden	14.5 weeks	60 days before birth	80%
Switzerland	16 weeks		Varies by canton
UK	6/26/52 weeks*	Up to 11 weeks before birth	90%/flat rate/unpaid

see text for more details of variations on these conditions

In Belgium, if a multiple birth is expected, nine weeks can be taken before birth; in addition, all but one week of before-birth leave is optional and can be taken after birth if there are complications. In the case of the death of the mother, post-natal leave can be changed to paternal leave under certain conditions. In France, the basic 16 weeks can be augmented under certain conditions: two extra weeks are permitted if medical complications are experienced during pregnancy; 26 weeks maternity leave are allowed for a third child (eight before confinement); 34 weeks (twelve before confinement) are allowed for twins and 46 weeks (24 before confinement) in the case of other multiple births. In Poland, length of maternity leave also depends on parity status: sixteen weeks are allowed for the first child, eighteen for each subsequent child and 26 weeks for multiple births. Up to 52 weeks maternity leave is allowable in the UK: the first 6 weeks are paid at 90 per cent, the following 20 are paid at a flat rate (currently £102.80) and the remaining 26 weeks are unpaid. It would appear from this information from this that the UK maternity leave allowances are not as generous as some countries but more generous than others.

Table 2.10 illustrates the situation with regard to parental leave entitlement (i.e. leave designed to enable parents to care for young children) in those countries within Europe from which it has been possible at this date to obtain information. Here, the UK would appear to offer less generous conditions.

Table 2.10: Availability of parental leave

Sources of information: O'Brien, 2004, based on Deven and Moss, 2002; Clearinghouse on International Developments in Child, Youth and Family Policies at Columbia University

	PARENTAL LEAVE ENTITLEMENT		
	Timing restrictions	Rate of payment	Specialconditions
Austria	Until 18/24 months	Flat rate	24 months if shared
Belgium	Up to 6 months	Low flat rate benefit	3 months per parent
Czech Republic	28 weeks	Unpaid	More for some parents*
Denmark	10 weeks	60%	Extra childcare leave*
Finland	26 weeks	Flat rate	Extra childcare leave*
France	Until child is 36 months	Flat rate	Varies by no. children
Germany	3 years until child is 8	Flat rate/ income related	Unpaid in 3rd year
Greece	3.5/7 months	Unpaid	3.5 months each parent
Hungary	Until third birthday	Flat rate/ income related	
Ireland	14 weeks	Unpaid	
Italy	10 months*	30%	20 months multiple births
Luxembourg	6/12 months*	Flat rate	+ annual family leave
Netherlands	6 months per parent*	Unpaid	+ family/care leave
Norway	52 or 42 weeks*	80% or 100%	Inc. maternity leave
Poland	24 weeks	Flat rate	36 wks for single parent
Portugal	6-24 months*	Unpaid	Family + special leave
Spain	Until child is 3	Unpaid	
Sweden	Until child is 2*	80%/flat rate/ unpaid	
Switzerland	Right to part-time work		Varies by canton
UK	13 weeks until child is 5*	Unpaid	18 weeks special needs

*see text for further details

In the Czech Republic, parents expecting multiple births and single parents are entitled to 37 weeks rather than the standard 28 weeks of parental leave. In Denmark, up to 52 weeks childcare leave can be taken by either parent up until the child's eighth birthday, with a 60 per cent payment entitlement. In Finland, additional child-rearing leave of absence is allowable until the child is three, although parents can also opt for home-care or childcare allowances until the child is seven. In Italy, unused parental leave can be taken up until the child's ninth birthday and there is also a fully-paid family sick leave entitlement of five days per year where children are aged between three and eight. In Luxembourg, parental leave is allowed for six months full-time or twelve months part-time until the child is five; in addition, two days per year are allowed for family leave. Parents are entitled to six months (per parent) unpaid parental leave with an additional ten days per year family leave and two days emergency leave. The arrangements for parental leave in the Netherlands are subject to a number of conditions and agreement with employers; the leave granted is only full-time under exceptional circumstances. Norwegian parents are also entitled to child-rearing leave, paid at a flat rate, until the child is two. Parents in Portugal can take up to 30 days per year family leave if they have children under ten and 15 days if they have older children; they are also entitled to up to four years' special leave if they have a sick child. Full parental leave is available to Swedish parents until the child is aged 18 months (80 per cent of full pay) and two further 3-month periods, the first paid at a flat rate and the second unpaid. In the UK, parents can take 13 weeks unpaid leave until children are five years old and are entitled to 18 weeks unpaid leave until the eighteenth birthday of a child with special needs.

To summarise this section so far then, Britain would appear to compare fairly well with other European countries but, as parental leave is unpaid, it clearly discriminates against lower paid parents who will often feel unable to take advantage of their entitlements. Many new initiatives have been introduced by the current UK Government and, in a number of ways, work conditions for mothers appear to be better (while it may not be possible to evaluate the impact of all the changes yet, it seems unlikely that they can make work more difficult). Nevertheless, even changes that make work less difficult for mothers may not necessarily make it convenient, congenial or even financially worthwhile. Throughout the twentieth century, men have earned considerably more than women. It is now almost three decades since the first Equal Opportunities legislation was passed. We wondered whether there was any evidence, over the period of interest to our report, of any greater equality in remuneration for men's and women's work.

In fact, evidence from birth cohort studies, and from other sources, appears to show that the gender pay gap may be decreasing, at least among younger generations: comparisons of wages of men and women in their 30s showed far greater similarity between men and women in the 1970 cohort than in the 1946 or 1950 cohorts (Dearden, Goodman and Saunders, 2003). Dearden et al. (2003) point to several possible reasons for this convergence: that women's educational attainments are

now more comparable with men's, that they are now more likely to secure employment in areas that are not characterised by low pay, that they take on occupations
which "are less distinctly 'female'" (p.158), that they stay in the workforce longer
because they start families later and that they return to work sooner after having
babies. However, childbirth-related career breaks still appear to be associated with
disadvantages for women, a point to which we return later in this chapter.

There appears to be some debate around the nature of the gender pay gap and the
factors associated with it. Using data from Labour Force Surveys, it is possible to
calculate women's average hourly rates of pay for full- and part-time work as a
percentage of men's earnings for full- and part-time work (Figure 2.2). The lower
percentage for all work is accounted for by the fact that part-time work is generally
paid at a much lower rate than full-time work. This method of calculation indicates
that, in agreement with the Department of Trade and Industry figures mentioned
earlier in this chapter, women in full-time employment earned around 80-85 per
cent as much as men over this time. However, it indicates that women appeared to
be earning as much as men for part-time work during most of this period (the DTI's
method, it may be recalled, assesses the gender pay gap by calculating women's
part-time average hourly rate as a percentage of men's *full*-time average hourly
rate). However, this method of calculation is likely to be rather less informative than
methods that take into account the type of work that men and women are engaged
in, i.e. whether they receive the same pay for the same job.

Harkness (1996), whose figures did take account of differences in many observable
characteristics, showed that women's full-time wages were 82 per cent of men's
while their part-time wages were 87 per cent. In another more recent report for the
Women and Equality Unit, Hurrell (2003) concluded that, for the period 1996/97
and 2000/01, there was a 65 per cent income gap between men and women's pay
among couples with children. Men earn the greater amount while women's earnings
rarely exceed those of their male partners.

As mentioned earlier, in spite of the upward trend in women's labour force participation and their greater success in gaining educational qualifications, the nature of
most paid work for women is still different from that of most men. However, Myck
and Paull (2001), on the basis of their time series analysis of the British Family
Expenditure Survey, argue that the sizeable gap that still exists between identical
workers is not accounted for by differences in either skills, qualifications or length
of work experience (indeed, they found that as length of work experience increased
and the correlation between length for women and men became higher, the pay
gap increased). Rather, the only factor they found to be associated with the size of
the pay gap was the number of returns to work that women made. It seems that,
although the gap has been narrowing among more recent cohorts, it is something
about the way that women are able, or not, to negotiate returns to work on wages
that are advantageous to them that results in their being disadvantaged.

Figure 2.2: Gender pay gap: Women's earnings as a percentage of men's, based on average gross hourly rates of pay
Source: Labour Force Survey, ONS

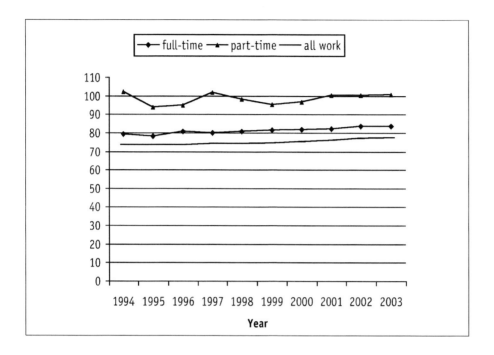

These findings were also confirmed by Gershuny (2001) whose investigation into the effects of work-breaks on women's career positions suggested that women who take substantial periods out of paid employment to care for their families show marked divergence in their career positions, and this applies both in comparison with their partners and in comparison with other partnered women who did not take similar breaks. McRae (2002), examining women's labour force behaviour during the period of family formation and its relationship to economic change, found that, during the 1990s, only 10 per cent of first time mothers maintained continuous full-time employment in the 11 years following the birth of their baby. Women who did maintain full-time employment were more likely to be employed in managerial or professional occupations, have smaller families, and experience more marital disruption than other mothers.

Negotiation of the return to work, therefore, despite government initiatives at the beginning of the twenty-first century, seems still to pose considerable difficulties for many mothers. Paull et al. (2002) suggest that, although some mothers may choose not to work, some may not be able to afford to work while still others may feel either unable to work at all or unable to take on the kind or amount of work that they would like because of constraints imposed by their responsibility for childcare. In the following section, we look at the issue of day care, its availability and how mothers feel about using it.

Meantime, to conclude this section, we can perhaps best summarise by saying that, although a number of aspects of women's work conditions appear to have improved, the choice of whether to work or not to work is still difficult for most women. For many women in the UK, balancing work and family life (which is often perhaps experienced as being torn between the demands of both paid and unpaid work) is a sizeable challenge. That this need not be the case seems evident from comparisons of experiences of working women in other countries (for example, France) where greater progress has been made in provision of social policy. However, it may be necessary to question whether all that is needed is workplace reforms that may often be designed with only the demands imposed by paid work in mind, as opposed to wider considerations such as the relationship between paid and unpaid work (Gregory and Windebank, 2000; Duncan et al., 2003).

2.6   How satisfactory is day care and nursery provision for children of working parents?

Earlier in this chapter we alluded to the cultural and historical context within which the experiences of working mothers in the UK are located. We identified a central theme in discourses on childcare as a belief that young children need to be physically close to their mothers. This theme has been central to debates about day care which have been markedly dominated by the question of whether mothers should leave their very young children with other people and what the effects might be if they do. These concerns have generally focused on the question of whether the use of day care might involve deprivation of critically important mother-child interactive experience. The theoretical basis for such concerns arises directly from the belief that it is only within mother-child interactions, with the particular intensity driven by a mother's biological investment in her child, that the child can begin to connect to other people and make sense of his or her own experiences (e.g. Schore, 2001). Deprived of these vital experiences, children are thought to develop a less than healthy sense of self which will manifest in later childhood, or adulthood, as less than optimal psychosocial adjustment, that is, behavioural and conduct disorders, emotional problems and difficulties in forming meaningful social relationships. Those who hold these views therefore see day care as a serious threat to children's psychological well-being.

Testing such theories is difficult for a number of reasons (Barrett, 2000; Rutter, in press). First, it is difficult to establish whether the use of day care necessarily constitutes deprivation of important mother-child interactive experiences to the extent that poor child outcomes might be expected. Second, poor outcomes may take some time to materialise, by which time it is likely to be difficult to track their origin. Third, it is almost impossible to employ a sufficiently controlled design to test whether, had children not been exposed to day care, she or he might have developed differently; problems may also arise in the case of children brought up by mothers who, for any of a number of reasons (e.g. isolation, depression, a sense of inadequacy, etc.), find it difficult to stay at home. Fourth, the day care environment itself may or may not provide supplementary interactive experience which, for some children, may be as rich as that which would have been obtained from the home; measuring the impact and quality of day care in all its variety, though, is a complex task.

Until recently, research on the effects of day care in the UK has tended to be piecemeal and small scale. While concerns were expressed (e.g. Jackson and Jackson, 1976; Bryant et al., 1980; Mayall and Petrie, 1977; Melhuish et al., 1990a, 1990b; Holterman, 1995; Melhuish, 2001), efforts to examine what the effects of day care might be were largely undermined by inadequate research methodologies (Barrett, 1991). By contrast, in the US, research has been carried out on a larger scale and, although there must be some question about the comparability of day care provision and thus about the extent to which findings from US studies might generalise to the UK, this research has effectively kept alive worries about the potential effects of day care on children's development.

In 1986, Belsky's re-evaluation of day care research findings initiated what since became known in the US as the 'day care war'. Specifically, Belsky identified an association between nonmaternal care in the first year for more than 20 hours per week and developmental difficulties in a small but significant minority of children (Belsky, 1986, 1987, 1988; Belsky and Rovine, 1988). Difficulties were manifested predominantly as a tendency towards increased incidence of avoidant attachment and some evidence of non-compliant behaviour towards adults, particularly in boys. There was insufficient evidence to conclude that these effects were directly attributable to any one aspect of day care such as quality, quantity or age of entry and Belsky suggested that they might better be seen as attributable to the ecology of day care (Belsky, 1988).

Belsky's initial claims were greeted with considerable resistance. They were challenged by many workers on a number of grounds, perhaps the most notable being that inappropriate conclusions had been drawn from attachment data (Clarke-Stewart, 1988; Fein and Fox, 1988) and that conclusions rested upon non-representative, poorly controlled studies, or unreliable findings (Thompson, 1988; Richters and Zahn-Waxler; 1988; Roggman et al., 1994). Subsequently, many of these issues began to be addressed by studies employing more sophisticated methods. Two main approaches have been used: large-scale studies which attempt to address sampling and measurement problems, and longer-term follow-up studies of children post-day care.

Representative of the first approach is a longitudinal study of 1,364 children, reports of which are still emerging from the US National Institute of Child Health and Development (e.g. NICHD, 1997, 1998, 1999, 2000a, 2000b). Unlike previous studies, in this study, a range of selection effects were monitored, including parents' education, child-rearing beliefs, race, economic and marital status and health-related measures such as parenting stress, maternal depression and separation anxiety. The scope of analyses has enabled consideration of factors such as children's gender and temperament, as well as many aspects of day care including type, quality, stability, quantity and age of entry. Outcome measures, where possible, have been based on multiple sources (observational, questionnaire, parent and teacher) with careful checks for inter-rater reliability. This increased design sophistication has made it possible to examine more closely relationships between parental, child and day care variables and their effects on children's development. Most importantly, it has thrown light on the fact that some effects attributed to day care by earlier workers (for example, avoidant attachment behaviour and behaviour problems) no longer appear to obtain once selection factors are entered into analyses.

However, the picture which has been emerging from this study has not been one of clear, consistent main effects across each of the five testing points (6, 15, 24, 36 and 54 months). Rather, different effects have emerged at different times and in association with different attributes. For example, although longer hours of care were found to be associated with lower maternal sensitivity (on one of the two measures taken) at 6 months and at 36 months, no significant associations were found at 15 or 24 months. Further, in a subsample of mother-child dyads who had more than 10 hours of care and where effects of quality of care were controlled, no significant association was found between amount of time spent in day care and maternal sensitivity. These findings led the authors to conclude that the effects they were seeing "may be due to other unmeasured family processes or to aspects of maternal functioning" (NICHD, 1999, p.1410). They also suggested that, for low income, single parent mothers, early age of entry to high quality day care may be associated with more positive mother-child interaction and more sensitive maternal care (NICHD, 2000). They found no effects in relation to ethnicity. Belsky, on the other hand, on inspection of the same NICHD data has reiterated his concerns and concludes that, for a small minority of children, day care does carry a risk. He argues (Belsky, 2000, 2001) that extensive day care, starting in the first year of life, still appears to be associated with the development of non-compliant behaviour and near-clinical conduct problems in a small but substantial minority of children. Belsky does not specify precisely the numbers of children that might be affected, but suggests that the quantity may be enough to add to classroom management difficulties. Since, to date, it has still not been possible to identify any one variable responsible for these negative effects (neither quality, amount, consistency of care nor interactions between these factors appear to account for effects), Belsky suggests that one clue may lie in family factors which are in some way influenced by the whole ecological system in which day care is located. More recently, he has raised the possibility that child attributes might provide a clue to what he has otherwise described as a "developmental mystery". He suggests that children who are emotionally highly reactive (that is, they become aroused relatively easily but are less easily calmed) may be more prone to negative effects of day care. This proposal has yet to be fully tested.

Follow-up studies of children post-day care have not thrown any more light on this question and have tended to produce rather inconsistent results. Using second generation data from mothers in the 1958 birth cohort of the UK National Child Development Study, Joshi and Verropoulou (1999) found no evidence that maternal employment beginning before school age was linked with increased anxiety or aggression in school-aged children (5-17). Rather, there was a tendency for children of mothers who worked while children were between the ages of one and four to score slightly higher than children of non-working mothers on a measure of "non-anxiety".

Although considerably more studies of the longer-term effects of day care on the development of children have been carried out in the US, to date, no consistent patterns of association between day care experience and children's behaviour appear to have emerged. Several analyses, which have included more stringent controls for sample selection effects, of data from the US National Longitudinal Survey of Youth (NLSY) have indicated associations between day care experience and negative adjustment in certain subsamples of children at some times of testing, but the reliability of these findings has not yet been established and the nature of possible underlying mechanisms has not yet been investigated to any great extent. Further, large-scale studies such as these may be limited due to lack of information in crucial areas such as that relating to the type or extent of early day care experience and mothers' employment status at the time of the child's birth (Joshi and Verropoulou, 1999). Failure to obtain information from multiple informants and variability in measures of adjustment may also pose threats to the validity of findings.

In the UK, findings from a large prospective study of day care, begun in 1997 (British Families, Children and Childcare Study; Sylva, Stein and Leach, 1997) have not yet, to the author's knowledge, appeared in the public domain. Within this study, observational data was to have been collected on a subsample (200-300) of the 1,200 infants and family members; fathers' involvement in childcare was to be assessed mainly via maternal interview. However, there are some indications from the Avon Longitudinal Study of Parents and Children (ALSPAC), which involves 12,000 families, that full-time day care begun within the first 18 months is associated with small negative child outcomes (Gregg et al., 2003). This study suggests that negative outcomes may be associated with quality of day care as well as with the amount of stress associated with mothers' full-time employment: children with mothers who have good social support and high quality care are less likely to experience later difficulties.

During the decade of this review, the nature of day care provision for young children in the UK has altered considerably due to a number of important Government initiatives. At the beginning of the 1990s, numerous research studies and campaign organisations were flagging up a strong sense of frustration among mothers about the general lack of affordable and accessible day care. Further, mothers often felt that they had no real choice about the kind of care they used and very little confidence in their ability to assess the suitability of their choice. Many used childminders because this was the only available option but would have preferred, even for small babies, to have used nurseries (Barrett, 1991). At this time, the number of children under three in the care of childminders was thought to be seven times higher than in other forms of day care (Pugh, De'Ath and Smith, 1994). A more recent study (Houston and Marks, 2000), however, reported that mothers felt quite strongly that maternal or family care was preferable for pre-verbal children. Nursery care was seen to be more beneficial once the child developed social awareness and a desire to play with other children. This seems to suggest that attitudes towards home-based care may have changed although more substantial research will be needed before this can be confirmed.

Evidence from a study by Burniston and Rodger (2003), who examined the experiences of lone parents from minority ethnic communities and their participation in the New Deal for Lone Parents (NDLP)[8], suggests that preferences among minority ethnic mothers may differ between cultures. Burniston and Rodger found that black lone parents tended to prefer nursery provision rather than childminders while Asian lone parents' preference was for someone from within the family to care for their children. Again, further research is needed before it is possible to establish the reliability of these findings.

Some of the reluctance on the part of parents to use childminders at the beginning of the 1990s was fuelled by the bad press given to childminders, but it was also driven by practical considerations, such as cost, fears about entrusting a stranger with care of a very vulnerable young infant, lack of information about what actually happens on a daily basis in the childminder's home, not knowing how to assess the quality of a childminder's care, the difficulty of finding cover when childminders were off sick or on holiday, etc.. These problems could be even greater for minority ethnic mothers, who were often unable to find affordable, culturally-sensitive care[9]. And the difficulties were, to some extent, compounded by provisions in the Children Act 1989, which placed emphasis on training for childminders and on annual inspection visits, as opposed to more regular and ongoing individual support and supervision.

Inspection and monitoring of home-based childcare in the UK, at the beginning of the 1990s, was highly problematic and, in many ways, it still is. Home-based childcare includes nannies, au pairs, registered and unregistered childminders. Only registered childminders are subject to official regulation and supervision. Although unregistered childminding is illegal, it is not a criminal offence and, for it to be prevented, it has to be proven that childminders (a) are not related to the children they are illegally caring for and that (b) they have the children in their care on a regular basis for more than a stipulated number of hours a week. Obtaining evidence of this kind that will stand up in court is too time-consuming for most local authority childcare officials to pursue. As a result, prosecution of unregistered childminders almost never happens and, for similar reasons, the incidence of unregistered childminding is not recorded in official statistics.

Although regulation and monitoring of most forms of home-based care in the UK still does not happen, procedures around registered childminders have changed considerably so that, by 2004, registered childminder services appear to be more publicly

---

8   For more information about this scheme, please see Appendix 2.2.

9   "It would be very good if, in this multinational society which you have, you could select childminders for foreigners... I would like to send her to an ethnic minority childminder... I don't like men around girls at all." Iranian mother (Barrett, 1991)

accountable and to have a greater air of professionalism. Key to these changes is the involvement of Ofsted in the registration and inspection of childminders. This has introduced the possibility of greater uniformity across the UK, in the sense of having a set of agreed standards and practices.

At the beginning of the 1990s, parents were articulating the request for access to inspection reports of home visits to childminders (Barrett, 1991). Ofsted reports are, in theory at least, in the public domain. Parents have always had the right to inspect the register of childminders, to check the status of women offering services. In practice, registers have neither been easy for the public to access nor always accurate or up-to-date. To some extent, this difficulty is being addressed by the provision of local authority websites, some of which provide information about vacancies with registered childminders. However, it would appear that the general move over the last decade has been to provide more nursery places for young children (tables 2.11 and 2.12), since monitoring the quality of care provided by these is less problematic.

Table 2.11: Day care places for children[1] (England, Wales & Northern Ireland), 1992-2001

Source: Department for Education and Skills; National Assembly for Wales; Department of Health, Social Services and Public Safety, Northern Ireland

(Thousands)	1992	1999	2000	2001
Day nurseries				
Local authority provided[2]	24	16	18	19
Registered	98	235	261	282
Non-registered[3]	1	12	2	2
All day nursery places[4]	123	262	281	304
Childminders				
Local authority provided[2]	2	9	3	3
Other registered person	275	360	349	331
All childminder places[4]	277	369	353	338

1 Under the age of 8 in England and Wales. Under the age of 12 in Northern Ireland.

2 England and Wales only.

3 England only before 2000; England and Wales only from 2000.

4 Figures do not add to totals. Total figures for England include an imputed figure for missing values.

Table 2.12: Number of registered childcare places in England by Ofsted region, March 31, 2004
Source: Ofsted website: http://www.ofsted.gov.uk/childcare/

	Providers	Places
Childminders	72,400	319,700
Full day care	11,000	456,300
Sessional day care	11,300	274,100
Out of school day care	9,200	326,700
Creche day care	2,200	38,000
All	**106,200**	**1,415,700**

There have also, more recently, been moves towards creating better links between home-based care and nurseries or 'children's centres' and to setting up mentoring schemes so that more experienced childminders can support others. These moves, it seems, will be welcomed by childminders, many of whom may prefer to take advantage of equipment, advice and support within a group setting[10]. It will be important to monitor the success of these initiatives, to see what impact they might have on the quality of services offered by registered childminders and to see whether co-temporal improvements in quality and number of nursery places will also result in higher quality provision overall.

A recent UK study indicates that mothers continue to identify childcare costs as a barrier to employment (costs, of course, increase in direct relationship to the numbers of children in the family). Even so, it seems that time costs are equally, if not more, important than childcare costs (Skinner, 2003). The working mothers in the study relied on a network of individuals offering informal, formal and back-up support with transporting children that was often additional to formal childcare.

Another recent UK study suggests that, for many minority ethnic mothers, lack of access to essential back-up support can make the search for appropriate childcare particularly stressful (Hall et al., 2004). Hall et al. (2004) found that the minority ethnic mothers in their study often relied on a combination of formal and informal childcare services. Generally, informal services were preferred as they were more culturally sensitive. Hall et al. (2004) identified needs for more minority ethnic carers, more affordable provision, services that were better geared to provide teachings about cultural beliefs and language, and that catered for the food preferences of minority ethnic families, and services that were more flexible in offering appropriate provision for children of different ages. They also identified a need for transport to be considered as an integral part of childcare provisions. Support from family,

---

10 Thematic analyses of childminder interviews (Barrett, 1991) revealed that isolation, expensive wear and tear on the home and lack of opportunity for career advancement were commonly experienced as problems by childminders

friends and the older children has also been found to be a crucial factor determining whether lone parents from Asian backgrounds in particular would attend both an initial NDLP (New Deal for Lone Parents[11]) interview and accept any subsequent decision to join NDLP. However, a report from the Daycare Trust (2003) found that only 79 per cent of black parents and 68 per cent Asian parents accessed any form of childcare. It would seem that particular attention is needed to ensure that suitable provision is available for parents from minority ethnic communities.

Summing up developments within early childhood services in the last decade, Pugh describes how many of problems identified in the 1980s and 1990s are beginning to be addressed "and, in many respects the Cinderella of the education system is now on her way to the ball" (Pugh, 2003: p, 186). However, she also observes that the number of new initiatives and the pace at which they have been introduced, though driven by a concerted effort to address issues associated with social exclusion (i.e. poverty and lack of support for families with young children), has still not produced a coherent overall policy in relation to day care services. She identifies needs for continued improvements in quality of childcare provision, including a review of pay and conditions across the pre-school sector to rectify inequalities which are leading to instability of services, improved access to in-service training and staff development, and greater reliance on long-term, sustainable funding. Further, she recommends that more attention be paid to the question of how to deliver services for under threes, so that these are better integrated with services for older children, are better integrated within themselves so that parents are not having to 'mix and match' to cover their need for flexible provision and so that the continuing severe shortage of places is addressed. In making these recommendations, Pugh also suggests that there remains an underlying ambivalence towards the status of day care in British society which needs to be finally laid to rest so that policies can be formulated on the basis of agreed understandings about what the purpose and role of early childcare really needs to be.

2.7   What do mothers feel about their ability to balance work and home life?

According to a report by Jarvis et al. (2000), based on inspection of British Social Attitudes survey data, most working women surveyed in 1998 did not feel that their work interfered with the rest of their lives although just under half (45 per cent of women with children under 16 and 47 per cent of those without) agreed with the statement "I make a point of doing the best I can, even if it sometimes does interfere with the rest of my life". The majority of women also stated that they were very satisfied (35 per cent) or fairly satisfied (45 per cent) with their work and this was true also of women with children under 16, 41 per cent of whom said they were very satisfied and 44 per cent fairly satisfied with their jobs. Nevertheless, only one in ten women surveyed in both 1989 and 1998 said that they never or hardly

---

11 More information about this scheme is to be found in Appendix 2.2

ever came home exhausted. In 1998, 12 per cent of women said they always came home exhausted, 29 per cent said that they often came home exhausted and the majority (49 per cent) said that they sometimes come home exhausted. Although there was a slight tendency for higher proportions of women surveyed in 1998 than of those surveyed in 1989 to state that they came home exhausted, the sample size (269) is too small to be confident that differences were attributable to more than chance variation.

Since more women have entered the workforce and usually appear to be expected to take as much responsibility for managing the family and home as ever, the question of how work and home life can best be juggled has begun to feature more highly on the agenda both of policy-makers and of some employers. Two types of work-family conflict have been identified: work interfering with family (WIF; also called 'negative spillover' in the literature) and family interfering with work (FIW). WIF has been shown to lead to psychological distress as well as to problems with family functioning, for example, poor parenting, family conflict, alcohol abuse, stress-related illnesses, etc. (Frone et al., 1992). Research has shown that perceptions of lack of control over one's workload (Duxbury, 1994; Parkes, 1989), job demand (Aryee et al., 1999), long hours (Negrey, 1993), flexible work schedules and supportive management (Thomas and Ganster, 1995) and job insecurity or instability are all associated with either the amelioration or aggravation of WIF conflict (Noor, 2003). Over the past decade, too, employers and policy-makers have realised how employees' perceptions can impact on productivity levels.

In a small-scale study of twelve 'four generation' families, Brannen et al. (2001) investigated inter-generational differences in perceptions of motherhood and maternal employment, using interviews with both men and women from the three older generations. Taking the grandparent generation as the pivotal marker, comparisons were made of people who had become parents in the forties, late sixties to early seventies, and nineties. A quarter of the great grandmothers had minimal or no experience of paid employment: either they had never worked or their employment had ceased at marriage or motherhood. The remaining three quarters of great grandmothers stopped work at parenthood, then resumed when their children were older, although over half reported working when at least one of their children was under five years. Their work tended to be low status, e.g. cooking and cleaning, with little opportunity for progression, and it involved part-time hours that could be fitted around the needs of the family.

A much higher proportion of the grandmother generation had what Brannen et al. termed 'interrupted employment paths': only one had hardly worked at all while only one had worked continuously. More grandmothers than great grandmothers, also, were employed full-time and worked when they had a child under five. Two-thirds of the grandmothers had been able to progress in their occupations after they had had their children.

Employment patterns for the mother generation continued the trend towards increased employment when children are young and, although only two mothers resumed work full-time after each birth, seven had worked continuously, or with only short breaks when having children. In contrast to the previous generations, five of the 12 mothers had already achieved professional or managerial jobs prior to becoming parents.

Thematic analyses suggested that, although the idea of motherhood as 'being there for children' was strong across all three generations, the meaning of 'being there' has been redefined as situations and contexts have changed. Normative ideas about motherhood obviously had an impact on each successive generation's decision about economic activity. However these were not necessarily universally agreed across generations: some great grandmothers stated that it was taken for granted that women stopped work at marriage or parenthood, whilst others maintained that it was usual for a mother to work to supplement men's low wages. The great grandmothers and grandmothers spoke about 'fitting work around the family', by ensuring that they could be home when the children where present, in order that children are cared for by 'family' rather than by 'strangers'. Working during school hours, or the father providing care before or after his work, were the two most common childcare arrangements in both the older generation groups, followed by other relatives and finally formal care. However, in the mother generation, to accommodate longer working hours, there was a slight shift to greater reliance on relatives and non-working fathers to supply childcare.

Brannen et al. (2001) proposed that the variations might be understood in terms of women making contextualised ethical decisions about their family responsibilities, influenced but not completely driven by constraints such as historical events, structural factors (e.g. changes in employment and education), economic demand, and normative ideas about motherhood. They also concluded that, contrary to the notion that it has become more acceptable for mothers to work, rather, mothers in successive generations have experienced increasing strain: they suggest that mothers have felt themselves increasingly caught between growing labour market demands for women's employment and pressures from a society which is still largely maternalistic in ideas about caring and responsibility for children, and which has little experience of providing good quality and readily accessible childcare services.

As already mentioned in our discussion of factors underlying the gender pay gap, taking time out of work to have a child appears to be the factor most closely and reliably associated with lack of career progression, or even demotion, for women (Paull et al., 2002). Considering data related to the strategies that women employ to resolve this situation, Gershuny (2001) postulated that there may be a growing polarisation between women who maintain a high attachment to the labour force and those who, for whatever reason, fail to maintain this high attachment. McRae (2002), however, concluded, in agreement with Brannen et al. (2001), that women's choices about balancing work and family life appeared to be best characterised as forming a continuum from completely work-centred to completely family-centred, rather than dividing women into distinct groups with particular preferences. In other words, there does not appear to be evidence to assume a fundamental polarisation between women with differing work histories, i.e. between career-orientated women and housewives or complementary earners.

On conducting a secondary analysis of data collected by the Work Life Balance 2000 Employee Survey (WLB2000, IFER/IFF, 2000), O'Brien and Shemilt (2003) reported that mothers, fathers, and other men and women appear to hold quite different attitudes toward the question of work life balance. While there is generally high verbal support for work–life balance among parents (85 per cent of mothers and 80 per cent of fathers agreed that everyone should be able to balance their work and home lives in the way they want), mothers and fathers seemed to differ quite considerably in what they expected from their employment conditions, what they wanted from them and how they put their work-life balance preferences into effect. Mothers' expectations about whether they would have access to specific work-life balance practices (identified as working from home, part-time work, flexible working hours, compressed week, annualised hours, shift work, working during term-times only, job sharing) were, in almost all aspects (with the exception of working from home, annualised hours and shift work) higher than fathers. Fathers tended not to expect that family-friendly working practices would be available to them and, as a consequence, tended both not to have found out about the options available to them and not to have taken advantage of the options that were in place (in this, they differed both from mothers and from men without families).

Not surprisingly, therefore, the time that fathers spent with their children ac-counted only for approximately one third of the total parental childcare time and this, combined with a long work hour culture, left mothers with responsibility for the bulk of childcare. In a minority of cases, where mothers worked full-time and particularly where they had a high income, fathers tended to be more highly involved in childcare and housework, suggesting that, in some families at least, cash versus care negotiations do happen. Nevertheless, both mothers and fathers appeared highly satisfied with the number of hours they worked, with the flexibility of their hours, and with their ability to balance work and non-work interests. Their main, and substantial, source of discontent was with childcare facilities. Having said this, parents working the longest hours were the least satisfied with all aspects of their work conditions and, as hours of work increased, mothers in particular were less likely to be satisfied.

O'Brien and Shemilt (2003) therefore concluded that there was evidence of sub-stantial unmet demand for more flexible working conditions among parents and emphasised that mothers and fathers may require their employers to put different flexible working strategies in place. They also flagged up a fairly general wariness on the part of employers towards family-friendly strategies (only 60 per cent of employers thought employees should be able to balance their work and home lives in the way they want and more than half did not offer any form of flexible work-ing). O'Brien and Shemilt therefore pointed to the need for more cost-effectiveness assessments to reassure, employers, particularly in smaller organisations, of the benefits of flexible arrangements.

Mothers employ a variety of additional strategies in order to juggle the demands of work and family. Bianchi (2000) described one common strategy as to 'shed load'. This involves spending less time on activities such as housework, sleeping or shopping so that more time is available for the children. Bianchi suggested that this might explain why the difference between working and non-working mothers in time spent on childcare is often not as great as might be expected.

Childcare is not just simply time spent looking after children, either by parents or child carers, but also includes related activities, not least of which is transportation to and from school, childminders, nurseries, after school activities and other leisure pursuits to mention just a few. In a small study of 40 mothers, including seven full-time, 21 part-time and 12 non-working mothers, living in two separate areas of a middle-sized city in England, Skinner (2003) found that the negotiations involved in coordinating work commitments around both the childcare that facilitates the possibility of paid employment and the plethora of other activities that children are involved in, can affect a mother's ability and willingness to work. These complexities were positively correlated with the number of children in the family, and could be multiplied where different-aged children used a range of services with varying opening times and locations. Within the study, six of the mothers working full-time used formal childcare which they supplemented with either formal or informal support in transporting the children on at least one occasion each day. All of the part-time working mothers used either formal or informal childcare, with 16 requiring additional support with transportation.

Inflexible employment conditions which fail to accommodate the fixed times of both pre-school and primary education and inefficient public transport/lack of access to private transport or support to get children to and from childcare and school were identified as deterrents to working by five of the non-working mothers. One of the conclusions that Skinner (2003) draws is that it is not necessarily lack of childcare that is a barrier to employment for mothers, but that the complexity of arrangements, especially in families with at least one child under five, is also a deterrent. Lack of support from others or lack of access to efficient transport considerably increased what Skinner identified as 'time costs' (Skinner, 2003).

Many mothers become self-employed because they believe this can offer working arrangements that make it easier to reconcile paid employment with family responsibilities, for example, enabling them to have more control over when, where and how often to work. However, Bell and La Valle (2003), whose study included a quarter of families with at least one self-employed parent, found that flexibility was not a deciding factor in most parents' decision to become self-employed. For many mothers, self-employment meant having more family–friendly working arrangements. However for some mothers and most fathers, self-employment meant working long, atypical hours with more frequent weekend working. Self-employed mothers with employees were more likely to use (non-parental) childcare and so relied on formal provision and had higher childcare costs. Among those without employees, levels of formal childcare use and expenditure were lower. Self-employed mothers with employees were more likely to work long atypical hours, while the majority of those without employees worked part-time. Self-employed mothers were more likely than their employee counterparts to report unmet childcare needs.

Finally, it seems important to remember that some mothers still choose not to go out to work. According to Dex (2003), mothers who did not go out to work mostly stated that they did not want to spend time away from their children. Almost a fifth of lone parents (19 per cent) also mentioned the cost of childcare as a barrier to work and 15 per cent mentioned a lack of available childcare. It is difficult to obtain meaningful data on women's choice not to work as the largest databases, e.g. most large household data surveys, are not set up to collect information on preferences and tastes (Paull et al., 2002). That not working could be a positive choice there-fore seems barely acknowledged, particularly in policy recommendations which are often preoccupied with the task of getting mothers into the labour force as a way out of poverty. Given the preference of a substantial number of parents, mothers and fathers, for spending more time with their children, and the potential benefits of this for children, there would appear to be clear indications that policy-makers might need to develop a greater range of routes out of poverty.

Author's note:

This chapter was researched and co-written with Carena Rogers, whose assistance was greatly appreciated. Responsibility for any errors is entirely my own.

References for Chapter 2

Ahmad, F., Modood, T. and Lissenburgh, S. (2003) *South Asian women and employment in Britain: The interaction of gender and ethnicity*. Bristol: Bristol University and the Policy Studies Institute.

Aryee, S. Luk, V., Leung, A. and Lo. S. (1999) Role stressors, interrole conflict, and well-being: the moderating influence of spousal support and coping behaviors among employed parents in Hong Kong. *Journal of Vocational Behavior*, **54**, 259-278.

Ashton, C., Primarolo, D. and Roche, B. (2002) *Inter-departmental childcare review: Delivering for children and families*. London: The Strategy Unit. Available to download at: http://image.guardian. co.uk/sys-files/Society/documents/2002/11/06/su-children.pdf

Barrett, H. (1991) *The social experiences of childminded children*. Unpublished PhD: Birkbeck, University of London.

Barrett, H. (2000) The politics and chemistry of early intervention. *Emotional and Behavioural Difficulties*, **5(2)**, 3-9.

Bell, A. and La Valle, I. (2003) *Combining self-employment and family life*. York: Joseph Rowntree Foundation.

Belsky, J. (1986) Infant daycare: A cause for concern? *Zero to Three*, **6**, 1-7.

Belsky, J. (1987) Risks remain. *Zero to Three*, 7, 22-24.

Belsky, J. (1988) The "effects" of infant day care reconsidered. *Early Childhood Research Quarterly*, **3**, 235-272.

Belsky, J. (1999) Quantity of nonmaternal care and boys' problem behavior/adjustment at ages 3 and 5: Exploring the mediating role of parenting. *Psychiatry*, **62**, 1-20.

Belsky, J. (2000) *Infant day care risks remain!* Paper presented to the Association of Child Psychology and Child Psychiatry, London.

Belsky, J. (2001) Developmental risks (still) associated with early childcare. *Journal of Child Psychology and Psychiatry*, **42**, 845-859.

Belsky, J. and Braungart, J. (1991) Are insecure-avoidant infants with extensive day-care experience less stressed by and more independent in the Strange Situation? *Child Development*, **62**, 567-571.

Belsky, J. and Rovine, M. (1988) Nonmaternal care in the first year of life and the security of infant-parent attachment. *Child Development*, **59**, 157-167.

Bianchi, S.M. (2000) Maternal employment and time with children: dramatic change or surprising continuity? *Demography*, **37(4)**, 401-414.

Bower, C. (2001) Trends in female employment. *Labour Market Trends,* **109(2)**, 107-118.

Bowlby, J. (1944) Forty-four juvenile thieves: their characters and home life. *International Journal of Psychoanalysis*, **25**, 19-52; 107-127.

Bowlby, J. (1951) *Maternal care and mental health*. World Health Organisation, Monograph Series, No. 2, reprinted in abridged version as *Childcare and the growth of love* (1953). Harmondsworth: Penguin.

Brannen, J., Moss, P. and Gilbert, E. (2001) *An intergenerational study of paid and unpaid work. Interim Report.* London: Institute of Education, Thomas Coram Research Unit.

Burniston, S. and Rodger, J. (2003) *An Evaluation of the New Deal For Lone Parents Innovation Fund 2001-2002*. York Consulting: Published online at http://www.dwp.gov.uk/jad/2003/156rep.pdf

Burns, A. and Scott, C. (1994) *Mother-headed families and why they have increased*. Hillsdale, NJ: Lawrence Erlbaum Associates.

Callender, C., Millward, N., Lissenburgh, S. and Forth, J. (1997) *Maternity rights and benefits in Britain 1996*. DSS Research Report, No. 67. Norwich: The Stationery Office.

Clarke-Stewart, K. A. (1988) 'The "effects" of infant day care reconsidered' reconsidered: Risks for parents, children, and researchers. *Early Childhood Research Quarterly*, **3**, 293-318.

Clegg, M. (2003) *Ethnic minority women in the UK*. London: Women and Equality Unit. Available online at: http://www.womenandequalityunit.gov.uk/publications/me_briefing_oct_2003.doc

Crompton, R., Brockmann, M. and Wiggins, R.D. (2003) A woman's place... Employment and family life for men and women. In A. Park, J. Curtice, K. Thomson, L. Jarvis and C. Bromley (Eds.), *Continuity and change over two decades* (161-187). British Social Attitudes, 20th Report. London: Sage.

Daycare Trust (2003) *Parents' eye. Building a vision of equality and inclusion in childcare services.* London: Daycare Trust.

Dearden, L,. Goodman, A. and Saunders, P. (2003) Income and living standards. In E. Ferri, J. Bynner and M. Wadsworth (Eds.), *Changing Britain, Changing lives: Three generations at the turn of the century* (148-193). London: Institute of Education.

Dennis, N. and Erdos, G. (1992) *Families without fatherhood*. London: Institute of Economic Affairs.

Department of Trade and Industry (2004) *Employment Matters: A lunchtime seminar series about employment relations and the world of work.* Presentation given on 25 February 2004, available online (April 2004) at: http://www.dti.gov.uk/er/emar/events.htm

Dex, S. (2003) *Families and work in the twenty-first century.* York: Joseph Rowntree Foundation.

Duncan, S., Edwards, R., Reynolds, T. and Alldred, P. (2004) Mothers and childcare: Policies, values and theories. *Children and Society, in press.*

Duxbury, L., Higgins, C. and Lee, C. (1994) Work-family conflict: a comparison by gender, family type, and perceived control. *Journal of Family Issues*, **15**, 449-466.

Fein, G.G. and Fox, N. (1988) Infant day care: A special issue. *Early Childhood Research Quarterly*, **3**, 227-234.

Frone, M.R, Russell, M. and Cooper, M.L. (1992) Antecedents and outcomes of work-family conflict: testing a model of the work-family interface. *Journal of Applied Psychology*, **77**, 65-78.

Furstenberg, F.F. and Kaplan, S.B. (2004) Social capital and the family. In J. Scott, J. Treas and M. Richards (Eds.), *The Blackwell companion to the sociology of families* (218-232). Oxford: Blackwell.

Gershuny, J. (2001) *Changing Times: Work and leisure in post-industrial society.* Oxford: Oxford University Press.

Gregg, P., Washbrook, E. and the ALSPAC Study team (2003) The effects of early maternal employment on child development in the UK. Preliminary results under project: Understanding the impact of poverty on children of the 90's. *CMPO Working Paper Series No. 03/070.*

Gregory, A. and Windebank, J. (2000) *Women's work in Britain and France.* Basingstoke: Palgrave.

Hall, K., Bance, J. and Denton, N. (2004) *Diversity and difference: Minority ethnic mothers and childcare. The role of childcare in women's labour market participation: A study of minority ethnic mothers.* London: DTI, Women and Equality Unit

Harkness, S. (1996) The gender earnings gap: Evidence from the UK. *Fiscal Studies,* **17(2)**, 1-36. Available online at : http://www.ifs.org.uk/publications/fiscalstudies/fsharkness.pdf

Hinds, K. and Jarvis, L. (2000) The gender gap. In R. Jowell, J. Curtice, A. Park, K. Thomson, L. Jarvis, C. Bromley and N. Stratford (Eds.), *British Social Attitudes. Focusing on diversity. The 17th Report* (101-113). London: Sage.

Holterman, S. (1995) *Investing in young children: A reassessment of the cost of an education and day care service.* London: National Children's Bureau.

Houston, D. M. and Marks, G. (2000) Employment choices for mothers of pre-school children: a psychological perspective. *ESRC Future of Work Bulletin*, **2**,6. Available online at: http://www.leeds.ac.uk/esrcfutureofwork/downloads/fow_bulletin_2.pdf

Hurrell, K. (2003) *Statistics on reasons for working part-time.* London: Equal Opportunities Commission. Information online (April 2004) at: http://www.eoc.org.uk/cseng/research/labour_force_survey.asp

Jarvis, L., Hinds, K., Bryson, C. and Park, A. (2000) *Women's social attitudes: 1983 to 1998.* London: National Centre for Social Research.

Joshi, H. and Verropoulou, G. (1999) *Maternal employment and child outcomes: Analysis of two birth cohort studies.* London: The Smith Institute.

Kasparova, D., Marsh, A., Vegeris, S. and Perry, J. (2003) *Families and children 2001: Work and childcare.* Research Report 191. Leeds: Corporate Document Services. Summaries available online at: www.dwp.gov.uk/asd

Lamb, M., Sternberg, K. and Prodromidis, M. (1992) Nonmaternal care and the security of infant-mother attachment: A reanalysis of the data. *Infant Behavior and Development*, **15**, 71-83.

La Valle, I., Arthur, S. Millward, C., Scott, J. and Clayden, M. (2002) *Happy families? Atypical work and its influence on family life.* Bristol: The Policy Press and Joseph Rowntree Foundation. [Cited in O'Brien and Shemilt, op cit.]

Lindley, J., Dale, A. and Dex, S. (2004) Ethnic differences in women's demographic, family characteristics and economic activity profiles, 1992 – 2002. *Labour Market Trends*, **112(4)**, 153-165. Available online at: http://www.statistics.gov.uk/articles/labour_market_trends/ethnic_differences.pdf

Martin, J. and Roberts, C. (1984) *Women and employment: A lifetime perspective.* London: HMSO.

McRae, S. (2002) *Mothers' Employment and Family Life in a Changing Britain.* Oxford: Oxford Brookes University.

Melhuish, E.C., Mooney, A., Martin, S. and Lloyd, E. (1990a) Type of childcare at 18 months: I. Differences in interactional experience. *Journal of Child Psychology and Psychiatry*, **31(6)**, 849-859.

Melhuish, E.C., Mooney, A., Martin, S. and Lloyd, E. (1990b) Type of childcare at 18 months: II. Relations with cognitive development and language. *Journal of Child Psychology and Psychiatry*, **31(6)**, 861-870.

Moss, P G., Brannen, J. and Mooney A. (2001) *An inter-generational family study of employment and care : looking forward and looking back.* University of London: Institute of Education.

Murray, C. (1990) *The emerging British underclass.* London: IEA Health and Welfare Unit.

Myck, M. and Paull, G. (2001) *The role of employment experience in explaining the gender wage gap.* London: Institute of Fiscal Studies [WP01/18]. Available online (April 2004) at: http://www.ifs.org.uk/workingpapers/wp0118.pdf

NICHD Early Childcare Research Network (1997) The effects of infant childcare on infant-mother attachment security: Results of the NICHD study of early childcare. *Child Development*, **68(5)**, 860-879.

NICHD Early Childcare Research Network (1998) Early childcare and self-control, compliance and problem behavior at twenty-four and thirty-six months. *Child Development*, **69(4)**, 1145-1170.

NICHD Early Childcare Research Network (1999) Childcare and mother-child interaction in the first 3 years of life. *Developmental Psychology*, **35(6)**, 1399-1413.

NICHD Early Childcare Research Network (2000a) The relation of childcare to cognitive and language development. *Child Development*, **71(4)**, 960-980.

NICHD Early Childcare Research Network (2000b) Factors associated with fathers' caregiving activities and sensitivity with young children. *Journal of Family Psychology*, **14(2)**, 200-219.

Negrey, C. (1993) *Gender, time and reduced work.* Albany: State University of New York Press.

Noor, N.M. (2003) Work and family-related variables, work-family conflict and women's well-being: some observations. *Community, Work and Family*, **6(3)**, 297-319.

O'Brien, M. and Shemilt, I. (2003) *Working fathers: Earning and caring.* Manchester: Equal Opportunities Commission.

ONS (2004) Statistics online (May 2004) at http://www.statistics.gov.uk/cci/nugget_print.asp?ID=463

One Parent Families (1998) *Social Security Committee submission – making work pay for lone parents.* [Unpublished document]. London: One Parent Families.

Parkes, K.R. (1989) Personal control in an occupational context. In S.L. Sauter, J.J. Hurrell and C.L. Cooper (Eds.), *Job control and worker health,* (21-47). Chichester: Wiley.

Paull, G., Taylor, J. and Duncan, A. (2002) *Mothers' employment and childcare use in Britain.* London: Institute for Fiscal Studies.

Popenoe, D. (1993) American family decline (1960-1990): A review and appraisal. *Journal of Marriage and the Family,* **55(3)**, 527-542.

Pugh, G. (2003) Early childhood services: Evolution or revolution? *Children and Society,* **17**, 184-194.

Pugh, G., De'Ath, E. and Smith, C. (1994) *Confident parents, confident children.* London: National Children's Bureau.

Richters, J. E. and Zahn-Waxler, C. (1988) The infant day care controversy: Current status and future discussions. *Early Childhood Research Quarterly,* **3**, 319-336.

Roggman, L., Langlois, J., Hubbs-Tait, L. and Rieser-Danner, L. (1994) Infant day care, attachment, and the "file drawer problem". *Child Development,* 1429-1443.

Rubery, J., Fagan, C., Grimshaw, D., Figueiredo, H. and Smith, M. (2004) *Indicators on gender equality in the European Employment Strategy.* EGGE – EC's Expert Group on Gender and Employment. Available online at: http://www2.umist.ac.uk/management/ewerc/egge/egge_publications/cff_indicators2001.pdf

Rutter, M. (in press) Environmentally mediated risks for psychopathology: Research strategies and findings. *Journal of the American Academy of Child and Adolescent Psychiatry.*

Schore, A.N. (2001) Effects of a secure attachment relationship on right brain development, affect regulation, and infant health. *Infant Mental Health Journal,* **22(1)**, 7-66.

Skinner, C. (2003) *Running around in circles: Coordinating childcare, education and work.* York: The Policy Press and the Joseph Rowntree Foundation.

Statham, J. and Mooney, A. (2003) *Around the clock: Childcare services at atypical times.* York: Joseph Rowntree Foundation.

Sylva, K., Stein, A. and Leach, P. (1997) *Families, children and childcare.* Unpublished draft.

Thomas, L.T. and Ganster, D.C. (1995) Impact of family-supportive work variables on work-emotional states. *Psychological Bulletin,* **96**, 465-490.

Thompson, R.A. (1988) The effect of infant day care through the prism of attachment theory: A critical appraisal. *Early Childhood Research Quarterly,* **3**, 273-282.

Work-Life Balance (WLB) Data Sets (2000). *Employee and employer surveys, IFER/IFF.* Archived at the ESRC Data Archive, Essex University. Available online at: http://www.data-archive.ac.uk/findingData/snDescription.asp?sn=4465

3 | Fathers' involvement in family life

In this chapter, we consider the role of fathers and the nature of their involvement in family life around the turn of the century. In particular, we focus our interest on questions pertaining to gender role relationships and examine evidence concerning the extent to which changes in these may have produced qualitative differences in relationships between fathers and their children. To set the context for this discussion, in the first section, we describe key policy and research issues which dominated the years immediately preceding the decade under review. Having sketched in this background, we go on to raise questions about the extent to which it may be possible to detect shifts in conceptualisations of the role of fathers throughout 1994-2004.

Defining fatherhood

Before embarking upon this discussion, we should note that we follow other researchers (e.g. Marsiglio, 1995; Hofferth, 2003) in adopting a broad definition of the term 'father' which encompasses married and unmarried biological fathers (whether co-resident or not and whether in contact with their children or not) and social fathers, including co-resident step-fathers, co-habiting partners and other resident and non-resident father figures.

The social and theoretical context of fatherhood in Britain

It is now widely accepted that fathers did not begin to feature to any conspicuous degree on the agenda of academics or policy-makers in the UK until the 1980s. Prior to this time, views on the role of fathers which had emerged from other sources, such as anthropological, ethological, sociological and psychoanalytical work, had produced a variety of models of family interaction. From anthropology and ethology came understanding of different types of society such as the hunter-gatherer (foraging) societies (Hewlett, 2004). In this type of society, the roles of mothers and fathers are clearly delineated: the father, as hunter, is responsible for exploring beyond the home base to procure provisions to support the family while the home-based mother's primary responsibility is to safeguard these provisions and to use them to promote the well-being of offspring. The more active bread-winner father dominates the family, earning his position of authority through his unique possession of considerable knowledge of the world beyond the home. He can impart worldly wisdom to his wife and children and act as family representative in the outside world. In this way, his social identity and responsibilities are rooted within a sphere of action which lies predominantly outside the family. The relatively uninformed mother passively respects her husband's superior wisdom, confines her attention to home-based interests and presents no challenge to her spouse's authority.

In early formulations of psychoanalytic theory, this imbalance of power was not only acknowledged but reinforced and legitimised: males, whose resolution of the Oedipal complex required them to subdue murderous impulses towards same-sex parents and to inhibit libidinous interests in opposite sex parents, were seen as capable of achieving a higher moral status than inferior females who were "weaker in their social interests" and "must be regarded as having little sense of justice" (Freud, 1933/1977, pp.168-169). A slightly different view came from other psychoanalysts, such as Donald Winnicott, who wrote that "father is needed to give mother moral support, to be the backing for her authority, to be the human being who stands for the law and order which mother plants in the life of the child" (Winnicott, 1964, p.115). Winnicott also recognised the mother's relative omnipotence in controlling father's access to children and in facilitating good father-child relationships: "I should say that it is mother's responsibility to send father and daughter, or father and son, out together for an expedition every now and again....it is very much in your power to make such a relationship possible, or to prevent it, or to mar it" (Winnicott, 1964, p.118).

That the roles of fathers and mothers were conceptually distinct had also emerged from sociological research, for example, fathers were described as fulfilling an 'instrumental-leader' function while mothers performed an 'expressive' function (Parsons and Bales, 1955). In theories of this sort, men tended to be viewed as active and engaged with the outside world while women were more passive and focused on internal, emotional matters. Dawkins (1976), from an ethological perspective, suggested that differences between mothers and fathers stemmed from contrary biological processes: in his view, fathers have a biologically-driven need to ensure the continuation of their own genes, which necessarily mitigates against investment in the stable, monogamous relationships that constitute the preferred child-rearing environment for mothers. It is perhaps not surprising that early formulations of attachment theory, which were heavily influenced by ethological and psychoanalytic traditions, attributed the quality of attachments between mothers and children to instinctive biologically-prepared responses (e.g. Bowlby, 1969) but initially provided no account of father-child relationships.

Within academic disciplines generally, until the end of the 1970's and the beginning of the 1980's, studies of the role of fathers were relatively rare. It was only at this point, in mainstream social and developmental psychology, that attention began to move beyond the mother-child dyad to the wider family context. Initially, inquiries were cast in 'mother-template mode': the tools which had been developed to explore mother-child relationships were used unquestioningly to examine father-child relationships and at the top of the research agenda was the question of how the role of fathers compared with that of mothers (Lamb, 1981; Lewis, 1987; Lewis and O'Brien, 1987).

In this literature, typically, mothers were conceptualised as having primary responsibility for the nurturing and care of children while fathers, by contrast, were seen as providing a valuable but less substantial supportive role as a secondary caregiver or 'alloparent' (Hrdy, 1999). A number of studies suggested that fathers' relationships with their children might be characterised as affiliative rather than as focused on attachment. In other words, the general view was that fathers related to their children as playmates while the role of carer was assigned to mothers who were better placed to respond to the immediate physical, emotional and social needs of their children.

Perhaps unsurprisingly, from this early research, a 'deficit model' of fathers began to emerge (Richards, 1982). It was recognised that, as principal breadwinners, fathers served a vital function in the family. However, their input in terms of the emotional life of the family did not appear anywhere near comparable in importance to that of mothers: they were more detached in many ways, less intuitively involved, considerably less skilled because less practised in childcare, biologically ill-equipped for breast-feeding and so disadvantaged from the point of view of early skin-to-skin contact and bonding, further disadvantaged because they possessed vocal organs designed to emit sounds of lower frequencies to those preferred by neonates and, finally, they almost invariably lacked experience of good same sex role models of care-giving. In short, fathers appeared to be very much in the shadow of the mother not only in relation to the decision to give birth to children but also with respect to almost every aspect of their children's upbringing.

Throughout the seventies and eighties, rising rates of separation and divorce, increased frequency of childbirth outside marriage, higher visibility of the effects of multiple relationships and changing attitudes towards gender role divisions had greatly complicated fathers' rights, roles and responsibilities towards sexual partners and children. Alternative models of fatherhood had begun to be put forward to encapsulate the nature of these relationships as well as to replace the patriarchal model which appeared to be under challenge. Dienhart (1998) describes some of these alternative models as follows: the *'new father'* who is highly nurturing of his children and much more involved in their care and in related household tasks (Lewis and O'Brien,1987); the *'hands-on'* father who, while not necessarily taking on equal responsibility for childcare, would in principle be as willing as his partner to undertake essential tasks such as changing nappies, etc. (Daniels and Weingarten, 1988); the *'enlightened father'* who, in theory, would be equally involved if it were not for institutional and work practices which mitigate against shared parenting; the *'modern father'* who is more expressive, more involved in daily life, more democratic and so less likely to be seen as an authority figure or hero (e.g. Giveans and

Robinson, 1985); the *'third-stage father'* (Barnett and Baruch, 1988) whose greater involvement in family can have positive benefits but may also produce problems if the gender roles are not satisfactorily re-negotiated.

Other typologies have emerged from sources such as Mori polls, focus group studies or content analyses of various sorts of literature and other media. Picking up on the different functions that fathers might have in relation to bread-winning, discipline, play and partnership, Haffer et al. (2002) suggested that fathers might be categorised as *'enforcer dads'* (those not involved in the everyday care of children but who envisage their role as a model and rule-setter for their children), *'entertainer dads'* (who provide a distraction for children while mother gets on with domestic chores), *'useful dads'* (who both entertain and help around the house, to a minimal extent) or *'fully involved dads'* (who share domestic and childcare tasks equally with their partners). The value of this typology, based on perusal of transcripts from focus groups carried out with fathers and employers in the north-west of England, remains to be tested.

From analysis of the content of 10 daily and 10 Sunday newspapers over four weeks in June 1994, a range of both negative and positive images emerged. The most frequently-occurring image appeared, from the details provided in the report, to have been of fathers as monsters (Lloyd, 1994: 38/90 references). Negative views are perhaps highly primed within the context of newspaper reports but need not emerge quite so readily from all other types of media. For example, an analysis of fathers in soap opera revealed a wide variety of father characters, ranging from caring, articulate and involved to aggressive, immature and irresponsible (Barrett, 2002). Analysis of novels, television documentaries, comic books, magazines and other media seems likely to produce a similarly varied range of father images.

Nevertheless, towards the end of the century, a negative view of fathers was emerging from another source for, as the financial consequences of the loosening connection between child-rearing and marriage were becoming more apparent, fathers were becoming increasingly noticeable to policy-makers by their absence (Hobson, 2002). In the US, the term *deadbeat dads* had been coined to reflect concern about the way in which fathers were failing to provide financial support to partners and children, particularly once a romantic relationship had ended.

In the UK too, between 1970 and 1990, the number of children born to unmarried mothers had trebled (from 10 to 31 per cent) and the number of lone parents claiming benefits had almost doubled. By contrast, the number of resident parents receiving child support from non-resident partners had halved (Bates et al., 2002). It had become increasingly evident that action was needed if the Government was not to be left with increasingly high bills for child support. The notion that fathers are unreliable, 'feckless' or 'ne'er-do-well' is purported to have emanated predominantly from Thatcherite days when prominent, even Prime, ministers berated fathers and vowed to change the culture which supported them in walking away from family responsibilities and allowed them to engage uncaringly in serial monogamous relationships (Burghes et al., 1997; Bradshaw et al., 1999).

At the outset of the period of interest to this report, then, negative images of fatherhood appeared to dominate much of the discourse related to policy and research yet, curiously, running counter to these images, was a sense that gender role boundaries had softened and that many fathers had been seeking, not without success, to become more involved as carers in the lives of their families. In the remainder of this chapter, we will attempt to make sense of this paradox, by examining evidence from recent reports on the nature of fathering in the last 10 years. Because the range of material available for this discussion is so vast, we have chosen to limit ourselves to seven questions which we hope will yield sufficient information to provide a reasonably balanced picture of the nature of fathering practices in the UK. The seven questions are as follows:

3.1 Have fathers become more involved in everyday childcare and household tasks?

3.2 How well do fathers care for their children?

3.3 What happens to relationships between fathers and children when parents separate?

3.4 Are fathers important for children's development anyway?

3.5 Is there any evidence that UK society has become more or less 'father-friendly'?

3.6 What do we know about life for teenage and lone parent fathers during this decade?

3.7 Has life for fathers in the UK really changed over the last decade?

As in previous chapters, where possible, we will also supply contextual material to discover social attitudes toward the role of fathers and to show how the situation for fathers in the UK might compare with fathers elsewhere in Europe.

3.1 Have fathers become more involved in everyday childcare and household tasks?

Midway through the decade of interest to this report, researchers drew attention to the long hours of work that were being expected of British fathers and the potential incompatibility of work with home life. Brannen et al. (1997) showed that British fathers were working nearer 47 hours on average compared with 42.7 hours among their European counterparts. As shown in chapter 2, fathers with children younger than 11 were also working the longest hours (O'Brien and Shemilt, 2003).

At around the same time, time use studies indicated that both mothers and fathers spend more time caring for their children than previous generations of parents, that the increase in time was greater for fathers than for mothers and that, as a consequence, the difference between mothers and fathers in the amount of time spent on childcare had reduced (Burghes et al., 1997; Gershuny, 2000; Gershuny and Sullivan, 2001). Nevertheless, mothers still carried most of the responsibility for looking after children and for housework, even when both parents were in full-time employment. Fathers still did most of DIY and mechanical maintenance tasks and few fathers undertook laundry or cooking. Further, as discussed elsewhere in this report, most mothers were still working less and earning less than fathers.

Evidence from American studies indicates that there is no direct correlation between the number of hours that fathers work and the extent to which they become involved in domestic chores or childcare responsibilities: men tend not to view housework as their responsibility regardless of the number of hours they are available to do it. However, on a more positive note, British Social Attitude survey reports (Gershuny and Sullivan, 2001) have suggested that there may be more sharing of tasks than simple counts of time use can reflect and that the nature of fathers' input may be more distal and thus not easy to capture using simple time use approaches. They also argue that this may account for discrepancies between self-reported attitudes and practice, where fathers have described themselves as having more input than observers have reported. They suggest that the discrepancy might reflect the nature of fathers' care rather than a lack of fathers' care. Clearly, this is an area where more information is needed.

Moss (1995) identified two apparently opposite trends in fathers' behaviour: some fathers appear to have become more caring and others more distant. In this connection, it seems likely that different processes might be at work among different populations of parents, that relationship dynamics between dual-earner couples and others might be qualitatively different and that variations may be found within different geographical and cultural populations. In this respect, time use studies have been limited in the extent to which they can inform about the processes involved in parents' negotiations around their use of time and how attitudes may have changed or impacted on parental relationships.

Birth cohort studies are a rich source of information about change and continuity of practices and experiences within and across families over time. Using data from three major UK birth cohort studies (1946, 1958 and 1970), Ferri and Smith (Ferri and Smith, 1996, 2003a, 2003b) investigated a number of aspects of family life, including work experience and childcare arrangements, responsibility for childcare and household tasks, and experiences of divorce and re-marriage. From inspection of 1958 and 1970 birth cohort responses when respondents were 33 and 30 respectively, Ferri and Smith (2003b) found that it was twice as common for parents to report that they shared childcare equally when both parents were working as compared with families where only one parent was working, a finding which agreed with their earlier conclusions in respect of the 1958 data (Ferri and Smith, 1996). However, they also rather surprisingly found that, contrary to the notion that the 'new man' caring father would be more prevalent in the later birth cohort, women born in 1970 were *less* likely than mothers in the 1958 cohort to report shared caring. And in both cohorts, there was a discrepancy between mothers' and fathers' reports of the extent to which fathers undertook shared responsibility for childcare. Ferri and Smith (2003b) suggest that two processes might account for this: first, the accounts given by men in the later birth cohort might be more heavily influenced by social pressures to appear to be doing more at home; second, working mothers might expect and need more from their partners and so be less inclined to accept less than equal input than previous generations had been.

Ferri and Smith (2003b) also confirmed their earlier findings with regard to the lack of a positive association between fathers' social class or education and involvement in shared childcare. They found that fathers with more educational qualifications were *less* likely to engage in shared childcare (only 37 per cent of fathers with higher degrees as opposed to 59 per cent of fathers with no qualifications) while fathers in professional and managerial occupations also engaged less in shared care than fathers in skilled or semi-skilled manual occupations (39 per cent vs 60 per cent, respectively). Ferri and Smith (2003b) further reported that fathers in the 1970 birth cohort worked longer hours than earlier cohorts and that this appeared to be having an impact on the extent to which they contributed to family life. They questioned whether this factor might also be implicated in the higher incidence of relationship difficulties in the 1970 cohort (Ferri and Smith, 2003a).

Warin, Solomon, Lewis and Langford, et al. (1999) report on a study which aimed to explore the extent to which housework and childcare tasks were shared in 'work-rich' and 'work-poor' families. Using as their base families living in Rochdale who had previously taken part in a 1986 survey, they selected 95 adults (53 women and 42 men) with children aged 11-16 for further follow-up interviews. The sample included 21 families from the Indian subcontinent (18 Punjabi, three Bengali). It also contained both biological and social fathers (with some children conceived using IVF and one child who was reared by grandparents). A variety of working arrangements was represented: in 22 per cent of families, both adults worked full-time while in 28 per cent of families neither parent was working; in 21 per cent of families, the father worked full-time and the mother part-time and, in the remaining families, only one adult worked (full-time: 19 per cent; part-time: 9 per cent).

Warin et al. (1999) found that, in just under three-quarters of dual-earner households in their sample, mothers did most of the housework, although 18 per cent of parents shared the burden equally and nine per cent of fathers were described as doing more housework than mothers. They described the majority of fathers as having a traditional view of their role in the family: they saw their ability to provide materially as of central importance and preferred to see their partner's contribution as relatively minor. The status conferred by father's ability to perform their provider role was seen to impact on self esteem so that men who were less able to be in control of material goods, for example, younger fathers or those who were not employed for any reason, experienced lower self esteem and saw themselves as less competent parents. Fathers who were unemployed or sick generally retained this view of their role and consequently did not take on any more childcare or housework even if they were available to do so.

Warin et al. (1999) further observed that fathers often experienced the dual role of carer and provider as a double burden and tended to rate their own involvement in the home as being rather less important than in their partners' view. Men's and women's attitudes toward paid employment and childcare differed considerably too. While fathers saw their paid employment as a financial imperative, mothers tended to value theirs because it was a way of gaining greater independence. Mothers also claimed more expertise in childcare and parenting issues and often viewed the father's role as somewhat peripheral to these tasks. In public, fathers in this sample liked to be seen as head of the family. A key message from this study, therefore, was that it provided little evidence of a move towards a new model of fatherhood. Rather, the suggestion was that role strain is created when pressure is put on fathers to fulfil more than the provider role which they feel they must try to maintain and which remains a key benchmark informing their self-assessment as competent parents.

These findings, then, provide little evidence of fathers having become more closely identified with the role of carer but, rather, reinforce the view that many fathers continue to espouse a more traditional view of their role. It is important to remember, though, that these conclusions are based on a small, qualitative study. While the kind of community from which the sample was drawn may not be atypical of rural England, it is possible that it reflects a location in the UK where work patterns and gender role relationships may not have changed as much over the last few decades as in other parts of the country. Also, it is not clear from the details given whether the participants drawn from minority ethnic groups were recent or later generation immigrants nor how typical their views might have been. For these reasons, it is perhaps wise to view these findings as valuable in their capacity to generate hypotheses for further checking rather than as conclusive evidence of contemporary trends.

Evidence from other sources, though, does seem to support the view that role strain in parents can have a detrimental effect on family relationships. DeFranc and Mahalik (2002) observed that children's perceptions of gender role strain in parents impacts on the quality of their relationships with parents. Also a growing literature indicates that 'negative spillover' (negative effects of work pressure on home life) produces poorer family relationships. Fathers who are satisfied with their work and who do not feel pressure to work long hours report greater satisfaction with family relationships (O'Brien and Shemilt, 2003).

It also seems possible that, in some parts of the UK, where mothers are able to earn as much or more than their partners, fathers may feel more free to take up alternative family roles. In support of this notion, O'Brien and Shemilt (2003) point out that mothers' income is a stronger predictor of father involvement than mothers' employment alone and that it is not until parents experience the gender pay gap as no longer being influential that fathers may feel free to relinquish the bread-winner role.

3.2   How well do fathers care for their children?

Summing up their assessment of how well fathers care for children, Lamb and Lewis (2004) conclude that there are qualitative differences between father-child and mother-child relationships and that the quality of fathers' relationships is best captured when investigations use tools which are developed to be particularly sensitive to the nature of the father's role. Since it is now well established that the nature of fathers' input is highly dependent upon social contextual factors (for example, family size, structure, mother's attitudes and social constraints such as culture and employment patterns), it is important that researchers take account of these factors when drawing comparisons between fathers and mothers.

Lamb and Lewis (2004) assert that fathers are as likely as mothers to adapt positively to parenting. However, they also point out that the quality of fathers' relationships with newborns is strongly associated with their own experiences of parental care and that it can be modified by post-natal depression (a condition which, in fathers, has received relatively little attention until recently). They draw attention to evidence showing that fathers experience hormonal changes around the birth of a first baby (Storey et al., 2000), and that mothers and fathers are quite similar in the extent to which they vary their speech and behaviour, both in interaction with babies or toddlers and in response to older children's preferences, age, understanding and interests.

On the other hand, Lamb and Lewis (2004) note that fathers have tended to be judged as less perceptive of their infants' states and as rather less effective than mothers in soothing their infants. It has also been observed that, by four months of age, infants usually prefer the higher pitched voices of mothers (Ward and Cooper, 1999) though it is not yet clear that any of these effects would obtain in the case of infants raised predominantly by their fathers from birth.

Differences between fathers and mothers in styles of play have been observed from the beginning of father-child interactions: fathers engage in a more stimulating style of interaction, are more prone to tease, more intrusive, more likely to engage in rough-and-tumble play and in arousing play, and are, in most though not all cultures, more likely to spend time on play than on caretaking (Lewis and Lamb, 2004). By adolescence, qualitative differences in children's relationships with each parent are also in evidence. In one UK study, although mothers and fathers were equally likely to help their children with homework (Solomon et al., 2002), teenagers reported spending more time with and feeling closer to mothers than to fathers, although there was a question about whether this closeness might have been moderated by the extent to which fathers were cast in the role of disciplinarian (Langford et al., 2001).

Perhaps unsurprisingly, given the relative control that fathers and mothers may feel they have over the quality of their relationship with their children, studies have found that fathers tend to feel less satisfied with their new role as parents than mothers (Dulude, Wright and Belanger, 2000). Fathers' satisfaction has also been found by some researchers to be closely correlated with their satisfaction with their relationship with the child's mother (e.g. Bouchard and Lee, 2000). After parental separation or divorce, these differences can become even more starkly apparent.

3.3 What happens to relationships between fathers and children when parents separate?

Outside the UK, a number of large-scale studies have investigated outcomes of parental divorce and separation in terms of children's psychosocial adjustment and their social, cognitive and emotional development (e.g. Amato and Booth, 1997; Amato and Rogers, 1997; Emery et al., 1999; Hetherington, 1999; Wallerstein and Blakeslee, 1989; Wallerstein and Corbin, 1989). These have suggested that it is the quality of the relationship before divorce that appears most predictive of the quality of relationships after parents separate, that older children have greater difficulty adjusting especially if they have had no warning of problems and have not been well informed about what was happening in the family, that boys react with more challenging behaviours than girls and that there are more serious consequences for children's adjustment if parents prolong co-residence where there is serious conflict. No consistent patterns have yet been identified in respect of amount or frequency of contact on the quality of the relationship between a non-resident parent and his/her children (Stewart, 2003).

Inside the UK, as in so many areas of social research, a substantial study into this important and complex area has yet to be conducted. Currently, very little is known about what happens to relationships between fathers and children when parental relationships break down. A daunting number of questions has yet to be addressed concerning, first, the nature of the relationship between the parents, second, the nature of the relationship breakdown and, third, the nature of subsequent arrangements. With regard to the nature of the relationship, account needs to be taken of whether the relationship involved cohabitation or marriage, whether it was a first or a later partnership, whether children were biologically or socially related to their carers, whether it involved violence or other anti-social elements, whether it began in adolescence or later, whether there were stresses to do with disability, unemployment or other social or personal disadvantages within the family, whether there were particular pressures pertaining to race or culture, or to do with the influence of extended family members, etc.. With regard to the nature of the relationship breakdown, aspects to consider include whether the separation was a mutual decision or primarily one person's choice, whether other adults were implicated, whether the decision to separate involved temporary separations before a final split, whether outside advice was sought and, if so, by whom, whether couples involved intermediaries such as solicitors or court welfare officers or other court officials to resolve differences over childcare arrangements. Finally, aspects relating to the nature of subsequent arrangements range through arrangements for access to and care of children, geographical proximity and housing arrangements, financial provision, as well as the personal circumstances of both parents. Another important matter about which very little is yet understood concerns cross-national divorce. In these situations, international differences are likely to complicate the process of negotiation both for parents and for professionals called upon to arbitrate in disputes.

Nevertheless, some data has emerged from UK birth cohort studies (e.g. Richards et al., 1997; Ely et al., 1999) as well as from other national and large-scale community studies (Kiernan and Hobcraft, 1997; Dunn, 2003) although, as these were not initially designed specifically to track the effects of divorce, the amount of information they can provide is necessarily somewhat limited. In addition, a number of small-scale, usually qualitative, studies has been conducted, based mainly on volunteer samples with the associated problems that these entail. Even so, these studies have produced indicative data in respect of important issues and so are useful pointers toward further areas in need of research.

As has already been emphasised earlier in this report, it was largely problems with financing families after parental separation and divorce that brought fatherhood onto the agenda of policy-makers in the UK. By the mid 1980s, it had become evident that many mothers following parental separation were living in relative poverty, were prone to more health problems and were not receiving maintenance from ex-partners (Haskey, 1998; Oppenheim and Harker, 1998; Benzeval, 1998; Shouls et al., 1999). Links between childhood poverty and poor educational and social outcomes for children reinforced a sense of the need for urgent action if the Government was not to be left to fill the shortfall which had resulted from the de-coupling of marriage and parenthood (Burns and Scott, 1994).

Fathers had become visible by their absence (Bradshaw et al., 1999; Burghes et al., 1997; Gingerbread, 2001). In an effort to reinstate fathers as the key providers for their children, in 1991, the Child Support Act was passed and this initiative was followed up, in 1993, by the setting up of the Child Support Agency (CSA). Its remit was (a) to trace non-resident parents, (b) to assess how much maintenance non-resident parents should pay, (c) to ensure that money is paid and, (d) to collect payments (from source) if necessary. These developments set the stage for a relationship between authorities and non-resident parents which has at times been characterised by acrimony and desperation worthy of the most bitter of parental relationships. New regulations in 1994 and a new Child Support Act in 1995 changed the formula for calculating CSA payments in an attempt to overcome the difficulties that the new Agency was experiencing. Nevertheless, the effectiveness of the CSA in achieving its intended goals is still unclear.

Bradshaw et al. (1999) report a survey carried out in 1995-96 in the initial phase of CSA. They found that the CSA appeared more often to be intervening in established payment arrangements rather than tracking down non-paying fathers and that almost all fathers who had contact with CSA were highly critical of it, believing that the payment assessment process was unfair. Most fathers felt that the CSA assessment had not taken account of their living expenses, nor of other costs or outstanding debts, e.g. the expenses incurred during visits to or by children. Of the fathers who were not paying maintenance fees set by CSA, 63 per cent were genuinely unable to pay. Only one third of mothers reported that they were receiving the full maintenance they were entitled to, that is, about the same proportion as before CSA was introduced.

As Bradshaw et al. (1999) point out, the CSA takes the approach that fathers have lifelong financial obligations to children from a previous marriage, who are assumed to be the fathers' legal responsibility. Many fathers disputed this obligation for a number of reasons. Perhaps the most compelling argument came from fathers who were dissatisfied with the arrangements made for contact with their children and who were also unhappy with the restrictions placed on their role in parenting their children. While fathers may value their role as providers for their children, the expectation that they will give unqualified support to a new regime, which is often presided over by a rival male, seems somewhat unrealistic. Legal and humane perspectives would seem to differ on this: the law views fathers' financial obligations as the right of the child regardless of parent-child relationships. The fathers, on the other hand, may resent an obligation which forces them to collude with a situation over which they feel they have little control, particularly if their relationship breakdown has involved loss of income and material status for them. They may wish to retain a more informal financial relationship, in which their gifting of financial support is appreciated on a more personal level by their children. It is not clear that, once the CSA has intervened to set levels of payment, fathers are left with sufficient resources to feel able to engage in this important, personally negotiated relationship.

Further information about the ability of couples to agree on financial management comes from a recent survey of couples by Direct Debit (BACS Payment Schemes, April 2004) which claimed that a third of couples in current relationships were 'financially incompatible'. Among all respondents, only 39 per cent of men and 34 per cent of women described themselves as jointly looking after household accounts. Complaints about partners' behaviour ranged from spending too much money (12 per cent men and 9 per cent of women complained about this), being disorganised and forgetting to pay bills (complained of by 9 per cent men and 11 per cent of women), being hopeless at saving (complaint by 4 per cent of men, 9 per cent of women), stretching the truth about how much they've spent (5 per cent of men and 4 per cent of women), being miserly with money (complained of by 5 per cent of men and 8 per cent of women). Although this survey cannot be said to be representative, it does suggest that there may be a rather high level of disagreement and non-cooperation over financial matters in relationships that have not broken down. It seems unsurprising that this level of apparent distrust might later translate into intractable problems once relationships have foundered. It also seems unlikely that a legal framework which uses the language of rights and duties will successfully address or unravel the complex emotional and personal issues which precede or compound disagreements.

In the early 1990s, Bradshaw and Millar (1991) estimated that 35 per cent of non-resident parents had no contact with their children. An earlier UK study (Simpson et al., 1995) also suggested that fathers were three times more likely to stay in touch with boys than with girls and that, overall, they had stayed in touch with around sixty per cent of their children. Burghes et al. (1997), reviewing evidence from UK studies, reported that, although contact was almost always reduced between fathers and children after separation, in the one in six cases where fathers were living apart from some or all of their biological children, the majority of fathers did retain contact.

How much contact fathers have with their children after parental separation is, however, difficult to assess objectively. Accurate assessments are complicated by difficulties associated with a general lack of agreement on how to define contact as well as by failure to incorporate adequate analysis of the effects of children's ages (an important matter given the natural variability in contact across the lifespan) and, in UK studies at least, there has been a lack of comparison data drawn from patterns of contact in intact families. As with time use studies, simple counts of the amount of time fathers spend with children often fail to inform about the quality of father-child relationships and almost always involve cross-sectional measures that neglect consideration of changes over time. Consistent direct relationships between frequency or amount of contact and quality of father-child relationships have not emerged from research studies and more recent research (Dunn, 2003; Maclean and Eekelaar, 1997) has tended to use more subtle measures of contact and to have concluded that failure to maintain any kind of father-child contact may be relatively rare. An accurate assessment of the actual situation, however, seems likely only to emerge on the basis of a representative study which does not rely on volunteer samples and which incorporates measurement of all relevant factors. Such a study has not yet been conducted in the UK.

Gender differences have not been found systematically across studies and speculation about direction of effects in the absence of sound empirical evidence (i.e. do children choose not to contact fathers or vice versa?) is unlikely to be informative. More important is information about perceptions of the nature of relationship breakdown and the impact of this on subsequent relationships (Gorrell Barnes et al., 1998; Geldof, 2003). Qualitative interviews with children and fathers, as well as information from a postal survey of fathers, have suggested complex and changing processes associated with children's and fathers' behaviour after parental separation (Barrett and Tasker, unpublished data): it was not unusual for children to report having varied their strategies in line with changing perceptions of parents' relationships (for example, refusing contact when contact appeared to escalate conflict between parents but re-engaging it when the situation between parents was less volatile); nor was it unusual for fathers to report having to 'hang in' for long periods of time with very little contact and often with little belief in their capacity to reinstate a meaningful relationship with their children; sometimes fathers only managed to establish a relationship once the children had become independent adults. Short-term small-scale studies are unlikely to capture these aspects which promise to contribute importantly to a fuller understanding of father-child relationships.

One recent qualitative study of 140 family members drawn from 61 families (48 resident parents, 35 'contact parents' and 57 children and young people with a mean age of 10.8 years) set out to investigate what might characterise 'working' and 'not working' contact arrangements. Three major categories of arrangements were identified: 'consensual committed' working arrangements, 'faltering' and 'conflicted' non-working arrangements (Trinder et al., 2002). 'Consensual committed' arrangements were characterised by relatively high commitment to contact by both parents and by children, relatively well controlled inter-parental conflict, more clearly defined parental roles and valuing of role of the non-resident parent in family life; 'faltering' arrangements were characterised by lower commitment to contact on the part of parents and children, some acceptance of the importance of the non-resident parent's input, little evidence of conflict but some evidence of mutual frustration due to a failure to address difficulties associated with making successful contact arrangements; 'conflicted' arrangements were characterised by asymmetric commitment to contact (with the non-resident parent often being blocked by the resident parent and with no evidence of reciprocal bargaining), mutual hostility and denigration, and subsequent failure to reach consensual agreements on most aspects of parenting. In summing up findings from this study, Trinder et al. acknowledge the difficulty of arriving at prescriptive solutions to cover the highly complex relationship issues surrounding contact arrangements and also question the validity of a default assumption that contact is beneficial. This position is not as extreme as that of some US researchers who have suggested that the non-resident parent's input is relatively unimportant but it does perhaps touch on a larger issue to which we will now turn concerning the importance of fathers to children's development more generally.

3.4   Are fathers important for children's development anyway?

Throughout the 1990s, the opinion has often been expressed, generally by commentators known for somewhat reactionary views though not only confined to these, that fathers have disappeared from family life and that their absence is responsible for rising youth crime as well as for other social ills (Murray, 1990; Dennis and Erdos, 1992; Popenoe, 1996; Phares, 1997). These rather polemical views are unlikely to be shared by researchers taking the view that direction of causal effects can only be confidently established through rigorously designed studies (e.g. Rutter, in press).

Nevertheless, since the issue of fatherhood came onto the policy agenda, it has become fairly common for campaign groups and other pro-father lobbyists to popularise the view both that fathers' involvement in family life is substantial and that it has positively beneficial outcomes for children. Typical claims include the following: children of involved fathers perform more highly on tests of cognitive functioning at most ages, tend to come from homes that are more cognitively stimulating and behave more appropriately at school (Pedersen et al., 1980; Radin, 1994; Cooksey and Fondell, 1996; William, 1997; Horn and Sylvester, 2002); they are also more likely to perform better on measures of peer interaction, psychosocial adjustment and work-related achievement (Field et al., 1995; Harris et al., 1998; Easterbrooks and Goldberg, 1990; McRae, 1999); involved fathers have higher self esteem, rate their satisfaction with their parenting role more highly and have better physical and psychological health (Snarey, 1993; Pleck, 1997); finally, involved fathers tend also to participate more positively in community life (Eggebean and Knoester, 2001). The particular advantages or disadvantages of father involvement or absence in relation to boy and girl children may also be highlighted, for example, in a study of 369 households (Hoffman and Youngblade, 1999), associations were found between greater involvement by fathers in childcare and children's school attainment: girls with more highly involved fathers tended to have less stereotypical views of parents' expectations about their own gender role behaviour while both girls and boys appeared to benefit from fathers' role as family mediator.

Encouraging though such findings may be, the combined risks of biased selectivity and over-generalisation need to be recognised. Fathers are by no means a homogeneous group and a more balanced approach may be needed if the diversity of roles and relationships among fathers and children, both young and old, throughout the UK is to be captured. It is also very important, as mentioned earlier, to bear in mind the fact that strong positive associations do not imply causality and that father-child relationships occur within social contexts that vary considerably. This often means that strong positive associations are mediated or moderated by mother-related influences and that, unless these processes are accounted for, the true nature of the father's influence may be inaccurately evaluated.

The above point reflects the view of workers like Palkovitz (1997) who criticise the assumption that fathers' involvement with their children is either qualitatively or quantitatively comparable with that of mothers. Arguing that the concept of involvement needs to be re-theorised, Palkovitz questions many conclusions traditionally drawn from comparisons of mothers and fathers and claims that research has been flawed conceptually, often, by faulty operational definitions. For example, he argues that level of involvement should not be measured in terms of amount of time spent on caring for children since it is possible to be involved without actually being physically present. He further argues that, to capture the true extent and quality of fathers' involvement, it is necessary to re-define involvement so that it incorporates more subtle forms of involvement which occur within the wider social context. This move toward a broader conceptualisation of fathers' involvement is also reflected in the notion of generativity (cross-generational influences) proposed by Hawkins and Dollahite (1997) and the more systems-oriented perspective of theorists like Biller (1993) who assert the need to see fathers' contribution in the context of the whole mother-father-child-system.

By way of practical example, in a UK study of differences on child outcomes among children reared in father-absent homes, Joshi et al., 2000 suggested that family structure accounted for very little of the variance related to children's cognitive performance and that long-term social disadvantages such as poverty and parents' own educational attainments were more strongly related.

Another recent study has shown that father involvement can be good or bad (Jaffee et al., 2001; Jaffee et al., 2003) and that anti-social fathers can have a very negative impact on children's development. Inspecting data from a longitudinal study carried out in Dunedin, New Zealand, Jaffee et al. (2003) showed that, although the incidence of behaviour problems in children was generally higher where fathers spent less time living with the family, this pattern only applied to fathers who did not exhibit antisocial behaviour: the length of time that children lived with an antisocial father was also strongly correlated with behaviour problems. Jaffee et al. (2003) suggest that children who live with an antisocial father may be doubly exposed to negative influences, from both genetic and environmental sources. On the basis of these findings, they further argue that "marriage may not be the answer to problems faced by some children living in single-parent families unless their fathers can become reliable sources of emotional and economic support" (Jaffee et al., 2003, p.109).

A UK study, based on data from the 1974 follow-up of the 17,000 children registered on a 1958 birth cohort study (the National Child Development Study), examined parental involvement with children in intact families (Flouri and Buchanan, 2002; Flouri and Buchanan, 2003a). Flouri and Buchanan (2002) found that, for boys only, IQ, father involvement and parental criminality were negatively related to being in trouble with the police at age 16; for girls, non-intact family structure in childhood was associated with being in trouble with the police. In their later paper, Flouri and Buchanan (2003b) reported that fathers were more likely to be highly involved when children were not assessed as behaviourally or temperamentally difficult and also more involved in their children's education when their children were doing well academically; further, they tended to be more involved in managing and undertaking outings with sons than with daughters.

Flouri and Buchanan (2003a) posit possible two-directional causal influences and suggest that fathers may find it easier to be involved with children who are not difficult while children may do better educationally when their fathers are more involved. However, the precise nature of causal influences remains unknown in the absence of a controlled study, and Flouri and Buchanan stress the need for further caution on the grounds of sample attrition and possible datedness.

In a separate study (Flouri et al., 2002; Flouri and Buchanan, 2003a), questionnaires were administered to adolescents aged 14 to 18. 2,722 adolescents responded to questions about their attitude to school and their experiences of the extent to which their parents took interest in their school work or spent time talking with them and listening to their worries. The adolescents also rated themselves on measures of happiness, self-efficacy and depression and indicated the existence of conflict at home. Again, the cross-sectional design prevented identification of causal influences.

However, the study indicated that father involvement was perceived as importantly contributing, independently of mother involvement, both to adolescents' emotional wellbeing and to their positive attitudes to education. These effects appeared to be as strong for boys as for girls.

In an effort to discover more about children's views on the importance of their father's role, O'Brien and Jones (1995) asked 3rd and 4th year secondary school children in East London (mean age 14 years 9 months) to fill in a questionnaire in the class-room and to keep a diary for one week on the time they spent with parents at home. Living arrangements varied: the majority of children (68 per cent) were living at home with both natural parents, a substantial minority were living in step-families (14 per cent) or in lone parent households (16 per cent: 12 per cent with mothers and 4 per cent with fathers). The majority of teenagers in this sample (reported by Clarke and O'Brien, 2004, to consist of 620 young people) were white (83 per cent), nine per cent were Asian, five per cent Black, and two per cent from other minority ethnic backgrounds

In this study, children were asked about their preferences for father involvement in a range of family situations. Their responses showed that the majority (95 per cent) thought their fathers should be present at the birth of a baby and that a somewhat smaller majority (70 per cent) also thought their fathers should have access to paid paternity leave. Reasons given for fathers' involvement at the birth of a baby included support for the mother (42 per cent), because it is a father's right (28 per cent) and to bond with baby (21 per cent). Very similar reasons were given for access to paid paternity leave: 52 per cent thought paternity leave was needed so that fathers could give mothers more support (a view more frequently expressed by girls than boys), 22 per cent thought it was the fathers' right and 20 per cent thought paternity leave would be valuable in helping fathers get to know the baby. However, a substantial minority of young people (30 per cent) were against the principle of paternity leave because they felt it was more important that fathers earned money (38 per cent), because they felt mothers, not fathers, needed a rest after childbirth (29 per cent), because they felt only one person was needed to care for a newborn baby (14 per cent) or because they felt caring for newborn babies was the mother's responsibility (13 per cent).

Fewer than a quarter of the girls (23 per cent) and fewer than half of the boys (44 per cent) felt that their fathers understood them well. Fewer than a quarter of the adolescents in the study said that they would seek their fathers' help with home-work (23 per cent) or with problems at school (17 per cent), although slightly more said that they talked to their fathers about money worries (44 per cent), problems with their mother (38 per cent) or sports (31 per cent). In addition, fathers were reported as rarely participating in household tasks, with the exception of organis-ing household bills (41 per cent), helping with shopping (29 per cent) and doing repairs (8 per cent). When asked what they felt their fathers should do, 34 per cent said that fathers should earn money, 27 per cent said that they should spend time caring for and being with their children while 25 per cent said fathers should undertake domestic activities. Only four per cent thought their fathers should be role models.

The authors concluded that these young people, who were predominantly from working class homes, appeared to endorse a *new father* model of fatherhood. Further studies would be valuable to test the validity of these conclusions and to assess how reliable the results might be in a larger, more representative sample of children in the UK.

3.5 Is there any evidence that UK society has become more or less 'father-friendly'?

Clarke and Roberts (2002) comment that British policies affecting fatherhood are formulated in response to political decisions, not research evidence, a finding that would seem to suggest that policy changes have not generally been based on consideration of the needs of fathers nor of the complex way in which these needs might be shaped by the fathers' social context.

In an attempt to explore how employers feel about paternity leave and other father-friendly employment practices, O'Brien and Shemilt (2003) elicited comments from a sample of employers. They found that large public sector organisations with a high percentage of female employees were more likely to offer family-friendly work conditions, i.e. to provide opportunities for job-sharing, working from home, or for employees to manage their hours of work flexibly in other ways. Few employers seemed to feel confident that their businesses could accommodate more flexible work practices and remain competitive, a finding which led O'Brien and Shemilt to comment on the need for a systematic cost-benefit analysis of the effects on employers of flexible working. They further commented on the difficulty for fathers of changing their work arrangements in isolation from their social context: if employers do not feel sufficiently secure to freely offer greater flexibility to employees, regardless of their legal obligations or of the human rights implications for fathers, fathers are unlikely to feel able to change their practices.

O'Brien and Shemilt (2003) also noted that fathers tend to have relatively low take-up of available services. One recent study of fathers' views on family services (Ghate, Shaw and Hazel, 2000) indicated that a mutual distrust may characterise attitudes between fathers and professionals: fathers were uneasy about using family centre services while family centre workers were similarly uneasy about their relationship with fathers. In a similar vein, Featherstone (2001) queried whether some professionals might be inclined to view fathers as more of a risk than a resource. Early reports of the success of Sure Start schemes in engaging fathers also point to the need for special efforts to be made if barriers are to be overcome (Lloyd, O'Brien and Lewis, 2003).

Looking at fathers' experiences of support from health services around the time of child birth, Singh and Newburn (2000) gave a slightly more optimistic account of fathers' involvement in events around their partners' pregnancy. Questionnaires were initially sent out antenatally via mothers to male partners and 817 were returned by these men (37 per cent of the total possible sample). These respondents were again contacted six months after the birth of a child when 463 complete questionnaires were returned. From the information given, the authors concluded that fathers typically want more information about their role during pregnancy and after childbirth, and that most fathers want to be more involved. This applied particularly to first-time fathers. Singh and Newburn concluded that fathers may benefit from single-sex antenatal classes, from more social and emotional support, from paid parental leave and from greater flexibility from employers. They suggested that time was the main constraint that prevented greater involvement. The relatively low rate of questionnaire return (just over 20 per cent), though, possibly limits the generalisability of these findings. Nevertheless, these findings would also appear to agree with those of other workers.

Quinton et al. (2002), in their study of young couples and health visitors in Bath, found both that fathers often felt excluded by health care professionals from involvement with ante-natal and post-natal care and that health service professionals knew little about the fathers, felt unsure about their skills in relating to them and did not always see fathers as relevant to their work. Also, in a small study of Black and minority ethnic men's use of family centres, Butt and Box (1998) found that referral processes to centres tended to make men feel marginalised. And, in a review of a number of studies, Bignall and Butt (2001) concluded that many minority ethnic fathers find it difficult to become involved in a range of different childcare settings, for a variety of reasons, including the nature of the organisations, the attitudes of staff, as well as the fathers' behaviour.

There would appear to be many cultural, social and legal factors that complicate relationships between men and their children. We noted earlier in this chapter the financial and practical difficulties that many fathers experience after parental divorce, and the particular difficulties faced by unmarried fathers. These problems would suggest that some, though by no means all, fathers might not experience legal services as very 'father-friendly', in spite of the considerable efforts that have been made by many professionals within the legal system to review and improve procedures. Other studies have also suggested that fathers often find it difficult to relate to staff in childcare settings and can feel marginalised. The workplace, within which the social identity of men is often closely tied is in many ways, due to its emphasis on productivity, set up almost in opposition to less immediate means-to-productivity aims such as rearing children. In some senses, it could be said that the most severe social pressures on men may encourage their acquiescence in a less involved parenting role. Also, as Lewis (2000) points out, men appear reluctant to receive support: they are reluctant to discuss problems in their parenting or relationships and this reluctance is compounded by the fact that services target mothers as users rather than fathers. These observations seem to indicate that, as many researchers and others have concluded, there is a need to develop strategies to enable fathers to be better integrated into childcare settings. But perhaps it is also even more important to consider how the work place ethos might be changed so that work and family life are less in competition?

Paternity and parental leave allowances

As was seen in chapter two, throughout European countries, policies on maternity and parental leave vary considerably. The same is true in respect of paternity leave. While, in most countries, some allowance is made for parents to take time off work to care for sick children (parental leave), this allowance is often limited in some way, for example, being a quota to be used by the family rather than by a specified parent, or being limited to only one parent. Where these limitations obtain, it has been found that the lower-earning parent or the parent with the least secure post, who is often the mother, will take parental leave when necessary (O'Brien, 2004). In at least half of Europe, this leave is unpaid and only available while children are very young: in the majority of countries, parental leave is only available for children up to one year old though a few extend this time limit to two (Austria) or three years (Germany, France, Spain, Sweden, Finland).

Until recently, the UK was among the countries in the European Union that resisted European Union recommendations with respect to paternity leave allowances. Paternity leave differs from parental leave in that its purpose is to enable fathers to be involved in childcare around the time of the birth of a baby. Typically, policies on paternity leave will recommend that employers allow between one or three weeks (though only two days in Spain). However, willingness on the part of governments to endorse policies on leave entitlement is not always shared by employers whose reservations may subtly influence employees to the extent that they feel unable to take advantage of their entitlement, even if they are aware of their rights to it which, often, they are not (O'Brien and Shemilt, 2003).

In the UK, fathers of children born on or after 6 April 2003 (or earlier than this if children are born before the expected arrival date), became entitled to two weeks' paid paternity leave on condition that (a) they had or expected to have responsibility for the child's upbringing, (b) they were either the child's biological father or the husband or partner of the child's mother, (c) they had worked continuously for their employer for 26 weeks ending with the 15th week before the baby was due, (d) they had informed their employer of their intention to take leave 15 weeks before the baby was due (unless this is not reasonably practicable). A flat rate payment of £100 per week is payable unless fathers normally earn less than this, in which case payment is 90 per cent of their normal wage. Fathers earning less than £75 per week (i.e. less than the lower earnings limit for national insurance) do not qualify for SPP (Statutory Paternity Pay) but may be eligible for Income Support.

Table 3.1: Paternity leave
Sources of information: O'Brien, 2004, based on Deven and Moss, 2002; Clearinghouse on
International Developments in Child, Youth and Family Policies at Columbia University

	PATERNITY LEAVE ENTITLEMENT		
	Amount	**Rate of payment**	**Other conditions**
Austria	10 days	Paid	
Belgium	3 days	100%	
Denmark	2 weeks	Earnings-related	Up to a "low maximum"
Finland	18 days	Under 70%	Proposed increase to 25 days
France	3 weeks	Earnings-related (100%)	
Germany	None		
Greece	None		
Ireland	None		
Italy	None		
Luxembourg	None		Could use family leave
Netherlands	2 days	Paid	
Norway	4 weeks	Unpaid	
Poland	None?		
Portugal	5 days	Earnings-related (100%)	
Spain	2 days	100%	
Sweden	2 weeks	Up to 70%	
UK	2 weeks	See text (above)	Take within 56 days of birth

Men rarely take parental leave within first year of child's birth (Moss and Deven, 1999) and it would appear that breast-feeding patterns may have considerable influence on the way couples negotiate use of parental leave at this stage. Bruning and Plantenga (1999) observed that, where parental leave is a family entitlement, it tends to be taken by mothers. Paternity leave is more likely to be taken by fathers if there is high wage compensation, if the entitlement is non-transferable, if the scheme is well-publicised and supported by the government and if its uptake allows for some flexibility (Smith, 2002).

The majority of fathers in most studies report satisfaction with the effects of having taken leave, either in terms of improved family relationships or of having more time to spend with the family. However, some studies suggest that, for a minority of fathers, the option of taking leave might increase stress (Haas, 1992) or that positive effects are only experienced in a context where parents are not experiencing pressure to work longer hours (Chuang et al., 2003).

3.6   What do we know about life for teenage and lone parent fathers during this decade?

Teenage fathers

In the early and mid nineties, concerns about high rates of teenage pregnancy in the UK (Botting et al., 1998) led to the formulation of the Government's 10-year Teenage Pregnancy strategy. This sets out to halve the rate of conceptions among teenagers under 18, to increase their rates of participation in education and training to 60 per cent and to reduce their risk of long-term exclusion by 2010. It also aims to set a firmly established downward trend in the rate of conceptions among under-16s by the same date. A nationwide survey has been instigated to track progress on the implementation of this strategy (the most recent report being BMRB International 2003) and this is yielding information drawn from around 750 teenagers aged between 13 and 21 about their sexual practices and knowledge.

Data from US studies have indicated a number of disadvantages associated with teenage fatherhood (e.g. Teti and Lamb, 1986; Marsiglio and Cohan, 1997). In comparison with older fathers, young fathers have been described as having less knowledge of child development, less experience of caring for young infants and less tolerance of temperamentally difficult infants (Marsiglio and Cohan, 1997). They are also less likely to have children in long-term, stable relationships and so more likely to be fathering in a relationship where there is tension and conflict. Since young fathers are thought likely still to be 'finding their feet' as young men, it has been argued that they may be rather more focused on establishing their status in a same sex peer group than in investing in a stable, intimate relationship (Lamb and Elster, 1986); these authors also suggest that young fathers may not be at a cognitive developmental level at which they find it easy to 'de-centre' and appreciate the needs of small children. Further observations suggest that adolescent fathers are more likely than same-age adolescent mothers to ignore infants' social bids (Frodi and Lamb, 1978; Nash and Feldman, 1981). Hawkins et al. (1993) also comment that younger fathers may be less likely to subscribe to the 'generativity' motive, that is, the wish to pass on values to a younger generation, since they are likely still to view themselves as the younger generation.

A number of studies show that the majority of teenage pregnancies are unplanned 'off-time' events and that a substantial number of teenage fathers do not live with their children. Data from the US National Longitudinal Survey of Labor Market Experience (NLSY) further indicated that young, unmarried fathers were more likely to have engaged in criminal activity, to have used hard drugs, to have higher rates of non-criminal problem behaviours (e.g. conduct problems, school drop-out) and to have come from economically and socially deprived family backgrounds. Additional difficulties for teenage fathers stem from the way the mother's family responds to their daughter's pregnancy. It is not uncommon for them to view the young man as a negative influence and to take steps to prevent his access to their child or grandchild. Marsiglio and Cohan (1997) observed that, whereas young Puerto Rican women were expected by their families to live with the father of their child, other communities were more likely to encourage the young parent not to marry but to continue with their education.

One recent prospective study of a New Zealand (Dunedin) birth cohort (Jaffee et al., 2001) identified that 60 per cent of young men who had experienced negative childhood environments (defined as having been exposed to five factors such as having a teenage or single parent mother, parents with criminal records, low socio-economic status, family conflict, harsh discipline, frequent changes of caretaker, etc.) had become fathers before the age of 26, in comparison with only 10 per cent of young men exposed to fewer than two environmental risks. Specifically, becoming a father before the age of 26 was associated with a stressful rearing environment, school difficulties, a history of conduct problems and precocious sexual behaviour. Further analyses showed that the fathers who spent the least time living with their offspring were most likely to have experienced difficulties in their own upbringing. Young men with a history of conduct disorder spent significantly less time living with their child compared to those with no such history. In fact, a history of conduct disorder and family difficulties including conflict, criminality and instability predicted the amount of time both teenage and older fathers spent with their children.

Jaffee et al. (2001) also found that a high proportion of the group of fathers who had had little contact with their children were, due to their own histories, prone to severe difficulties in forming close, mutually respectful relationships with partners and also prone to seriously negative behaviours, such as drug addiction, impulsivity and violence which, in its turn, would present difficulties for partners and children. Jaffee et al. (2001) therefore argued that father absence in these cases may be preferable since, for higher levels of contact to be beneficial, it would first be necessary to expend considerable efforts to alter deep-seated problems in the father's behaviour.

UK data on teenage parenting has been rather slow to emerge. It has also focused heavily on teenage mothers and has a tendency to be more concerned with delineating incidence and factors associated with incidence rather than with identification of processes of adaptation. Typically, teenage pregnancy has been depicted as arising from social disadvantages such as being in care or homeless, being offspring of young or teenage parents, being in need of educational support (Dawson, 2000; Horgan, 2001) or living in areas of social disadvantage (Hobcraft and Kiernan, 1999; Roberts, 2000). It has also been associated with poor health outcomes for mothers and children, including more post-natal depression, less breast-feeding, high infant and child mortality, high infant and childhood rates of hospital admission and low birth weight (Social Exclusion Unit, 1999).

One small UK study (Phoenix, 1991), focused predominantly on teenage mothers, questioned the view that adolescent parents were less able or less committed to bringing up children. More recently, Quinton and colleagues (Quinton et al., 2002) interviewed young first-time parents in Bath (92 women and 74 men aged 17-23) and later re-interviewed a number of these young people (79 women and 52 men). They concluded that, although the majority of families were ambivalent about the pregnancy and a third of the young people's parents responded negatively to news of the pregnancy, five months into the pregnancy, 71 per cent of couples seemed positive about the pregnancy. In addition, most couples were also positive about their relationship: most described themselves as compatible, moderately to highly committed to each other and felt that their relationship was moderately or even highly stable. Nine months after the birth of the child, 69 per cent of the young couples were living together and 63 per cent of the fathers were involved in childcare. The youngest men were those least likely to be involved: only 20 per cent of 17 year olds, 65 per cent of 18-19 year olds, 56 per cent of 20-21 year olds and 76 per cent of 23-23 year olds were much involved. Quinton et al. stressed that it was the quality of the relationship between the couple rather than the history of the young people's family or social development that best predicted fathers' post-natal involvement. They argued that successful intimate relationships can provide a positive turning point in young men's lives. This is perhaps more optimistic than conclusions from workers on the New Zealand study and it seems important to acknowledge that the size and length of the study, its methodology and the nature of attrition between time one and two interviews might suggest the need for caution in generalising its conclusions. Nevertheless, it seems worth noting that a substantial number of young couples does seem able to provide sound child-rearing environments, that others may benefit from greater support and encouragement, while the behaviour of a smaller minority may give cause for concern.

Lone fathers

As many researchers emphasise, studies of lone fathers are relatively rare: although approximately 11 per cent of lone parent households in the UK in the 1990s were headed by fathers (representing only two or three per cent of all families), statistical reports and other studies of lone parents have either treated lone parents as a homogeneous group or have tended to focus almost exclusively on lone mothers. This relative neglect of lone fathers is highly compatible with a research culture that favours small-scale focus-group approaches or larger-scale surveys designed to discover the views of 'Mr. Average UK Dad': even a representative sample of 200 fathers (of whom approximately two per cent would be lone parents) might capture only about five or six lone fathers and would not provide an adequate basis for generalisation while larger-scale surveys, unless they were designed specifically to examine the situation of lone fathers, may include questions that are not sensitive to the complex social circumstances of these fathers.

Data from the 1958 birth cohort study (Payne and Range, 1998) included only a very small sample of lone fathers (just over one per cent of all men and around two per cent of all men who were fathers by age 33) but indicated that, compared with other men who had become fathers by age 33, lone fathers had lived with more partners and had entered their first relationship earlier than other fathers. They also tended to have more children living with them than lone mothers, and their children tended to be older. Of the lone fathers in this sample who were in work (87.5 per cent), very few worked part-time.

Gingerbread (2001) carried out a small-scale study of fathers using Gingerbread, a telephone advice helpline and support network for lone parents. A volunteer sample of 115 lone fathers completed survey questionnaires and 360 calls to the helpline were also analysed. The majority of lone fathers in this sample felt that society had a negative view of lone fathers (61.1. per cent) although 14 per cent expressed the contrary opinion and 7 per cent were divided about whether their status was viewed positively or negatively. Few fathers in this study had been the main carer before becoming a lone father (fewer than two per cent). The most common sources of support for fathers during the transition to lone parenthood came from friends and neighbours (45.2 per cent) or family members, either grandparents (50.4 per cent) or other family members (34.7 per cent). A few fathers reported having received support through work colleagues (13 per cent) although a substantial minority (22 per cent) reported that they had no social support at all. A quarter of fathers stated that becoming a lone parent had had a negative impact on their careers and 80 per cent said that they were worse off financially, attributing this to loss of their partner's income (27 per cent), reduced work hours or employment (24.5 per cent) or unemployment (17.9 per cent).

Numerous studies have established the existence of a strong association between lone parenthood and poverty. Associations between poverty, poor mental health and anti-social behaviour are also well-established. In October 1998, the New Deal for Lone Parents was implemented with the aim of facilitating the transition to work of lone parents with school-age children. In connection with the inception of NDLP, NatCen was commissioned to discover more about employers' perceptions of the needs of lone parents as well as about possible barriers to retention of employment by lone parents (Lewis et al., 2001). These matters were further investigated in a report focusing on parents living in London (O'Connor and Boreham, 2002) which drew attention to differences in patterns of employment for different minority ethnic lone parents but failed to uncover reasons for non-participation in the labour market. Neither report presented analyses of data relating to mothers and fathers separately (possibly due to the fact that NDLP has tended to be taken up, in the main, by mothers). Lewis et al. (2001) comment that it was striking how little lone parents were viewed by employers as a distinct, cohesive group and that employers had quite a range of responses to lone parents: while some preferred not to employ lone parents, others saw them as valuable staff members; some felt that they did need to make allowances for lone parents whilst others did not. Lewis et al. point to the need for employers to recognise the special needs of lone parent fathers but suggested that this might need to be done through broader parent-friendly initiatives as opposed to initiatives directly aimed at NDLP lone fathers, since the latter might increase the propensity for stigmatisation.

3.7 Has life for fathers in the UK really changed at all over the last decade?

This question can be looked at from several perspectives: first, we can ask whether the ways that fathers behave or think about themselves have changed over the last ten years; next, we can ask whether peoples' attitudes and expectations of fathers have changed; third, we can ask whether the social circumstances of fathers have changed.

With regard to the first question, the studies that we have presented in this chapter suggest that there have not been revolutionary changes in men's behaviour or self-image: fathers continue to see their main responsibility as being to provide for the family, they continue to be less likely than women to talk about feelings or to do the housework and, in general, they do not take as much responsibility for childcare as mothers. But to stop there would be to see only part of the picture.

Ten years is not a long time for changes in long-established behaviours and attitudes to be noticed. Subtle, gradual changes may have been occurring to which surveys and studies have not been sensitive. Indeed, large changes may have been occurring among some fathers which have not been captured either by larger scale surveys or by qualitative studies. It is even possible that changes may be happening but are being met with resistance, i.e. the real changes are being masked, though, if this is the case, it is difficult to imagine how research could delve under the surface to measure this sort of covert change.

Frosh et al. (2002), reporting on a study of boys' experiences of being themselves, convey a sense of the struggle that 11-14 year old boys have to try out ways of not inhabiting the hard, masculine identities that they feel peers and others expect of them. They depict young people who act with bravado to cover a sense of loss connected with their inability to interact with other boys or with their fathers in an emotionally fulfilling way. They suggest that boys feel pushed into less mature behaviour than girls because they feel already written off by society. Boys who do not naturally fit a mould of being tough and masculine often experience homophobic bullying or other forms of social isolation. But, across all the boys, there was variety in the degree to which they espoused hard, apparently uncaring attitudes and, in private, the boys were sometimes able to be articulate and emotionally literate in ways that showed their awareness of alternative modes of being.

This view of boys' experiences as dynamic and conflicted seems to provide considerable insight into what it is like to grow up as a male in the UK. It gives an idea of the complexity of the influences of class and ethnicity and the interplay between these influences and boys' behaviour, and asks how it might be possible to help boys to construct a less problematic view of themselves.

This question and the study it arises from seem very pertinent to a consideration of fathers and the way fathers view themselves in relation to mothers and to their children. Perhaps fathers, like sons, in many parts of UK society still find it difficult to show softness and to engage in more caring, expressive relationships with their children. But perhaps, like their sons, they experience this way of being as fluid and changing, not fixed and rigid. In other words, the options for engaging with different ways of being will seem more or less possible for different fathers in different social settings and at different times.

This leads into the second question, whether expectations of fathers have changed over the last decade and, again, it only seems possible to answer that expectations may have changed in some ways but not in others and that this is probably the case in some sections of society and in some parts of the UK more than others. Evidence from many sources suggests that there are wide variations among fathers, both within and between different social classes and minority ethnic groups, in attitudes towards family life and child rearing. Berthoud (1999), for example, described differences in family formation across ethnic groups: three fifths of Pakistani and Bangladeshi men in his study were married, had children and held more 'traditional' attitudes towards family life whereas only one fifth of Caribbean fathers lived with both a partner and children.

Goulbourne and Chamberlain (2001) also stress the importance of recognising the fact that the extent to which fathers are physically present can vary considerably from one culture to another. They point out that, in Caribbean families, the norm for fathers is more likely to be serial parenting and low participation in family life: as a result, families are often headed by mothers whose children have different fathers. This family form has been supported by social traditions and kinship networks that have evolved over many generations, often through periods of social change and difficulty, and across countries as well as across generations. However, as Hall (1991) indicates, "new ethnicities" evolve as immigrant communities interact with other cultures. Within these, fathers' roles may also change and evolve.

Finally, in reply to the question of whether fathers' social circumstances have changed in the last decade, it seems we should acknowledge that, while during this decade some aspects of life for fathers in the UK have changed, these changes have generally not been without precedent and nor have they affected only fathers. For example, developments in birth control, the expansion of service industries and the reduction of traditionally 'male' jobs, the increased diversity of family forms consequent upon changed patterns of family formation as well as upon different ways in which post-divorce families have evolved, etc., all these things impact upon both mothers and fathers. And, for some mothers and fathers, they have meant that family life is different now to how it was before the 1990s. For others, though, there may be little difference.

Some developments are unique to this decade: such as the particular state of technological advance (e.g. the stage of internet use and development, the increased availability of television channels, the availability and use of DNA testing, etc.), the impact of campaign groups on policies affecting fathers (e.g. the inauguration of Fathers Direct, the recent successes achieved by Stonewall in inching slowly towards greater equality for gay and bisexual fathers), European directives on use of physical punishment, etc.. Gauging the extent to which such changes have affected the lives of fathers in the UK in this decade is tricky: for some individuals, the impact may be enormous; others may appear unaffected.

In a sense, because the role of the father in families is so dependent on social context, and because mothers are still responsible for the bulk of childcare, the father's role during the last decade may not seem to have changed. On the other hand, families and family relationships are not and never have been static so, to some extent, it is in the nature of the father's role that it must be continually changing and adapting. But perhaps one of the most striking ways in which the role of fathers has changed is that it has become more visible. This visibility in itself seems likely to impact on the experience of fathering in the UK today and may well be bringing with it a greater awareness of the complexity of relationships between fathers and children within constantly evolving family forms.

References for chapter 3

Allen, S. and Daly, K. (2002) The effects of father involvement: a summary of the research evidence. *Newsletter of the Father Involvement Initiative – Ontario Network*, **1**, 1-11.

Amato, P.R. (2000) The consequences of divorce for adults and children. *Journal of Marriage and the Family*, **62**, 628-640.

Amato, P.R. and Booth, A. (1997) *A generation at risk: Growing up in an era of family upheaval.* Cambridge, MA: Harvard University Press.

Amato, P.R. and Rogers, S. (1997) A longitudinal study of marital problems and subsequent divorce. *Journal of Marriage and the Family*, **59**, 612-624.

BACS Payment Schemes Limited (23 April 2004) *Press release: Till debt do us part. One in three British couples are financially incompatible.* Online at http://www.directdebit.co.uk/news/cpr_story54.php

Barker, R.W. (1994) *Lone fathers and masculinities.* Aldershot: Avebury.

Barrett, H. (2002) Soaps and the Family. London: National Family and Parenting Institute.

Barnett, R.C. and Baruch, G.K. (1988) Correlates of fathers' participation in family work. In P. Bronstein and C.P. Cowan (Eds.), *Fatherhood today* (66-78). New York: John Wiley.

Bates, G., Hutchinson, D., Robertson, T., Wadsworth, A. and Watson, R. (2002) *Identifying the cause of the Child Support Agency's problems.* Online at <http://www.childsupportanalysis.co.uk/guest_contributions/newcastle_paper/history.htm>

Benzeval, M. (1998) The self-reported health status of lone parents. *Social Science and Medicine*, **46**, 1337-1353.

Berthoud, R. (1999) Young Caribbean men and the labour market: a comparison with other ethnic groups. York: Joseph Rowntree Foundation.

Bignall, T. and Butt. J. (2001) *Supporting fathers as parents*. Black and Minority Ethnic Families Policy Forum, Discussion paper 3. London: REU.

Biller, H.H. (1993) *Fathers and families: Paternal factors in child development*. Westport, CT: Auburn House.

BMRB International (2003) *Evaluation of the Teenage Pregnancy Strategy. Tracking survey. Report of results of nine waves of research*. London: BMRB International. Online at www. teenagepregnancyunit.gov.uk

Botting, B., Rosato, M. and Wren, R. (1998) Teenage mothers and the health of their children. *Population Trends*, **93**, 19-28.

Bouchard, G. and Lee, C.M. (2000) The marital context for father involvement with their preschool children: The role of partner support. *Journal of Prevention and Intervention in the Community*, **21(2)**, 37-54.

Bowlby, J. (1969) *Attachment and Loss: Vol.1: Attachment*. Harmondsworth: Penguin.

Bradshaw, J., Stimson, C, Skinner, C. and Williams, J. (1999) *Absent fathers?* London and New York: Routledge.

Bradshaw, J. and Millar, J. (1991) Lone parent families in the UK. London: HMSO.

Brannen, J., Moss, P., Owen, C. and Wale, C. (1997) *Mothers, fathers and employment: Parents and the labour market in Britain, 1984-1994*. London: Department for Education and Employment.

Bruning, G. and Plantenga, J. (1999) Parental leave and equal opportunities in eight European countries. *Journal of European Social Policy*, **19(3)**, 195-210.

Burgess, A. (1997) *Fatherhood reclaimed*. London: Vermilion.

Burghes, L., Clarke, L. and Cronin, N. (1997) *Fathers and fatherhood in Britain*. London: Family Policy Studies Centre.

Burns, A. and Scott, C. (1994) *Mother-headed families and why they have increased*. Hillsdale, NJ: Lawrence Erlbaum Associates.

Butt, J. and Box, L. (1998) Family Centred: a study of the use of family centres by black families. London: REU.

Chuang, S., Lamb, M.E. and Hwang, C.P. (2003) Internal reliability, temporal stability and correlates of individual differences in paternal involvement: A 15-year longitudinal study in Sweden. In R. Day and M.E. Lamb (Eds.), *Reconceptualizing and measuring fatherhood* (129-148). Mahwah, NJ: Lawrence Erlbaum Associates.

Clarke, L. and O'Brien, M. (2004) Father involvement in Britain: The research and policy evidence. In R.D. Day and M.E. Lamb (Eds.), *Conceptualizing and measuring father involvement* (39-59). Mahwah, NJ: Lawrence Erlbaum Associates.

Clarke, L. and Roberts, C. (2002) Policy and rhetoric: The growing interest in fathers and grandparents in Britain. In A. Carling, S. Duncan and R. Edwards (Eds.), *Analysing families: Morality and rationality in policy and practice* (165-182). London: Routledge and Kegan Paul.

Cooksey and Fondell, 1996 [Cited in Allen and Daly, 2002, op. cit.]

Daniels, P. and Weingarten, K (1988) Reshaping fatherhood: Finding the models. *Journal of Family Issues*, **14**, 510-530.

Dawkins, R. (1976) *The selfish gene*. Oxford: Oxford University Press.

Dawson, N. (2000) Education and occupational training for teenage mothers in Europe. University of Sheffield: http://www.shef.ac.uk/uni/projects/tme/ [Cited in Tabberer, S. (2003), *op.cit.*]

DeFranc, W. and Mahalik, J.R. (2001) Masculine gender role conflict and stress in relation to parental attachment and separation. *Psychology of Men and Masculinity*, **3(1)**, 51-60.

Dennis, N. and Erdos, G. (1992) *Families without fatherhood*. London: Institute of Economic Affairs.

Deven, F. and Moss, P. (2002) Leave arrangements for parents: Overview and future outlook. *Community, Work and Family*, **5**, 237-255.

Dienhart, A. (1998) *Reshaping fatherhood: The social construction of shared parenting*. London: Sage.

Dulude, D., Wright, J. and Belanger, C. (2000) The effects of pregnancy complications on the parental adaptation process. *Journal of Reproductive and Infant Psychology*, **18**, 5-20.

Dunn, J. (2003) Contact and children's perspectives on parental relationships. In A. Bainham, B. Lindley, M. Richards and L. Trinder (Eds.), *Children and their families: Contact, rights and welfare* (15-33). Oxford and Portland, Oregon: Hart Publishing.

Dunn, J., Davies, L. and O'Connor, T. (2000) Parents' and partners' life course and family experiences: Links with parent-child relationships in different family settings. *Journal of Child Psychology and Psychiatry*, **41**, 955-968.

Eadley, N. and Wetherell, M. (1999) Imagined futures: Young men's talk about fatherhood and domestic life. *British Journal of Social Psychology*, **38**, 181-194.

Easterbrooks and Goldberg, 1990 [Cited in Allen and Daly, 2002, op. cit.]

Eggebean and Knoester, 2001 [Cited in Allen and Daly, 2002, op. cit.]

Ely, M., Richards, M.P.M., Wadsworth, M.E.J. and Elliott, B.J. (1999) Secular changes in the association of parental divorce and children's educational attainment – evidence from three British cohorts. *Journal of Social Policy*, **28**, 437-455.

Emery, R., Waldron, M., Kitzmann, K.M. and Aaron, J. (1999) Delinquent behavior, future divorce or nonmarital childbearing, and externalizing behaviour among offspring: a 14-year prospective study. *Journal of Family Psychology*, **13**, 568-579.

Featherstone, B. (2001) Putting fathers on the child welfare agenda: A research review. *Journal of Child and Family Social Work*, **6(2)**, 179-186.

Ferri, E. and Smith, K. (1996) *Parenting in the 1990s*. London: Family Policy Studies Centre and Joseph Rowntree Foundation.

Ferri, E. and Smith, K. (2003a) Partnerships and parenthood. In E. Ferri, J. Bynner and M. Wadsworth (Eds.), *Changing Britain, Changing Lives: Three generations at the turn of the century* (105-132). London: Institute of Education.

Ferri, E. and Smith, K. (2003b) Family life. In E. Ferri, J. Bynner and M. Wadsworth (Eds.), *Changing Britain, Changing Lives: Three generations at the turn of the century* (chapter 5, 132-147). London: Institute of Education.

Field et al., 1995 [Cited in Allen and Daly, 2002, op. cit.]

Flouri, E. and Buchanan, A. (2002) Father involvement in childhood and trouble with the police in adolescence. Findings from the 1958 British Cohort. *Journal of Interpersonal Violence,* **17(6)**, 689-701.

Flouri, E., Buchanan, A. and Bream, V. (2002) Adolescents' perceptions of their fathers' involvement: significance to school attitudes. *Psychology in the Schools*, **39(5)**, 575-582.

Flouri, E. and Buchanan, A. (2003a) The role of father involvement and mother involvement in adolescents' psychological well-being. Research Note. *British Journal of Social Work*, **33**, 399-400.

Flouri, E. and Buchanan, A. (2003b) What predicts fathers' involvement with their children? A prospective study of intact families. *British Journal of Developmental Psychology,* **21**, 81-98.

Freud, S. (1933/1977) *Femininity. Lecture 33: New Introductory lectures on psychoanalysis.* Harmondsworth: Penguin.

Frodi, A.M. and Lamb, M.E. (1978) Sex differences in responsiveness to infants: A developmental study of psychophysiological and behavioral responses. *Child Development*, **49**, 1182-1188.

Frosh, S., Phoenix, A. and Pattman, R. (2002) *Young masculinities. Understanding boys in contemporary society.* Basingstoke: Palgrave.

Geldof, B. (2003) The real love that dare not speak its name. In A. Bainham, B. Lindley, M. Richards and L. Trinder (Eds.), *Children and their families: Contact, rights and welfare* (171-200). Oxford and Portland, Oregon: Hart Publishing.

Gershuny, J. (2000) *Changing times: Work and leisure in post-industrial society.* Oxford: Oxford University Press.

Gershuny, J. and Sullivan, O. (2001) Cross-national changes in time-use: Some sociological (hi)stories re-examined. *British Journal of Sociology*, **52(2)**, 331-347.

Ghate, D., Shaw, C. and Hazel, N. (2000) *Father and family centres: Engaging fathers in preventative services.* York: Joseph Rowntree Foundation.

Gingerbread (2001) *Becoming visible: focus on lone fathers.* London: Gingerbread.

Giveans, D.L. and Robinson, M.K. (1985) Fathers and the pre-school age child. In K. Hanson and F.W. Bozett (Eds.), *Dimensions of fatherhood* (115-140). Beverly Hills, CA: Sage.

Gorell Barnes, G., Thompson, P., Daniel, G., and Burchardt, N. (1998) *Growing up in stepfamilies.* Oxford: Clarendon Press.

Goulbourne, H. and Chamberlain, M. (Eds.) (2001) *Caribbean families in Britain and the Trans-Atlantic world.* London and Oxford: Macmillan.

Grossmann, K., Grossmann, K.E., Fremmer-Bombik, E., Kindler, H., Scheurer-Englisch, H. and Zimmerman, P. (2002) The uniqueness of the child-father attachment relationship: Fathers' sensitive and challenging play as a pivotal variable in a 16-year longitudinal study. *Social Development*, **11(3)**, 307-331.

Haas, L. (1992) *Equal parenthood and social policy: a study of parental leave in Sweden.* New York: State University of New York Press.

Haffer, W., Vintner, L. and Williams, R. (2002) *Dads on Dads: Needs and expectations at home and at work.* Manchester: Equal Opportunities Commission.

Hall, S. (1991) Old and new identities, old and new ethnicities. In A.D. King (Ed.), *Culture, globalisation and the World-System*(41-68). Houndmills: Macmillan.

Harris et al., 1998 [Cited in Allen and Daly, 2002, op. cit.]

Haskey, J. (1998) One-parent families and their dependent children in Great Britain. *Population Trends*, **91**, 5-14.

Hawkins, A.J. and Dollahite, D.C. (Eds.) (1997) *Generative fathering: Beyond deficit perspectives.* Thousand Oaks, CA: Sage.

Henwood, K. (2001) *Masculinities, identities and transition to fatherhood.* ESRC End of grant report. Online at http://www.esrc.ac.uk

Hetherington, E.M. (1999) *Coping with divorce, single parenting, and remarriage: A risk and resiliency perspective.* Mahwah, NJ: Lawrence Erlbaum Associates.

Hewlett, B.S. (2004) Fathers in forager, farmer, and pastoral cultures. In M.E. Lamb (Ed.), *The role of the father in child development*, (182-195). 4th edition. Hoboken, NJ: Lawrence Erlbaum Associates.

Hobcraft, J. and Kiernan, K. (1999) *Childhood poverty, early motherhood and adult social exclusion.* Case paper 28. London: London School of Economics Centre for Analysis of Social Exclusion.

Hobson, B. (Ed.) (2002) *Making men into fathers: Men, masculinities and the social position of fatherhood.* Cambridge: Cambridge University Press.

Hofferth, S.L. (2003) *Measuring father involvement and social fathering: An overview.* Paper presented in session on Fathering and social involvement, conference on Measurement Issues in Family Demography, 13-14 November, Bethesda, M/D.

Hoffman, L. and Youngblade, L. (1999) *Mothers at work: Effects on children's wellbeing.* Cambridge: Cambridge University Press.

Horgan, G. (2001) *A sense of purpose: The views and experiences of young mothers in Northern Ireland about growing up.* Belfast: Save the Children.

Horn and Sylvester, 2002 [Cited in Allen and Daly, 2002, op. cit.]

Hrdy, S.B. (1999) *Mother nature: A history of mothers, infants, and natural selection.* New York: Pantheon.

Jaffee, S.R., Caspi, A., Moffit, T.E., Taylor, A. and Dickson, N. (2001) Predicting fatherhood and whether young fathers live with their children: Prospective findings and policy reconsiderations. *Journal of Child Psychology and Psychiatry*, **42(6)**, 803-815.

Jaffee, S.R., Moffitt, T.E., Caspi, A. and Taylor, A. (2003) Life with (or without) father: The benefits of living with two biological parents depend on the father's antisocial behavior. *Child Development*, **74(1)**, 109-126.

Joshi, H., Wiggin, D. and Clarke, L. (January, 2000) The changing home: outcomes for children. *ESRC Children 5-16 Research Briefing, Number 6.* Available online at www.hull.ac.uk/children5to16programme/

Kiernan, K. and Hobcraft, J. (1997) Parental divorce during childhood: age at first intercourse, partnership and parenthood. *Population Studies*, **51**, 41-55.

Lamb, M.E. (Ed.) (1981) *The role of the father in child development.* New York: Wiley.

Lamb, M.E. and Lewis, C. (2004) The development and significance of father-child relationships in two-parent families. In J. Scott, J. Treas and M. Richards (Eds.), *The Blackwell companion to the sociology of families* (272-306). Oxford: Blackwell.

Langford, W., Lewis, C., Solomon, Y. and Warin, J. (2001) *Family understandings: Closeness and authority in families with a teenage child.* London: Family Policy Studies Centre.

Lewis, C. (2000) *A man's place is in the home: Fathers and families in the UK.* York: Joseph Rowntree Foundation.

Lewis, C. and O'Brien, M. (Eds.) (1987) *Reassessing fatherhood. New observations on fathers and the modern family.* London: Sage.

Lewis, J. (2002) The problem of fathers: policy and behaviour in Britain. In B. Hobson (Ed.), *Making men into fathers: Men, masculinities and the social position of fatherhood* (125-149). Cambridge: Cambridge University Press.

Lewis, J., Mitchell, L., Woodland, S., Fell, R. and Gloyer, A. (2001) *Employers, lone parents and the work-life balance.* Report ESR64, Employment Service.

Lewis, M. (Ed.) (1987) *Beyond the dyad.* New York: Plenum Press.

Lloyd, N., O'Brien, M. and Lewis, C. (2003) *Fathers in Sure Start.* National Evaluation of Sure Start Implementation Report, No. 2. London: DfES. Online at http://www.surestart.gov.uk/_doc/index.cfm?document=417

Lloyd, T. (1995) Fathers in the media: An analysis of newspaper coverage of fathers. In P. Moss (Ed.), *Father figures* (41-51). Scotland: HMSO.

McRae, S. (1999) *Changing Britain: Families and households in the 1990s.* Oxford: Oxford University Press.

Maclean, M. and Eekelaar, J. (1997) *The parental obligation.* Oxford: Hart.

Marsiglio, W. (1995) *Fatherhood: Contemporary theory, research and social policy.* Thousand Oaks, CA: Sage.

Marsiglio, W. and Cohan, M. (1997) Young fathers and child development. In M.E. Lamb (Ed.), *The role of the father in child development* (227-244). New York: John Wiley and Sons.

Moss, P. (Ed.) (1995) *Father figures: Fathers in the families of the 1990s.* Edinburgh: HMSO.

Moss, P. and Deven, F. (Eds.) (1999) *Parental leave: Progress or pitfall? Research and Policy issues in Europe.* The Hague and Brussels: NIDI/CBGS Publications, Volume 35.

Murray, C. (1990) *The emerging British underclass.* London: IEA Health and Welfare Unit.

Nash, S. C. and Feldman, S. S. (1981) Sex-role and sex-related attributes: Constancy and change across the family life cycle. In M.E. Lamb and A.L. Brown (Eds.), *Advances in Developmental Psychology* (1-35). Hillsdale, NJ: Lawrence Erlbaum Associates.

O'Brien, M. (2004) Social science and public policy perspectives on fatherhood in the European Union. In M.E. Lamb (Ed.), *The role of the father in child development* (Chapter 5, 121-145). 4th edition. Mahwah, NJ: Lawrence Erlbaum Associates.

O'Brien, M. and Jones, D. (1995) Young people's attitudes to fatherhood. In P. Moss (Ed.), *Father figures* (27-39). Scotland: HMSO.

O'Brien, M. and Shemilt, I. (2003) *Working fathers: Earning and caring.* Manchester: Equal Opportunities Commission.

O'Connor, W. and Boreham, R. (2002) *Investigating low labour market participant among lone parents in London: A review of methods.* London: HMSO.

Oppenheim, C. and Harker, L. (1998) *Poverty: the facts.* London: Child Poverty Action Group.

Parsons, T. and Bales, R. (1955) *Family socialization and interaction process.* New York: Free Press.

Palkovitz, R. (1997) Reconstructing "involvement": Expanding conceptualizations of men's caring in contemporary families. In A.J. Hawkins and D.C. Dollahite (Eds.), *Generative fathering: Beyond deficit perspectives* (200-216). Thousand Oaks, CA: Sage.

Payne, J. and Range, M. (1998) *Lone parents' lives: An analysis of partnership, fertility, employment and housing histories in the 1958 British birth cohort.* DSS Research Report No. 78. London: HMSO.

Pedersen et al., 1980 [Cited in Allen and Daly, 2002, op. cit.]

Pels, T. (2000) Muslim families from Morocco in the Netherlands: Gender dynamics and fathers' roles in a context of change. *Current Sociology,* **48(4)**, 75-93.

Phares, V. (1997) *Fathers and developmental psychology.* New York: Wiley.

Phoenix, A. (1991) *Young mothers?* Cambridge: Polity Press.

Pleck, 1997 [Cited in Allen and Daly, 2002, op. cit.]

Popenoe, D. (1996) *Life without father: Compelling new evidence that fatherhood and marriage are indispensable for the good of children and society.* New York: Free Press.

Pickford, R. (1999) *Fathers, marriage and the law.* London: Joseph Rowntree Foundation and Family Policy Studies Centre.

Quinton, D.L., Pollock, S.B., Anderson, P. and Golding, J. (2002) *The transition to fatherhood in young men: Influences on commitment.* End of award ESRC report.

Radin, 1994 [Cited in Allen and Daly, 2002, op. cit.]

Richards, M., Hardy, R. and Wadsworth, M.E.J. (1997) The effects of divorce and separation on mental health in a national UK birth cohort. *Psychological Medicine*, **27**, 1121-1128.

Roberts, H. (2000) *What works in reducing health inequalities in child health.* London: Barnardo's.

Rutter, M. (in press) Environmentally mediated risks for psychopathology: Research strategies and findings. *Journal of the American Academy of Child and Adolescent Psychiatry.*

Shouls, S., Whitehead, M., Burstrom, B. and Diderichsen, F. (1999) The health and socio-economic circumstances of British lone mothers over the last two decades. *Population Trends*, **95**, 41-46.

Simpson, B., McCarthy, P. and Walker, J. (1995) *Being there: Fathers after divorce.* Newcastle Upon Tyne: Relate Centre For Family Studies

Singh, D. and Newburn, M. (2000) *Becoming a father: Men's access to information and support about pregnancy, birth, and life with a new baby.* London: National Childbirth Trust.

Smith, A. (2002) *The role of the state in encouraging male parenting: lessons from Europe.* Paper presented at Women in Politics conference, Birkbeck, University of London. [Cited in O'Brien and Shemilt, 2003, *op. cit.*]

Snarey, 1993 [Cited in Allen and Daly, 2002, op. cit.]

Solomon, Y., Warin, J., Lewis, C. and Langford, W. (2002) Helping with homework? Homework as a site of tension for parents and teenagers. *British EducationalResearch Journal*, **28(4)**, 603-22.

Stewart, S.D. (2003) Nonresident parenting and adolescent adjustment: The quality of nonresident parent father-child interaction. *Journal of Family Issues*, **24(2)**, 217-244.

Storey, A.E., Walsh, C.J., Quinton, R.L. and Wynne-Edwards, R.E. (2000) Hormonal correlates of paternal responsiveness in new and expectant fathers. *Evolution and Human Behavior,* **21**, 79-95.

Tabberer, S. (2002) Teenage pregnancy and teenage motherhood. In J. Bradshaw (Ed.), *The well-being of children in the UK* (187-197). London: The Save the Children Fund.

Teti, D. M. and Lamb, M. E. (1986). Sex-role learning and adolescent fatherhood. In A.B. Elster and M.E. Lamb (Eds.), *Adolescent fatherhood* (19-30). Hillsdale, NJ: Erlbaum.

Trinder, L., Beck, M. and Connolly, J. (2002) *Making contact: How parents and children negotiate and experience contact after divorce.* York: Joseph Rowntree Foundation.

Trinder, L., Beck, M. and Connolly, J. (2001) *The contact project, first year report.* York: Joseph Rowntree Foundation.

Trinder, L. (2003) Working and not working contact after divorce. In A. Bainham, B. Lindley, M. Richards and L. Trinder (Eds.), *Children and their families: Contact, rights and welfare* (387-406). Oxford and Portland, Oregon: Hart Publishing.

Wallerstein, J.S. and Blakeslee, S. (1989) *Second chances: Men, women, and children after a decade of divorce.* New York: Ticknor and Fields.

Wallerstein, J.S. and Corbin, S.B. (1989) Daughters of divorce: Report from a ten-year follow-up. *American Journal of Orthopsychiatry*, **59**, 593-604.

Ward, C.D. and Cooper, R.P. (1999) A lack of evidence in 4-month-old human infants for paternal voice preference. *Developmental Psychobiology*, **35**, 49-59.

Warin, J., Solomon, Y., Lewis, C., Langford, W., et al. (1999) *Fathers, work and family life*. London: Family Policy Studies Centre for Joseph Rowntree Foundation.

William, 1997 [Cited in Allen and Daly, 2002, op. cit.]

Winnicott, D.W. (1964) What about fathers? In D.W. Winnicott, *The child, the family, and the outside world* (113-118). Harmondsworth: Penguin.

4 | Parent-child relationships: Socialisation and empowerment

"When you are younger you think it's like they're the thing you look up to, as all things good and everything... But then as you get older you find they are just human beings and they become more like really good friends.."
(14 year-old boy)

"I am actually very open with my mum and dad, like I said I am very lucky, I can tell them almost anything ... it's because they're very honest with me, I think."
(14 year-old girl)

These two quotes are from a recent study focused on relationships between teenagers and their parents (Langford et al., 2001). They illustrate the views of young people who appear not to have difficulty communicating with parents who make them feel that their opinions will be respected. This seems a far cry from the Victorian dictate that *"Children should be seen and not heard"* and may appear to reflect the possibility that family relationships in modern Britain are based on more democratic principles of mutual respect than was the case in the past. But whether the facts can really support this position is highly debateable (Gillies, 2000).

In this chapter, we will try to uncover which attributes might characterise family life in the last decade in UK and whether, indeed, it is possible to identify issues or concerns that are unique to these times. As in previous chapters, to assist us in focusing our discussion, we have devised a set of questions which we feel are pertinent to key debates within UK society. They are listed overleaf:

4.1 Has it become more difficult for parents to control their children?

4.2 How do families in the UK differ from families in other parts of the world?

4.3 Has parenting become more dominated by consumerism?

4.4 Do market forces have more influence than parents on children?

4.5 Is new technology making it more difficult for parents to communicate with their children and to monitor their safety?

4.6 Are sexual behaviours among children changing?

4.7 Are children becoming independent earlier or later?

4.1 Has it become more difficult for parents to control their children?

"In the UK, the continued existence of the defence allowing parents to use 'reasonable chastisement' when disciplining their children remains a barrier to fully respecting children as human beings in their own right – developing citizens, the responsibility, and not the property, of their parents." (Boyson and Thorpe, 2002)

A Victorian ruling, made by Chief Justice Cockburn in 1860 in a case where a father had beaten his son to death, made it legal to hit children if it could be shown that only "reasonable chastisement" was intended. The defence of "reasonable chastisement" was included in the 1933 Children and Young Persons Act and remains on the statute books in spite of a 1998 ruling by the European Court of Human Rights stating that English law was failing to protect children from beatings.

A recent Populus poll reported in *The Times* (12 April 2004), based on responses from 1,045 adults, indicates that the majority of respondents (59 per cent) would oppose a change in the law to ban smacking and to give children the same protection as adults from being hit or assaulted. Although, among respondents aged between 18 and 24, 59 per cent thought that smacking should become a criminal offence, nevertheless a substantial minority of this group (38 per cent) was also opposed to a change in the law.

Men and women were equally opposed to a ban: only 36 per cent of women and 33 per cent of men were in favour of a change in the law. Perhaps somewhat surprisingly, opposition to a ban was slightly stronger among upper (AB and C1) than lower classes (C2 and DE): 64 per cent of upper and 52 per cent of lower class respondents stated that they would oppose a ban. Overall, just under three-quarters of respondents (72 per cent) thought that a public information campaign to inform about alternatives to physical punishment would be useful (75 per cent AB/C1; 69 per cent C2/DE). Younger respondents were more in favour of such a campaign than respondents aged over 44.

One interpretation of these findings may be that, while people oppose a move to criminalise the use of physical punishment on children, they would not support its use if effective alternative actions could be agreed. They may also reflect the possibility that adults in the UK are in general reluctant to extend police powers into the home rather than a determination to retain the right to hurt children. Another possible interpretation is that these findings may be artefactual, that is, due to factors such as how questions are asked or who is asked, etc. In support of this notion are findings from a MORI poll commissioned by the Children are Unbeatable! Alliance between 26 February and 2 March, 2004. Responses were obtained from 2004 adults of whom 71 per cent were in favour of changing the law so that children are given as much protection from being hit as adults. Only 10 per cent were opposed to such a change while 74 per cent of parents, 76 per cent of adults under 24 and 73 per cent of women were in favour. Almost a third of survey respondents (29 per cent) endorsed the view that "children should be given more legal protection from being hit than adults". However, there was still very little agreement in respect of whether "it is wrong for someone to hit a child in their family": just over a half agreed (56 per cent) but almost a third disagreed (31 per cent).

Whatever surveys such as these may indicate, the fact remains that the UK has neither a very good record on child protection nor a reputation for being a child-friendly nation. The most cursory glance at social history records attests to this. The question that we would like to address here though is whether there are any signs that this situation may be changing in modern Britain?

Psychological and sociological studies of the use of physical discipline have consistently shown that it is both ineffective and can be counter-productive since it is likely to be associated with higher incidence of antisocial behaviour, including other forms of parental domestic violence, and other negative psychological effects (Gershoff, 2002). Numerous international laws have been passed acknowledging that physical punishment constitutes a breach of the rights of children and recognising that parents benefit from support and education to help them find alternative ways of socialising their children. Chief among the laws passed are the UN Convention on the Rights of the Child 1989, the European Convention on Human Rights 1950 and the Human Rights Act 1998. The latter act is applicable in all courts in the UK.

Boyson and Thorpe (2002) document steps taken in 10 countries (Sweden, Finland, Norway, Austria, Cyprus, Denmark, Latvia, Croatia, Israel and Germany) which have put legislation in place to protect children from experiencing violence from their parents. In most of these countries, legislation has taken place in stages, with the first step being to ban corporal punishment in public institutions such as schools, followed by the removal of the defence that parents were using "reasonable punishment" in attacking their children, and finally by a total ban on the use of physical discipline. Appendix 4.1 details the wording of this legislation and shows the legal situation in the UK.

Boyson and Thorpe (2002) describe a range of common pre-legislation worries which include fears that the state will intervene too much in domestic affairs, that parents will be imprisoned for minor transgressions and that children will become out of control. Although access to accurate data is difficult in this sensitive area, Boyson and Thorpe (2002, p.2) cite evidence to show not only that these fears were unfounded but that "No negative effects have been documented following legal reform, and such reform has helped to foster a culture in which children are accorded greater respect, have greater equality, and enjoy greater protection from violence."

In 2002, Wales became the first country in the UK to prohibit the use of corporal punishment in all forms of day care. Scotland and the UK Government followed in 2003 (Appendix 4.2).

Studies of discipline and control

Ghate et al. (2003) surveyed 1,250 parents of 0-12 year old children across Britain, using a Computer Assisted Personal (and Self) interviewing programme (CAPI/CASI) with the aim of enabling respondents to feel free to give more honest answers. Disciplinary acts were measured using the Misbehaviour Response Scale which is a form of the American Conflict Tactics Scale (Straus et al., 1998) modified by the authors for a British sample. The Strengths and Difficulties Questionnaire (Goodman, 1997) was used to measure children's behaviour. Further in-depth interviews with 20 pairs of parents and eight focus group discussions with children aged 8-12 were also included.

Preliminary findings indicated that 67 per cent of the parents surveyed had used physical punishment (slapping, smacking on the limbs or bottom, etc.) within the past year while 88 per cent admitted to having ever used it. Nevertheless, 40 per cent of parents stated that physical punishment was never acceptable and only half thought it was sometimes acceptable, though a rather worrying one in ten parents considered that it was always permissible to smack a child, under any circumstances. At least one in seven parents, therefore, had used physical punishment in spite of their not being, in theory, in favour of it.

Severe methods of discipline (hitting with an implement, slapping or hitting around the face or head, etc.) had been used by nine per cent of respondents in the past year and by 16 per cent of parents ever. Ghate et al. (2003) found that parents who resorted to physical methods of discipline most often also used a wide range of non-physical disciplinary measures. Most parents who had used physical methods reported feeling distressed immediately after the event and almost all parents were, in principal, opposed to the use of an implement. Parents who used harsher discipline also tended to describe their relationship with their child as more critical or hostile, or as less warm and involved, and they were more likely to describe their pre-school child as 'difficult'; in addition, they were also more likely to describe themselves as having an unsupportive partner.

Although Ghate et al. (2003) claimed to have found some evidence in support of the notion that parents who had experienced harsh discipline themselves were more likely to visit the same practices on their children, they also suggested that changing social attitudes and negative appraisal of one's own negative experiences appeared, in some cases, to have the potential to disrupt patterns of intergenerational transmission. These conclusions can only be established or tested when evidence from longitudinal studies using larger, more representative samples and more rigorous controls is available: such a study design would have greater power to examine causal relationships across generations.

Anderson et al. (2002) employed a similar interview schedule to that used by Ghate et al. (2003). Their study aimed to examine parents' views on imminent changes in Scottish law, which propose that it should be made an offence to smack a child under three or to hit or strike a child of any age with an implement or to shake a child of any age; they also wanted to find out what parents knew of the law relating to discipline, what forms of discipline (physical and non-physical) parents used, how parents' use of discipline relates to their own experiences as children (i.e. changes over time) and what means of discipline parents considered appropriate for children of different ages. A range of data-gathering methods was used, including conventional focus groups with non-familiar peers, focus groups with familiar peers, interviews with couples and individual depth interviews (five interviews of each type). These interviews were followed up by a survey of 692 parents (496 mothers, 196 fathers; 518 parents in couple, 174 single parents; 372 in professional, managerial and clerical occupations, 320 in skilled and unskilled manual occupations or economically inactive) carried out in interviewees' homes, with responses mostly recorded by interviewers (though more sensitive questions about experience and use of discipline methods were self-keyed).

Anderson et al. (2002) report that 72 per cent of parents perceived themselves to be under greater pressure than their own parents and generally felt that they were less strict than their own parents; they particularly stressed the difficulty of maintaining a satisfactory work-life balance, the loss of routine family life and the pressure both from themselves and from their children to acquire material possessions. In addition, many parents felt that children nowadays are more assertive, less obedient and less respectful of their parents. Many parents appeared to welcome this more equal relationship but many also felt unsure of themselves as parents. Even those who felt unable to control their children's behaviour were wary about accepting advice from 'experts' outside the family and tended to feel that no-one could understand their situation sufficiently to intervene effectively. Added pressure for parents came from their awareness of the possibility that they might be penalised for their children's misbehaviour.

These reports of current practice and past experience, though, were not subjected to any statistical analysis, which means that it is not possible to draw any firm conclusions in relation to comparisons over time or generation. Parents who recalled having been physically chastised by their parents were also reported as being more likely to use physical discipline with their own children, a finding which the authors claim, somewhat arguably, lends support to intergenerational transmission of punitive child-rearing practices.

A lower proportion of parents in professional, managerial and clerical occupations reported that they would use physical discipline with their own child than parents in lower class occupations and a similar difference between occupational groups emerged in relation to parents' perception of whether all or most of their friends and family would smack a child. Although the report does not explicitly state this detail, it would appear than each parent answered questions about their use of physical discipline within the past year and the past week in respect of one child only. Table 4.1 shows the distribution of their responses.

Table 4.1: Use of physical punishment by age of child (per cent respondents)

	Child's age			
	Under 3	3-5	6-10	11+
Within past week	18	20	9	2
Within past year	46	77	57	34
Base = 692	n = 131	n = 116	n = 219	n = 226

While this report seems to lend support to popular beliefs about changes in parenting practices and confirms the view that parenting is qualitatively different from the experiences of respondents' own parents, it may be wise to treat these conclusions with some caution for a number of reasons. First, the sample, though recruited using methods typically thought capable of generating a representative sample, was rather small. Second, descriptive statistics only are reported rather than tests for differences which would need to be accompanied by probability and confidence levels and estimates of effect sizes in order for readers to ascertain whether the effects reported were substantial, statistically significant or reliable; this point is particularly relevant to assertions relating to class and gender differences. Third, no test-retest results are reported, making it difficult to have confidence in the validity or reliability of the measures employed. Fourth, although a number of methods were used in an effort to access information that many parents may feel unprepared to divulge, there is no guarantee that any of these methods was successful in tapping parents' actual behaviours. Nevertheless, bearing these reservations in mind, the report does suggest many possible avenues for further investigation.

In their now classic study of parenting practices (Newson and Newson, 1963, 1968, 1976), the Newsons elicited the views of parents about discipline, amongst other things. They found that a substantial majority of parents smacked their children (approximately 60 per cent of parents of one-year-olds, 80 per cent of parents of four-year-olds and around 73 per cent of parents of seven-year-olds). Resemblances between these findings and those of the more recent English or the Scottish studies seem to preclude any conclusions that British parents are more skilled or more confident about their ability to manage their children's behaviour. If anything, it would appear that parents feel as insecure as ever in this area.

Before leaving the subject of discipline, it seems valuable to remark that studies such as those described above tend to focus exclusively, often for reasons to do with policy, on situations in which parents exert control over their children's risky or troublesome behaviour. In doing this, they not only have the limitation of being self-report-based and inevitably prone to social response biases but they also overlook the wider context within which children's social development is being nurtured. This means that they are likely to afford only limited insight into the nature of parenting socialisation practices. For example, suppose a professional father is rarely at home when his three-year-old is awake whereas an economically inactive father is both at home and depressed, what meaning might the use or non-use of physical discipline have for each father? Both fathers might, in theory, ascribe to the same view that physical discipline is better avoided but successful avoidance may be more achievable by the father with the least direct contact or personal stress. An assessment of possible class differences in practice or attitudes may benefit from taking account of possibly influential contextual effects.

Similarly, it may not be wise to read too much into concurrent reports by parents of physical chastisement in their own past and similar treatment of their own children. There may be a genuine link but these are not sufficient grounds for establishing the existence of a causal link. At best, such evidence might point to the existence of an association but, without a representative sample, even this cannot be established with any confidence. This brings to mind that, while approximately 80 per cent of violent criminals might report having been abused as children, this cannot lead to the conclusion that 80 per cent of the total population of abused children are violent: an assessment of continuity needs to be based upon a representative population of all children, which would include a more representative sample of abused children (i.e. those who do not become violent criminals as well as those who do). In other words, to establish support for the intergenerational transmission assumption, more needs to be known about the processes involved both in repetition and in non-repetition of past insult. Attitudinal surveys run the risk of reproducing popular dogma rather than tapping into often very complex underlying processes. Parents across many generations may believe that their social situation is more challenging than that of their forebears or that they are more sophisticated than their forebears and these perceptions are, in their own right, of great interest. What they actually tell us about the real nature of change, though, is limited.

4.2 How do families in the UK differ from families in other parts of the world?

Kagitcibasi (1990, 1996) suggests that family structures and interactions might be mapped onto their social context in a fairly systematic way: rural agrarian cultures tend more towards extended, patrilineal structures while urban industrialised cultures are more strongly associated with nuclear families. In the rural agrarian social context, women's status tends to be low, preference for sons is usually high as are fertility rates, and the value of children lies very much in their capacity to contribute to often precariously low levels of subsistence. Parenting styles in these cultures tend to be authoritarian: children are expected to be obedient, to care for ageing parents as a duty and to be highly loyal to the family group. Wealth can be seen to flow toward the parent who will be in charge of its distribution. In this family context, children's sense of self grows from experience of relationships in which their individual needs and personality are subservient to the needs of the family group.

By contrast, as cultures become more affluent (i.e. urban, industrialised societies), Kagitcibasi (1990) notes that they are more likely to consist of nuclear families. Within the nuclear family structure, the developing sense of self is more autonomous and may either be formed through family interactions characterised by authoritative parenting (a warm, child-centred style of parenting in which the child is respected as an individual though is seen as being in need of firm guidance particularly in the early developmental stages) or through more permissive dynamics where children are encouraged to be self-reliant and to make decisions for themselves at relatively early ages. Kagitcibasi (1990) initially speculated that the permissive parenting style might be most closely associated with societies characterised by the most advanced technology. In both types of industrialised society, women's status is higher, fertility tends to be low, there is not so much evidence of preference for sons and the child is valued more for psychological than for material reasons. Wealth flows toward the children whose sense of self is formed either relatively independently of the family (in the case of permissively parented children) or in relation to the emotional context of the family (in the case of authoritatively parented children).

Within UK society, a number of minority ethnic communities ascribe to more patriarchal family patterns. Among these communities, parental expectations of obedience as well as beliefs and values in respect of child-rearing often contrast with those of the more technologically advanced 'host' culture. Where this is the case, intergenerational strain seems possible alongside considerable anxiety for parents who may view materialism and lack of respect for elders as a sign of serious moral failure. For newly arrived refugee families, the difficulties associated with this disparity may well be exacerbated by pressures evoked by adjusting to school (Hyman et al., 2000). All these factors might make adult-child communication more difficult for some minority ethnic groups.

4.3 Has parenting become more dominated by consumerism?

It would appear that modern Western societies may have undergone a further transformation since these schema were proposed or that the concept of the nuclear family may need to be replaced by a concept of families containing several nuclei. There has been some debate about whether children's identity may increasingly be being formed not in terms of the family group but more through peer group social comparison processes (e.g. Harris, 1999), and through their knowledge and possession of material goods which may be influenced by something approaching dictatorship by marketing manufacturers. In this model of social and family transactions, in contrast to contributing wealth to support their parents, children seem more likely to drain wealth away from parents as they engage in a process of self-aggrandisement. Parents, too, in this consumer culture are not immune from social pressures to possess high status possessions and may well feel pressured to create homes that can match up to their children's high expectations. The relatively recent deluge of terrestrial TV channels with programmes focused on home buying, decorating, maintenance, cleaning and related life-style matters, e.g. gardening, cooking, cars, clothes, etc. seems both to feed and to fuel pressing preoccupations with the need to project the 'right' image and social identity. As Dittmar (2004, p. 210) puts it, "to have is to be".

Anderson and Dittmar (2002) describe a small-scale study of teenagers' understanding of the social symbolism of different sets of brand name goods and conclude that teenagers are not only more knowledgeable about and desirous of brand name goods but they are very skilled at 'reading' other people through their ownership of branded goods. Dittmar (2004) draws attention to research which suggests that there are increasing tendencies for children of younger ages to construct their identity on the basis of material possessions, and worrying indications that young people are engaging in high levels of excessive spending. Rindfleisch et al. (1997) suggest that higher levels of spending may be a consequence of family breakdown, though finding evidence to support the actual direction of causality must remain problematic. As Benson (2000) suggests in a book entitled "I shop, therefore I am", social identity in consumer cultures may depend more on material wealth than on inter-family relationships. If this is the case, then parenting in such a context is likely to involve quite distinctive dilemmas or concerns, including, possibly, greater vulnerability of parents and children to the influences of mass media advertising than in the past.

4.4 Do marketing forces have more influence than parents on children?

Across continents as different as Asia, the Americas, Australia and Europe, children's fashions are being influenced by media marketing. In different parts of the UK, different terms have been coined by children to describe their peers who are adherents of name brand culture ("Nikeys", "Pikeys", etc.). Parents appear to have become increasingly aware of the social pressures placed on even their youngest children to own socially-approved commodities (usually either particular products or brands) and awareness of the pressure that is exerted on their children can oblige parents, often very reluctantly, to give in to what has become known as 'pester power', that is, the child's ability to pester their parent into purchasing goods.

There has been some debate about whether 'pester power' is a meaningful entity (McNeal, 1999) and there is currently no operational definition of the construct. Nevertheless the term seems to have become a popular one and has become associated with a sense that children's opinions are being allowed more weight in family decision-making that in the past. This hypothesis is, of course, difficult to test in the absence of relevant comparative data.

Children from very young ages are exposed to media and advertising and concern has been expressed about the extent to which advertisers target children, through free gifts, jingles, portrayal of child actors, humour, bright colours, child-oriented gimmicks such as cartoon characters, etc.. However, very few countries have restricted television advertising targeting children. Sweden and Norway have banned advertising directed at children under 12 and have disallowed advertising during children's programmes. Austria does not allow advertising during children's programmes and Australia does not allow advertising during programmes targeting pre-school children. Recently, the National Family and Parenting Institute recommended that television advertising to children should be better regulated in the UK.

Attempts to assess the impact of advertising on children's consumption are often hampered by the serious practical problems associated with manipulation of the independent variable (exposure to advertising) as well as difficulties involved in measuring effects. With variables that are so difficult to control, clear identification of cause and effect is problematic. For this reason, it is almost impossible to judge whether the consumer choices and behaviours of parents and children in modern society are really any more strongly influenced by advertising than in the recent past. What seems more likely is the possibility that family decision-making processes may have subtly altered so that parents are less inclined to exert their authority and to override the opinions of their children.

Earlier studies of the development of consumer behaviours in young children suggested that, until around 11, children are more strongly influenced by parents than by peers or by television (Ward, 1974). However, more recent studies have shown that children as young as two may have begun to make consumer choices and, from four onwards, will have begun to develop clear preferences as consumers and to use information from media advertising to inform their choices (McNeal, 1992a, 1992b; McNeal and Yeh, 1993).

Some research (e.g. Carlson and Grossbart, 1988) has suggested that different parenting styles impact on children's consumer preferences. For example, authoritative parents (defined as those who are child-centred, warm but firm in setting rules and explaining the necessity for rules) will tend to monitor children's exposure to adverts, will exert control over their children's spending on consumer goods and will be concerned to protect children from the effects of advertising and peer pressure; permissive parents will allow their children much more freedom to buy what they like though they will discuss preferences with them; authoritarian parents are likely to expose their children to outside pressures through their inability to recognise or discuss relevant issues with them.

Acknowledging parents' concerns about pressures on them from consumer culture, the Food Advertising Unit in 1996 published *ParentPower*, a booklet designed to help parents to deal with the difficulties inherent in raising children in a commercial world. In this publication, they identify pressures on modern parents that may not have influenced their own upbringing: the pressure, for example, for mothers to go to work rather than to stay at home and look after children, the advantages offered by labour-consuming devices not previously available but the sense that life needs to be lived at a faster pace because it is more competitive, and the inevitable and far greater exposure of family members to advertising. From the basis of these premises, *ParentPower* goes on to advise parents to engage in discussion, to control choice, to compromise and negotiate, to delay gratification and decision-making and to watch television together with their children. The overall message to parents appears to be that, unless parents put in the effort to keep channels of communication open with their children, their ability to influence their children's consumer-related behaviours will very likely be reduced.

4.5 Is new technology making it more difficult for parents to communicate with their children and to monitor their safety?

Data from General Household surveys indicates that, since 1984 when householders were first asked about possession of home computers, ownership has steadily risen, from fewer than 10 per cent in 1984 to approximately 20 per cent in 1990 and around 25 per cent in 1994. Since this time, ownership of home computers has doubled, standing at 50 per cent by 2001. Access to the internet from home has also increased although questions on this topic were not asked until 2000 when it was found that a third of all households had internet access, usually through home computers (31 per cent of all households). By 2001, this figure had risen to 39 per cent; by 2002 to 46 per cent, and by 2003 to 47 per cent (Expenditure and Food Survey Estimates; ONS, 2003). The UK is now thought, along with Germany and Italy, to have one of the largest at-home Internet populations (29 million).

Hanley (2002) identifies a number of areas from which parents' concerns seem to stem in relation to their children's use of new media: first, they can find it difficult to know how to monitor their children's television-viewing and internet surfing without either being neglectful or intrusive; second, they may not have consistent, effective or fully thought-through plans on how to monitor their children's media usage; third, they may feel unsure about what might constitute a danger to children.

In relation to television viewing, a substantial minority of parents had a number of concerns about both pre- and post-Watershed programmes, such as sexual content, strong language, violence, illegal drug use and blood and gore. They employed a variety of strategies to monitor their children's television usage such as banning or encouraging certain programmes, switching off the TV or changing channels, sending children out of the room, or more proactive methods such as watching the television with children. Although most parents seemed to feel that their children's viewing was under control, a substantial minority of children was left to watch unsupervised for quite large amounts of time and there was some anxiety about whether, as more channels became available, it would be more difficult for parents to keep tabs on what their children were being exposed to.

More serious worries appeared to be connected with children's internet usage, especially among parents who were not internet-experienced themselves. Only a minority of parents were knowledgeable about the scope or nature of available technological aids. As children are developing a deeper understanding of the messages conveyed by brand names than their parents and, via internet chatrooms and the use of mobile phones, are acquiring new skills in developing technologically-oriented languages (e.g. Merchant, 2001), some parents may feel they are losing touch, feel unsure about how to monitor their children's activities and worry about risks to their children from theft, bullying, etc. (National Opinion Poll, 2001; Hanley, 2002).

Thurlow and McKay (2002) assert that there are many benefits to be gained from the greatly increased use of new technology by young people, and that many of the risks are exaggerated, including "the wildly exaggerated, popular idea that young people are completely reinventing, and thereby destroying, standard (English) language use" (Thurlow and McKay, 2002, p. 116). They recommend research to discover what people actually do online, for example, how different intellectual interests might or might not be advanced, how 'safe spaces' are used, especially by 'at risk' young people, and the way in which the net might have altered more traditional ways of communicating.

Serious fears have come from the possibility that the internet may give dangerous people access to children. For example, O'Connell (2003) drew attention to the fact that children would become increasingly vulnerable to the activities of cyber groomers, particularly as internet access via mobile phones becomes more widely available. Amid mounting concern (e.g. Van Meeuwen et al., 1998; Barnardo's, 2002; Chase and Statham, 2004), a new definition of grooming was formed (Home Office, 2002) and this year a law has been introduced which aims to limit the danger to children of internet grooming.

The threat from negative media influences is likely to be multiplied in families in which communication and control issues are already somewhat problematic but the task of maximising protection for all children is not small. Recognising this, O'Connell (2003) recommends action on a number of fronts to reduce the risks to children. These strategies are aimed at a number of levels, including legislative procedures and legal practices, training of police and criminal justice professionals, improved network monitoring practices, public education and awareness raising, product development and marketing, and research to monitor closely the ways in which children and parents use the Internet as well as to find out as much as possible about the behaviour of people who might pose threats.

Communication

Communication between adolescents and their parents has been implicated in risk-taking behaviour such as experimenting with drugs, alcohol and sex (Karofsky et al., 2001). Although relationships between teenagers and parents have typically been portrayed as hampered by poor communication, considerable research now exists testifying to adolescents' communicative competence and the existence of mutually satisfying relationships between the majority of teenagers and important adults in their lives (Thurlow, 2002; Williams, 2002; Drury, 2002).

According to Gillies et al. (2001), popular deficit accounts of teen-parent relationships often overlook the complexity of the range of relationships between parents and older teenagers. In a small, qualitative study, Gillies et al. interviewed 32 teenagers (aged 16-18), 31 fathers and 30 mothers (of the 93 individual in-depth interviews carried out 39 were obtained from 14 family clusters). Results suggested that, contrary to popular stereotypes, parents and teenagers were in close communication with each other. However, in some areas, such as risk-taking behaviour, there was some disparity, for example, where parents assumed that their children had not experimented with drugs and sex, teenagers stated that the contrary was true.

Evidence gathered via self report from a much larger sample of young people (4,048 people aged 12-20 years) also lends support to a picture of greater communicative competence than stereotypes might suggest (Drury et al., 1998): young people assessed their bad communication experiences as having occurred more frequently outside the family than within it, and were usually able to give explanations and attributions for perceived poor communication.

Both the above studies are limited in that they rely on self-report but they do suggest that good relationships between parents and children might be less uncommon than negative stereotypes imply. There are also indications that, when communication is good, it can protect adolescents against risky behaviour, for example, Wellings and Wadsworth (1999) concluded that being able to talk with parents about sex appears to protect against teenage pregnancy.

4.6   Are sexual behaviours among children changing?

As mentioned in the section on advertising to children, the late twentieth century has witnessed the growth of concern about the degree to which marketing to children may have encouraged precocious interest in social comparison processes and inappropriate sexualisation of young children. That younger-aged children have become the target for market advertisers is apparent from the coining of the term 'tweens' for pre-teenage children. And this newly-created population of approximately 7-11 year old children is rumoured to have become fashion- and body-shape-conscious in a way unheard of in previous generations. However, just as researchers (e.g. Brannen et al., 1994) have emphasised that the concept of adolescence is a relatively recent and predominantly Western notion, it seems important to recognise that the same is even more true for the concept of 'tweenage'.

In truth, young children have probably shown interest in mothers' lipsticks ever since mothers first used lipstick and other cosmetic accoutrements. Possibly, in the days when men powdered their hair and fixed or painted on charmingly lumpy hairy moles, offspring may have mimicked these alluring paternal behaviours too. Most 'normally developing' young children show interest in their own images and will experiment with dressing up. And it is also normal for young children to be curious about parents' behaviour, to wonder where babies come from, and to want to find out about and compare each other's bodies.

However, concern about the sexualisation of young children's behaviour and the sense that childhood has somehow got shorter appears to touch on deeper worries about ways that market forces and differences in information networks may have impacted on children's lives in the twentieth century. It also has clear links with fears about the particular vulnerability of young girls (and boys, too, though this concern surfaces slightly less readily) to predatory older males, whether through the Internet or via other means.

Unfortunately, it is not possible to test whether there are sound empirical grounds for the belief that children nowadays are under more severe pressure to engage in sexual behaviours at an earlier age, nor is it easy to assess whether parents' concerns are greater now than they were in the past. It is probably true to say that parents have always been aware of the more serious consequences for daughters of early sexual experiences though this has not always meant that they have been able, or willing, to protect their children against sexual abuse from within or outside the family. In some respects, it seems unlikely that much has changed apart from the way that these matters are aired, i.e. the degree to which they feature in various forms of media discussion. However, this conclusion, too, is not easy to test.

Even the question of whether what is called the 'secular trend' in onset of puberty, that is, the tendency across generations for the onset of menarche to be earlier, is disputed among experts, on the grounds that data relevant to testing this hypothesis is not available. For a long time, the chief source of information about the onset of puberty came from a rather small UK study of 192 English girls (Marshall and Tanner, 1969): even if more recent studies have suggested greater variability and earlier onset (e.g. Herman-Giddens et al., 1997), the conclusion that qualitatively different processes are at work would be unsound. They may be, but the empirical evidence has not been gathered which can conclusively prove the argument one way or another.

On the other hand, information is available concerning associations between the onset of puberty and malnutrition, and there have also been a number of studies exploring links between the onset of puberty and factors such as obesity, stress and race (Herman-Giddens et al., 1988; Ellis et al., 2000; Kaplowitz et al., 2001; Chumlea et al., 2003). Information is also available from a number of sources allowing comparisons to be made between British teenagers and those in other countries in respect of ages and rates of conception and abortion. Recent British Social Attitudes surveys also provide some information about changing attitudes in relation to sexual behaviour.

Teenage pregnancy

During the 1990s and early 2000s, rates of teenage birth fell slightly but the relatively high incidence, in a context where education has been available (to varying degrees) and birth control is relatively easy to access, has remained a matter of concern. A report by UNICEF (UNICEF, 2001), based on Eurostat Labour Force Survey data gathered in 1998, drew attention to the fact that the UK then had the highest teenage birth rate in Europe (16.6 per thousand among 15 to 17 year old women and 51.8 per thousand among 18-19 year olds). Alongside this, the report also noted that the UK teenage birth rate was four times the European average. More detailed information about rates of conception, abortion and birth are given in Appendix 4.3 of this report.

A report by the Social Exclusion Unit (SEU, 1999) suggested that three negative processes might account for failure to avoid pregnancy during adolescence: low expectations (e.g. lack of job prospects), ignorance (e.g. not being aware of the consequences of unprotected sex or of the difficulties associated with bringing up children) and mixed messages (e.g. finding it difficult to know whether they are expected to engage in sexual behaviours or not). This none-too-flattering account of young people's state of knowledge appears to have formed a key part of the Government's Teenage Pregnancy Strategy which was launched in 1999. This set out to "reduce the rate of teenage conceptions with the specific aim of halving the rate of conceptions among under-18s, and to set a firmly established downward trend in the rate of conceptions among under-16s, by 2010" (Health Development Agency, Teenage Pregnancy Unit, 2004) and to increase teenage parents' rates of participation in education and training to 60 per cent by 2010 with the intention of reducing the risk of their long-term social exclusion. The Strategy involves a four-part action plan including a national information campaign, preventive measures (renewed efforts to deliver more effective sex education and to encourage safe sex practices, particularly among young men), more support for pregnant mothers and their partners, and joined-up action across local and government departments to co-ordinate the strategy.

At almost the same time as the Teenage Pregnancy Strategy was introduced, as part of its British Social Attitudes survey series, NatCen carried out a survey of attitudes towards teenage pregnancy (Clarke and Thomson, 2001/2002). From this, it appeared that the majority of respondents endorsed a distinctly negative view of teenage pregnancy: the majority agreed that teenage pregnancy was a problem, that one of the main causes of teenage pregnancies is lack of morals among young people, that teenagers in stable relationships should not have a child, that bringing up children is too difficult for most teenagers to do alone, that television and advertising put teenagers under too much pressure to have sex before they are ready, that teenage girls living in run down areas are more likely than others to become teenage mothers, that teenage girls who want to get on in life do not usually become teenage mothers, that Britain's welfare system all too often rewards teenage mothers and that there would be fewer teenage pregnancies if there was better sex education and if parents talked to their children more about sex, relationships and contraception (fuller details of responses to individual items are presented in appendix 4.4).

The base number of respondents from which these answers were obtained was 2,980. They were recruited using a method designed to achieve a representative sample and there appeared to be a fairly even distribution of respondents across the range of ages (from 18 to 65+). No details were given relating to respondents' ethnicity and the sample size, though substantial, was perhaps not sufficiently large to enable very meaningful analysis of differences by class, ethnic group or age. From the survey, a picture seemed to emerge of a UK population that is, by and large, opposed to teenage parenting, and these findings would appear to lend more support to Government moves to discourage the phenomenon.

Nevertheless, there does seem to be room for some doubt about the reliability and validity of a survey of this sort. The first worry, as already mentioned, is whether the survey included views of minority ethnic communities, particularly Caribbeans, and respondents from the Bangladeshi and Pakistani communities who may need translation and interpretation. A second concern is about the nature of questions which, since they often appear to reflect prejudices against teenage parents, stand in danger of eliciting responses which seem highly likely to be prone to social desirability effects. A third, rather fundamental, query relates to the validity of questions about 'teenage pregnancy' for it is not at all clear what the term means, nor how likely it was that all respondents were defining it similarly. Adolescence stretches across a wide age range: how useful is it to ask questions that assume that the situation of a 17-19 year old woman in a relationship with a similarly aged or perhaps slightly older man is the same as that of a 13-16 year old girl? In view of these difficulties, it seems that more useful information might be obtained if questions were re-framed with the aim of discovering more, for example, about the educational and support needs of teenage parents at different ages.

There is some debate in the research literature about the nature of teenage pregnancy and its effects. While some argue that negative consequences of teenage pregnancy are over-stated (Berthoud and Iacovou, undated), others have pointed to associations with poverty and a range of social, educational and employment disadvantages. The majority of teenage births in the UK occur outside marriage (90 per cent, 92 per cent and 93 per cent among all women under 20 in 1990, 1995 and 2001 respectively). They are also more common among women from lower social classes: the rate was found to be 10 times higher for girls from social class V families than for girls from social class I families (Botting et al., 1998). Concern has also focused on the incidence of unplanned pregnancies, the tendency for young mothers themselves to have been born to teenage mothers and on evidence of less than optimal levels of self-health care, for example, not practising safe sex, having higher than average smoking rates and poorer health in later life (Wellings et al., 1996; Allen and Bourke Dowling, 1999; Hamlyn et al., 2002). Teenage mothers are also less likely to complete their education or training (Manlove, 1997), are less likely to find satisfactory employment (Kiernan, 1995) and more likely than other teenage girls of their age to experience social isolation and depression (Botting et al., 1998).

Additional risks to the infants and children of teenage mothers have also been identified, including higher rates of infant mortality, increased rates of congenital anomalies, lower birth weight and poorer chances of survival compared with similar birthweight babies of older mothers (Botting et al., 1998), increased numbers of hospital admissions in connection with accidents involving poisoning and burns (Peckham, 1993) and a higher likelihood of being brought up in poverty (Kiernan, 1995).

Berthoud and Iacovou (undated) draw comparisons between European countries and argue that, while there are high risks that teenage mothers will experience poverty, this experience is not inevitable: there is only a weak association between teenage parenting and poverty in Austria, Italy and Spain, a very high risk in the Netherlands and substantial risk in the UK. The existence of such wide variations between countries points to the possibility that the cultural context of teenage parenting may be as important an influence as parents' age per se. It is not clear, for example, that in countries and cultures where marriages are arranged during late (18-20) or middle (15-17) teenage, where social support is more forthcoming and social disapprobation is less rife, the young people concerned do experience any of the disadvantages purported to exist in disapproving Western cultures. Medical evidence does not suggest, either, that child-bearing in the late teenage years is associated with poor health either in mothers or in children, unless it is linked to pre-existing social disadvantage, which may be the case for some young people in Britain.

One recent report (Berthoud, 2001) has examined variations between ethnic groups on rates of childbirth among mothers under 20. Using data from Labour Force Surveys (1987 to 1999), Berthoud calculated the annual rate per thousand births to mothers by ethnic group. For mothers aged 15-19, rates were highest among Bangladeshi mothers (75 per thousand), the next highest rate was among Caribbean and Pakistani mothers (44 and 41 per thousand, respectively), the rate for White mothers in this age group was 29 per thousand while Indian mothers had the lowest rate (17 per thousand). Closer inspection of these data showed that, while Bangladeshi women at all ages had the highest rates of birth, differences between ethnic groups do not emerge until age 17, which would correspond closely with the age at which marriages typically take place in this community. It is not perhaps surprising, therefore, to find that a much higher percentage of young South Asians mothers (Indians, Bangladeshis and Pakistanis: 85 per cent) were married, compared with only 47 per cent of white and 15 per cent of Caribbean mothers. Looking at patterns across time, Berthoud demonstrated that rates of births to young mothers appeared to be falling among the Indian, Pakistani and Bangladeshi communities but this decline was not mirrored by White or Caribbean mothers. These findings seem to point to a very different social context for younger mothers in the different communities and suggest that policy initiatives which aim to reduce numbers of teenage pregnancies need to be sensitive both to the social and cultural context of motherhood as well as to differences between older and younger teenage mothers.

Currently, it seems fair to say that it is still too early to know what the impact of recent government initiatives might be in respect of support for teenage and young parents across the UK but that, in the coming decade, considerably more information of good quality should be available to inform future policies. It will, though, of course be important to recognise the diverse nature of the teenage and young adult population in the UK and to ensure that young people who choose to start their families at the age of 17 receive the support that they might want to pursue the lifestyle of their choice and to maximise opportunities for their children also to make their own choices.

4.7   Are children becoming independent earlier or later?

Studies of children's transitions to young adulthood and independence appear to be showing that these transitions have changed qualitatively within recent decades. There no longer appears to be a "normative ordering along a single pathway (comprising a school-to-work transition followed some years later by a household-and-family-formation transition)" (Jones, 2002)[12]. Rather, transitions often involve 'back-tracking' as young people move backwards and forwards between family and the outside world. Many young people, at the same time as seeking greater autonomy and psychological independence, stay at home longer so that their financial and physical dependency is prolonged.

As a result, the significance which used to be attached to key transition periods, such as leaving school, finishing education or going to university, seems to have altered: going to university, for example, which used to involve a step towards independence that was, for some young people, a major life event may now, for some people, seem more like a continuation of school, especially if parents maintain a consistent level of involvement across both settings. These changes appear to be associated with trends towards later family formation, with wider access to education and training but with slower transitions between training and employment (Bynner and Pan, 2002), and with the greater instability of families with young children.

---

12 This pattern of transition is thought by many social historians/scientists to have been a pattern unique to the early 1950s and 1960s

They also appear to have created patterns for young people in more or less affluent or 'work-rich' families that are quite distinct from those of young people from lower income or no income families.

While children appear to be seeking and, often, acquiring greater financial autonomy than in the past while still living at home, many middle and upper working class parents are finding that their adult children are not choosing to move out into independent accommodation in the way that they might have expected from their own experiences. Not only that, they are finding that adult children who have moved out are moving back in again, and this behaviour, again, constitutes something of a violation of expectations. This pattern, however, is not apparent across all levels of the social structure and young people from the most deprived areas of society appear to be the least likely to stay at home, instead leaving at a point where they risk homelessness, and exposure to other disadvantageous lifestyles.

Jones (2002) offers a number of possible explanations as to why these changes may have come about. She suggests that the 'slow-track' pattern, where children delay setting up their own homes, that occurs within middle class and, increasingly, affluent working class families, may be influenced as much by factors such as lack of affordable housing, ineligibility for benefits, wariness of commitment to relationships, and unstable relationships, as by lifestyle choices. Whereas in the past young adults may have been prepared to set up independent homes with very little material resources and gradually, under their own steam, build up material goods, there is a tendency now for this option to be seen as less than desirable, in fact, as somehow 'infra dig', wrong and unnecessary. Instead, while still living with their parents, many young people have grown accustomed to a lifestyle which they could not easily, until their careers have developed further, sustain independently. She suggests that the emphasis placed by recent governments on encouraging families to support themselves may have increased the tendency for young people to rely on within-family transferences of material resources. In other words, the strengthening of processes of inter-generational transmission of goods may have led both to prolonged and constricted dependency. These, in turn, will have widened the gap between rich and poor.

'Fast-track' patterns, by contrast, involve children leaving home precipitately and, because of the erosion of much welfare support (e.g. welfare benefits, grants and adequate minimum wages for people at the outset of work careers), being exposed to considerable risk, perhaps leading eventually to their social exclusion. However, Jones (2002) argues that the most vulnerable of these young people do not form a static, homogeneous group and therefore their needs will not be met by processes that attempt to identify them as a targetable entity or as a stereotyped or stigmatised 'tip of the iceberg'. Rather, she urges that it will be far more productive to address more widely the needs of all those young people who are trying to survive on scarce resources.

Jones claims that this should involve accepting that previously held beliefs about young people need to change to accommodate the changed realities of their social context. Out-dated assumptions include notions such as that young people who do not make transitions at key times are dysfunctional, that parents should be expected to retain financial responsibility for children until their mid-20s, that young people will aspire to middle class social positions or lifestyles, that economic incentives or disincentives are effective controls of young people's behaviour. She suggests, instead, that more holistic approaches will need to be employed, such as extending the take-up of education by means of creative approaches sensitive to the specific requirements of young people and their families in all sections of society, easing the transition into work for those who have left the education system early, abolishing the transitional national minimum wage so that all over 18s are entitled to adult rates, improving the recently introduced sex education programme, taking serious steps to provide accommodation as well as assistance to parents who house their children, and researching alternative forms of support that can supplement family care.

Many of the reforms that Jones (2002) proposes may contribute considerably to the relief of pressure on young people and their parents, and some moves in the directions proposed have come from recent government initiatives, for example, through the work of the Connexions services. These provide personal development advice, support and opportunities to children aged 13-19, without the requirement of parental involvement. More recently, a raft of recommendations contained in the recent review of financial support to 16-19 year olds (HM Treasury, 2004) directly addresses many of the concerns about financial support to young people.

References to Chapter 4

Allen, I. and Bourke Dowling, S. (1999) Teenage mothers: Decisions and outcomes. In S. McRae (Ed.), *Changing Britain: Families and households in the 1990s* (333-353). Oxford: Oxford University Press.

Anderson, N. and Dittmar, H. (September 2002) *Shopping for identity*. Paper presented at the BPS Social Psychology Section of the British Psychological Society Conference, Hull. [Cited in Dittmar, op cit.]

Anderson, S., Murray, L. and Brownlie, J. (2002) *Disciplining children: Research with parents in Scotland*. Edinburgh: Scottish Executive Central Research Unit.

Barnardo's (2002) *Stolen childhood: Barnardo's work with children abused through prostitution*. Barkingside: Barnardo's.

Benson, A. (Ed.) (2000) *I shop, therefore I am: Compulsive buying and the search for self*. New York: Aronson.

Berthoud, R. (2001) Teenage births to ethnic minority women. *Population Trends*, **104**, 12-17.

Berthoud, R. and Iacovou, M. (undated) *Diverse Europe: Mapping patterns of social change across the EU*. Swindon: ESRC. Online (March, 2004) at: http://www.esrc.ac.uk/esrccontent/news/diverse_europe.asp

Botting, B., Rosato, M. and Wren, R. (1998) Teenage mothers and the health of their children. *Population Trends*, **93**, 19-28.

Boyson, R. and Thorpe, L. (2002) *Equal protection for children: An overview of the experience of countries that accord children full legal protection from legal punishment*. Online (March, 2003) at: http://www.nspcc.org.uk/inform/downloads/EqualProtectionForChildren.pdf

Brannen, J., Dodd, K., Oakley, A. and Storey, P. (1994) *Young people, health and family life*. Buckingham: Open University.

Bynner, J. and Pan, H. (2002) Understanding transition. *Young people's changing routes to independence* (27-36). York: York Publishing Services for the Joseph Rowntree Foundation.

Carlson, L. and Grossbart, S. (1988) Parental style and consumer socialisation of children. *Journal of Consumer Research*, **15**, 77-94.

Chase, E. and Statham, J. (2004) *The commercial sexual exploitation of children and young people: An overview of key literature and data*. London: Thomas Coram Research Unit.

Chumlea, W.C., Schubert, C.M., Roche, A.F., Kulin, H.E., Lee, P.A., Himes, J.H. and Sun, S.S. (2003) Age at menarche and racial comparisons in girls. *Pediatrics*, **111(1)**, 110-113.

Clarke, L. and Thomson, K. (2001/2002) Teenage mums. In A. Park, J. Curtice, K. Thomson, L. Jarvis and C. Bromley (Eds.), *British Social Attitudes: Public policy, social ties* (59-79). London: National Centre for Social Research.

Dittmar, H. (2004) Are you what you have? *The Psychologist,* **17(4)**, 206-210.

Drury, J. (2002) Adolescents' communication with adults in authority. In *Draft report of the task force on language, social psychology and adolescence, International Association of Language and Social Psychology* (47-61). Online (March, 2004) at: http://www.cf.ac.uk/encap/clcr/ialsp/reports/

Drury, J., Catan, L., Dennison, C. and Brody, R. (1998) Exploring teenagers' accounts of bad communication: A new basis for intervention. *Journal of Adolescence*, **21(2)**, 177-196.

Ellis, B.J. and Garber, J. (2000) Psychosocial antecedents of variation in girls' pubertal timing: Maternal depression, stepfather presence, and marital and family stress. *Child Development*, **71(2)**, 485-501.

Gershoff, E. T. (2002) Corporal punishment by parents and associated child behaviours and experiences: A meta-analysis and theoretical review. *Psychological Bulletin*, **128(4)**, 539-579.

Ghate, D., Hazel, N., Creighton, S., Finch, S. and Field, J. (2003) *The national study of parents, children and discipline in Britain: Summary of key findings*. London: Policy Research Bureau.

Gillies, V. (2000) Young people and family life: Analysing and comparing disciplinary discourses. *Journal of Youth Studies*, **3(2)**, 211-228.

Gillies, V., Ribbens McCarthy, J. and Holland, J. (2001) *Pulling together, pulling apart: The family lives of young people*. London: Family Policy Studies Centre.

Goodman, R. (1997) The Strengths and Difficulties Questionnaire: A research note. *Journal of Child Psychology and Psychiatry*, **38(5)**, 581-588.

Hamlyn, R., Brooker, S., Oleinikova, K. and Wands, S. (2002) *Infant feeding, 2000*. London: TSO.

Hanley, P. (2002) *Striking a balance: the control of children's media consumption*. Internet: BBC Broadcasting Standards Commission and ITC.

Harris, J.P. (1999) *The nurture assumption: why children turn out the way they do*. New York: touchstone Press.

Herman-Giddens, M.E., Slora, E.J., Wasserman, R.C., Bourdonoy, C.J., Bhapkar, M.V., Koch, G. and Hasemeier, C.M. (1997) Secondary sexual characteristics and menses in young girls seen in office practice: A study from the Pediatric Research in Office Settings Network. *Pediatrics*, **99**, 505-512.

Herman-Giddens, M.E., Sandler, A.D. and Friedman, N.E. (1988) Sexual precocity in girls: An association with sexual abuse. *American Journal of Disabled Children*, **142**, 431-433.

HM Treasury (2004) *Supporting young people to achieve: towards a new deal for skills.* Norwich: HMSO. Online at: http://www.hm-treasury.gov.uk

Hyman, I., Vu, N. and Beiser, M. (2000) Post-migration stresses among Southeast Asian refugee youth in Canada: A research note. *Journal of Comparative Family Studies*, **31(2)**, 281-293.

Jones, G. (2002) *The youth divide. Diverging paths to adulthood.* York: York Publishing Services for the Joseph Rowntree Foundation.

Kagitcibasi, C. (1990) Family and socialization in cross-cultural perspective: A model of change. In J. Berman (Ed.), *Cross-cultural perspectives: Nebraska symposium on motivation, 1989* (135-200). Lincoln, NE: Nebraska University Press.

Kagitcibasi, C. (1996) *Family and human development across cultures: A view from the other side.* Hillsdale, NJ: Lawrence Erlbaum.

Kaplowitz, P.B., Slora, E.J., Wasserman, R.C., Pedlow, S.E and Herman-Giddens, M.E. (2001) Earlier onset of puberty in girls: Relation to increased body mass index and race. *Pediatrics*, **108**, 347-353.

Karofsky, P.S., Sen, L. and Kosorok, M.R. (2001) Relationship between adolescent-parent communication and initiation of first intercourse by adolescents. *Journal of Adolescent Health*, **28(1)**, 41-45.

Kiernan, K. (1995) *Transition to parenthood: Young mothers, young fathers. – Associated factors and later life experiences.* Welfare discussion paper 113. London: London School of Economics.

Langford, W., Lewis, C., Solomon, Y. and Warin, J. (2001) *Family understandings: Closeness, authority and independence in families with teenagers.* London: Family Policy Studies Centre for the Joseph Rowntree Foundation.

McNeal, J.U. (1992a) The littlest shoppers. *American Demographics*, **14(2)**, 48-53.

McNeal, J.U. (1992b) Growing up in the market. *American Demographics*, **14(10)**, 46-50.

McNeal, J.U. and Yeh, C.H. (1993) Born to shop. *American Demographics*, **15(6)**, 34-39.

McNeal, J.U. (1999) *The Kids' Market: Myths and realities.* Ithaca: Paramount Market Publishing.

Manlove, J. (1997) Early motherhood in an intergenerational perspective: the experiences of a British Cohort. *Journal of Marriage and the Family*, **59**, 263-279.

Marshall, W.A. and Tanner, J.M. (1969) Variations in the pattern of pubertal changes in girls. *Archives of Disease in Childhood*, **44**, 291-303.

Merchant, G. (2001) Teenagers in cyberspace: An investigation of language use and language change in internet chatrooms. *Journal of Research in Reading*, **24(3)**, 293-306.

Newson, J. and Newson, E. (1963) *Patterns of infant care in an urban community.* Harmondsworth: Penguin.

Newson, J. and Newson, E. (1968) *Four years old in an urban community.* Harmondsworth: Penguin.

Newson, J. and Newson, E. (1976) *Seven years old in the home environment.* Harmondsworth: Penguin.

O'Connell, R. (2003) *A typology of child cybersexploitation and online grooming practices.* University of Central Lancashire, Preston.

Peckham, S. (1993) Preventing unplanned teenage pregnancies. *Public Health*, **197**, 125-133.

Rindfleisch, A., Burroughs, J.E. and Denton, F. (1997) Family structure, materialism, and compulsive consumption. *Journal of Consumer Research*, **23**, 312-325.

Straus, M.A., Hamby, S.L., Finkelhor, D., Moore, D.W. and Runyan, D. (1998) Identification of child maltreatment with the Parent-Child Conflict Tactics Scale: Development and psychometric data for a national sample of American parents. *Child Abuse and Neglect*, **22(4)**, 249-270.

Health Development Agency, Teenage Pregnancy Unit (2004) *Teenage pregnancy: An overview of the research evidence.* London: Health Development Agency.

Thurlow, C. (2002) Adolescents *in* communication, adolescents *on* communication. In *Draft report of the task force on language, social psychology and adolescence, International Association of Language and Social Psychology* (16-29). Online at: http://www.cf.ac.uk/encap/clcr/ialsp/reports/

UNICEF (2001) *A league table of teenage births in rich nations.* Innocenti Report Card, No. 3. Florence: UNICEF Innocenti Research Centre. Available online at www.unicef-icdc.org/publications/index.html

Van Meeuwen, A., Swann, S., McNeish, D. and Edwards, S.S.M. (1998) *Whose daughter next? Children abused through prostitution.* Basildon, Essex: Barnardo's.

Ward, S. (1974) Consumer socialisation. *Journal of Consumer Research*, **1**, 1-14.

Wellings, K, Wadsworth, J., Field, B. and Petruckevick, A. (1996) *Teenage sexuality, fertility and life chances*. London: School of Hygiene and Tropical Medicine.

Wellings, K. and Wadsworth, J. (1999) Family influences on teenage fertility. In S. McRae (Ed.), *Changing Britain: Families and households in the 1990s* (319-333). Oxford: Oxford University Press.

Williams, A. (2002) Adolescents' relationships with older family members. In *Draft report of the task force on language, social psychology and adolescence, International Association of Language and Social Psychology* (30-46). Online at: http://www.cf.ac.uk/encap/clcr/ialsp/reports/

5 | Kinship ties, community and family support

Throughout the twentieth century, increased geographical mobility and the disappearance of some industrial communities, combined with the changing nature of the general population (population ageing, the shrinking child population, changing family structures and, on average, increased fitness among older people) appear to have led to different patterns of family interaction.

As has been mentioned in previous chapters, some commentators have deplored what they see as the demise of the family. In their view, family support networks have been eroded and families have become dispersed, whether through parental divorce, through people moving away from the location of their family of origin, or due to pressures from the increasingly uncontrollable social context in which families are situated. They see traditional patterns of family exchange as having broken down and older generations as incapable of offering solutions to the new sorts of problems now facing their children. Families' support networks at various stages of development have broken down and new sources of informational (advice, knowledge, etc.), material (finance, property, goods), emotional and practical advice are needed. In other words, family members can no longer count on each other for assistance but have to look elsewhere.

As Giddens (1999b), and many others, have pointed out, there are reasons to doubt the premises on which the 'demise of the family' account is founded. Chief among these is the belief that families in the past were self-contained, self-sufficient and well-regulated. We need only turn to statistics on child abuse, delinquency, mental health, and the need for education, welfare, health and justice systems to find evidence to the contrary. Yet, despite this implausibility, a strong oral tradition (in the media as well as in the public imagination) seems to support the notion that communities are more unstable, that the youth of today are out of control, that society is a far more dangerous place than it ever was and that families are finding it more difficult to cope.

In this chapter, we focus particularly on the place of the family in its wider context and ask whether relationships between families and society have altered over the past 10 years.

Specifically, we address the following questions:

5.1 What is the effect of increased geographical mobility on family interaction?

5.2 How do minority ethnic families fare in terms of family functioning and community support?

5.3 Has the role of grandparents in family life altered?

5.4 Has it become less safe to raise children in Britain?

5.5 Is Britain becoming less family-minded as increasing numbers of women choose not to raise children?

5.6 Do parents need more or different forms of support and guidance from sources outside the family?

5.7 Should the Government intervene more to ensure that parents' rights and responsibilities are more clearly defined?

5.1 What is the effect of increased geographical mobility on family interaction?

As families become more dispersed, it has often been thought that family support networks come under increasing strain. Underlying this view is an assumption that physical proximity is needed for families to exchange the practical, material, emotional and other forms of social support that might normally be found in less mobile family units. Alongside this, is an understanding that geographical mobility is associated with community instability which, in turn, is associated with problems such as family break-down, crime, mental illness, social alienation, etc..

Arguably the most highly geographical mobile families in the UK are to be found in minority ethnic communities among whom families can be stretched across boundaries spanning several countries. The processes involved in the evolution of migrant families (e.g. the development of 'new ethnicities': Hall, 1991) are highly complex and diverse, and have been and continue to be the subject of much research. It is not possible within the limits of this report to describe this work but, nevertheless, it seems useful at this point to indicate that this research tends to show that family ties can be maintained and that many people experience a need to retain a sense that they are still part of the family and culture that they left behind (Vertovec, 1999). Some similar patterns have also been found among families that move within countries: both Grieco's (1987) study of Scottish migrants to Corby in the Midlands and Baumann's study of migrants in the Southall district of London (Baumann, 1996) showed that family members made positive efforts to maintain kinship contact.

Mobility which is internal to the UK is often related to employment. Higher geographical mobility tends to occur in social classes with higher education and also among young people with higher educational qualifications. Generally, this kind of mobility confers benefits on young, upwardly mobile family members. However, there is some evidence that there might be difficulties for dual-earner geographically mobile families, particularly for females who move at the expense of their own employment because their partners have found work (Bonney and Love, 1991; Cooke and Bailey, 1999). These effects were confirmed in Green and Canny's study (Green and Canny, 2003) on family re-location. Green and Canny point out that re-location changes lives as well as jobs and that, while some younger parents might be prepared for the disruption involved, older parents (fathers and mothers) tend to find the necessity to relocate more difficult to cope with. Green and Canny particularly draw attention to the effects upon family members at different life stages: parents worry about the disruption of school age children's education; adolescents and young adult find moves difficult as it disrupts their developing relationships with peers, which in turn may interrupt or distort the process of becoming independent (for example, resulting in premature home-leaving); and older relatives lose contact with familiar social networks of friends and others.

Nevertheless, there is information from other sources which indicates that distance between family members need not imply loss of contact or support. Grundy (1999) used data from the 1999 Omnibus Survey to examine the extent to which families were in touch with each other, across four generations. She found that, of those respondents who had a parent or an elder child alive, half or more made contact at least once a week and half of the people making contact lived within a half hour's journey of each other. She also found considerable reciprocity of exchange between parents and their eldest children (the only child asked about): two thirds of mothers and almost half of the fathers both provided help and were recipients of it. Similar findings also emerged from the 1986 and 1995 British Social Attitudes surveys. These indicated that, although frequency of contact had reduced by 1995 (possibly largely due to changes in employment patterns), the same family members were turned to when important life events took place, regardless of physical distance.

Research from the US lends further support to these findings. Several studies have shown that older people and their children have regular contact and exchange social support even though they are geographically distant (e.g. Lye, 1996). Findings from other studies (e.g. Bengston, 2001) indicate that intergenerational family support is usually provided when needed and that exchanges do not depend on co-residence or even physical proximity (Silverstein and Bengston, 1997). Riley and Riley (1993) proposed the existence of a system they term the 'latent kin matrix' to explain how distal family relationships might work: in this model family relationships within extended or 'extended-modified' families remain latent when they are not needed but quickly become activated when they are needed, for example, if one family member has a crisis.

Geographical distance between family members, then, need not dilute the importance of relationships. Neither is it a phenomenon that is exclusive to the last decade or even to the latter half of the twentieth century. It would also seem that some extension and permeability in family boundaries can be beneficial, in order to maximise the family's potential to take advantage of resources in the wider community and to reduce pressure on the family (Crow and Maclean, 2004).

5.2 How do minority ethnic families fare in terms of family functioning and community support?

Elsewhere in this report, we have drawn attention to the diverse nature of minority ethnic communities in the UK. In a recently published National Family and Parenting Institute report, Becher and Husain (2003) drew attention to the fact that families from these minority groups have as much need as families from other communities for support (Qureshi et al., 2000), that the kind of support that they might require will differ both between and within different minority communities (Ahmed et al., 1986; Ballard, 1994; Bose, 2000; Lau, 2000) and that much of the support that is available has often been difficult for them to access or has not been sufficiently sensitive to the particular situation of individual families (Butt and Box, 1998).

Becher and Husain identify culture as comprised of multiple, overlapping components including, for example, traditions and individual biographies, ethnicity and race, religion, spirituality, morality and artistic production. They argue that it is inaccurate to assume that, either within majority or minority communities, culture is a static, hegemonic entity or that ethnic identities are other than "fluid, shifting, reconstituted and interactive" (Becher and Husain, 2003, p. 11). Bearing this definition in mind, they point to varying patterns of need among different minority ethnic communities in respect of health services (psychological and physical needs), police and legal services (for example, in relation to effects of employment discrimination and other forms of racism), educational provision and family support.

There is now a very substantial literature, based on studies conducted in many different parts of the world, which has addressed the question of the nature of cultural integration among immigrant populations. From time to time, theories have emerged from this body of work which suggest that conflict between first and later generation family members is common as younger members more readily absorb values from the host culture and seek to move away from the values espoused by older members and to identify more closely with their peers. If this is an accurate account of acculturation processes, then it would seem to follow that communities with a longer history of settlement in Britain (e.g. Caribbean families) might be less prone to intra-family stress than more recent immigrants (e.g. Bangladeshi families). It would also suggest that traditional family support systems would be increasingly likely to come under strain as they are 'invaded' by the host culture and that difficulties would emerge quite predictably in areas where attitudinal differences between immigrant and host cultures are most marked, for example, in connection with attitudes to arrangements preceding marriage, the role of women, divorce, childlessness, etc..

Recent studies of these processes, however, do not appear to support a simple linear account but, rather, more complex accounts that accommodate greater variability and the possibility of more individual negotiation. For example, they allow for the fact that some people may, more or less deliberately, choose to adhere to more traditional customs, values and beliefs while others may take up a range of alternative practices and views (Halstead, 1994; Dosanjh and Ghuman, 1996). However, as recognised by a number of key workers in this area, there is currently in the UK, in general, a dearth of information about the nature of family and community networks among minority ethnic families. This is largely due to the fact that, where social research has been undertaken, it has rarely been specifically focused on minority ethnic communities and nor has it been undertaken on a scale which would capture sufficient numbers for minority ethnic people to be represented. As a result, it is not possible to gauge with any great precision whether, over the last 10 years, family structures, relationships, attitudes, customs and practices have changed much at all.

Recognising these difficulties, Becher and Husain (2003, p. 76) recommend the use of a 'communicative model of family support' to identify the service needs of minority ethnic communities. The aim of this model is to provide a conceptual framework for the development of culturally sensitive services which respond to individual and family needs and which mainstream those needs as opposed to allowing them to be subordinated to the needs of the 'majority' population. To achieve this, service providers and stake-holders at all levels would need to adopt strategies that would enable them to be effectively responsive to the needs of minority ethnic communities. This would involve self-monitoring closely: to ensure that communicative channels were in situ and effective; to enable the views of minority ethnic people to be heard; to facilitate maximal articulation and understanding of those views (i.e. to disseminate information as widely as possible); to efficiently counter discrimination and racism; to assess the adequacy of available services and to check that access to services is optimised.

Becher and Husain (2003) emphasise that this would require a co-ordinated approach across all levels of decision-making and most particularly the political will to ensure appropriate and sufficient allocation of resources (funds, training, staff, resource materials, interpretation and translation services, outreach work, etc.). The National Family and Parenting Institute is currently developing a 'tool kit' for the use of people working with minority ethnic communities which is intended to provide information to facilitate greater understanding and cultural sensitivity.

5.3   Has the role of grandparents in family life altered?

As mentioned elsewhere in this report, traditional stereotypes of intra-familial relationships have often shown the roles of male and female family members as clearly demarcated: males have been portrayed as guardians of the boundary between the family and society, negotiating the relationship between resources outside the family and those within it, being prepared to explore, assert and, if necessary, aggress to protect their territory; females, by contrast, have been portrayed as more inward-looking, nurturant and focused on the care of younger, weaker members. Similarly, gendered family roles have also been thought to characterise older generation family members: grandfathers have been conceptualised as the 'head' of the family, safeguarding its history and values while grandmothers have been equated with the 'heart', providing wisdom as well as emotional support and care (Kornhaber and Woodward, 1981).

It is difficult to gauge what bearing these stereotypes might currently have or, indeed, might ever have had on reality. Until the last two decades, very little empirical research had been carried out on grandparenting, either in the UK or abroad. Even at the present time, most available information comes from studies carried out in the United States. How this work translates to the situation of grandparents in the UK is unclear: although some work has begun on the investigation of social and cultural variations, much yet remains unknown (Smith and Drew, 2002).

There seems to be some evidence that maternal grandparents generally have closer relationships than paternal grandparents with their grandchildren and that step-grandparents have a tendency to be more remote than biological grandparents. These patterns have been found in a number of countries including, for example, Poland, Germany, Canada, Italy and the USA. It also seems to be widely accepted nowadays that the story-book image of grandmother as white-haired, bespectacled and frail may better describe great-grandmother, since the average age of becoming a grandparent, in US samples at least, is 50, for women, and 52 for men. As has already been mentioned, surveys have shown that, even over distance, the majority of grandparents are able to maintain contact with their grandchildren, that most grandchildren feel quite positive about this contact, and that most people consider grandparents to have an important role to play, even though many parents do not feel that grandparents should be closely involved in decisions about how children are brought up (ONS, 1998; AARP, 2001; Smith and Drew, 2002).

Nevertheless, the general consensus is that, overall, grandparents are by no means a heterogeneous group. Variations in individual attributes, such as personality, child-rearing style, gender, age and health, and in geographical, social and cultural attributes, including physical distance, wealth, mobility, family size, family structure, social organisation, work patterns and other patterns of communication and relating, all make for enormous diversity.

Further, as mentioned in the earlier chapters of this report, UK family sizes, structures and the relationships within them may have subtly altered. Decreasing family sizes, alongside other demographic changes, have given rise to a phenomenon sometimes referred to as the 'beanpole effect'[13], where families tend to contain fewer peer-group relatives such as aunts and uncles and rather more older or younger generation rela-

---

13 As opposed to the three- or four-generation 'pyramid' in which the youngest generation is the most numerous, the parent generation less numerous, the grandparent generation least numerous, etc.

tives, that is, there has been an increase in the number of three- or even four-generation families (ONS, 2001). Also, as already mentioned, the population is ageing and life expectancy has increased: at the beginning of the twentieth century, boys born in 1901 could expect to live to 45 and girls to 49 whereas boys and girls born in the year 2000 can now expect to live until 75 and 80 respectively. According to Lane (2003, p.1), these demographic changes are expected to continue so that, by the middle of the twenty-first century, "the old and the young will represent an equal share of the world's population." It is also anticipated that this 'ageing population' phenomenon will be present in both developing and developed countries.

The combined effect of these changes suggests that the role of grandparents within families in the UK may have been changing in recent years. Traditionally, grandparents have played an important part in helping to care for grandchildren, especially if the children have special needs or if daughters, and less often sons, have experienced problems in caring for their own children, for example, because they are teenage parents or because they are experiencing serious health problems or other difficulties. In more recent decades, though, in response to changing conditions of employment and to childcare needs created by family breakdown and births outside marriage, the kind of care that grandparents are required to offer appears to be becoming more integral to the economic and emotional functioning of family members. Whereas, in the past, grandparents may have seen themselves as involved on a voluntary and relatively casual basis, they now increasingly appear to be looked upon as the chief source of stability and continuity for grandchildren after parental divorce and separation (Dunn and Deater-Deckard, 2001). Also, research is beginning to show that the demands made by some working parents for provision of substantial day care services can place some grandparents under obligations which can cause immense stress (Minkler and Fuller-Thomson, 1999; Arthur, Snape and Dench, 2002). Recent research suggests that, where grandparents feel ambivalent about the demands placed upon them, they often feel unable to express these ambivalent feelings openly (Clarke and Roberts, 2002).

There is evidence, too, that the support needs of grandparents may change as a result of changing social conditions, for example, as they cope with the double trauma of watching an adult child (usually a son) lose contact with his children while dealing with the grief associated with their own loss of contact with grandchildren (Drew, Richard and Smith, 1998).

Several questions arise about the possible effect of these social changes for grandparents. First, there is the notion that, just as many single parent mothers, given the choice, may not wish to use full-time day care for their very young babies (Harper et al., 2002), so some grandparents may feel resentful of pressures from adult children to provide full-time day care. Similarly, a proportion of custodial grandparents may be extremely reluctant to accept the obligation to care for their grandchildren while others, though not reluctant, may feel inadequate or may find themselves over-stressed by the demands of young children and uncertain about how to deal with the problems created by adult children who are unable to care for their own offspring. Either of these scenarios seems potentially likely to lead to deficiencies in the quality of care given to the grandchildren and so may be a source of concern for policy-makers.

A substantial number of middle-aged women also undertake the care both of grand-children and of their own parents. Given differences in health status and longevity between men and women, some of these women are also caring for ill or disabled partners. Sometimes described as "sandwich grannies", this group of women, who may or may not be in paid employment outside the home, can therefore be faced with heavy demands to provide care at a time in their lives when they might have expected to have more time for themselves. They may also find themselves faced with financial burdens related to the cost of care for elderly parents or the obliga-tion to help single parent offspring with childcare costs. Since it seems likely that women will continue to choose to defer the age of giving birth to a first child, as the population continues to age, this population of women is likely to grow.

The role of paternal grandparents, too, has undergone a qualitative change in the last few decades. When families break up, the already less robust relationship between paternal grandparents and their grandchildren often comes under greater threat. Where their relationships are sustained, these grandparents can become a stable element, anchoring an otherwise fragmenting family, perhaps even helping separated parents to negotiate relatively non-acrimonious arrangements for sharing care (Dunn and Deater-Deckard, 2001). But the legal system rarely acknowledges them and few attempt to appeal to courts to re-establish lost contact, for fear of exacerbating poor relationships and due to prohibitive legal costs (Barrett and Tasker, unpublished data). Both paternal and maternal grandparents will need help to cope with the grief associated with loss of contact with grandchildren and with the distress associated with a child's divorce. Whether relation-ship breakdowns continue at the current rate or increase, it seems that grandparents will continue to be caught up in these situations over which they have rarely have much control and from which they have no escape. This combination of obligation and helplessness is thought to predispose to depression (Seligman, 1975; Miller and Norman, 1978; Abramson et al., 1978; Garber and Hollon, 1980; Burger, 1984) and so is likely to increase demands for mental health services. However, if provision could be made for both paternal and maternal grandparents to retain contact with grandchildren, this source of support or interest may provide a greater sense of stability for the grandchildren as well as, possibly, a sense of connection with cultural roots. As there is not much empirical evidence to show that this kind of connection does confer benefits on grandchildren, it would seem that this might be a fruitful avenue for future research.

In summary, as society continues to evolve, it would appear that, compared to their non-childbearing peers, the 'social capital'[14] exacted from grandparents is likely to grow and the demands placed upon them are likely to cause considerable strain.

---

14 Furstenberg and Kaplan (2004, p.219) have this to say about the term 'social capital':
"Simply put, our argument is that the idea of social capital, while attractive, is being used so promiscuously that it is on the verge of becoming quite useless in empirical research". We would agree and use it here in rather a loose sense..

Clearly, research is needed to monitor this situation, to discover more about the needs of grandparents across the full range of geographical, social and cultural situations and to consider whether there might be better ways of generating relevant social capital from other sources, so that the load is more evenly spread. It is likely that new social policies, support systems and funding mechanisms will need to be developed if adequate support is to be put in place. Already some grandparenting education and support services have begun to be set up in the UK but it seems likely that, as the population of UK residents over 60 increases, far more provision will be needed in this area.

5.4   Has it become less safe to raise children in Britain?

Since the 1970s, the view from some academics has been that fear of crime and incidence are not synchronous (e.g. Cohen, 1970, 1976). However, numerous surveys indicate that fear of crime is high, particularly in some local areas and in some sections of society, and a recent British Crime Survey reports that fear of crime does, to some degree, relate to the risk of being victim to crime (Simmons and Dodd, 2003, p.132). Also according to Simmons and Dodd, fear of crime over the last decade has to some extent reflected a downward trend which accords with the account they give of figures for actual crime. Table 5.1 illustrates some of the differences between 1994 and latest 2003 British Crime Survey responses on worry about violent and property crime (though it is not quite clear whether these figures represent endorsements on being very worried or at all worried, the downward trend still seems remarkable).

Table 5.1: Trends in worries about crime (1994-2004)
Source: Simmons and Dodd (2003), British Crime Survey

Worry (Percentages)	1994	1998	2003
Mugging	21	17	14
Rape	32	29	23
Burglary	26	19	15
Theft of a car	25	21	16
Theft from a car	20	16	13

Simmons and Dodd (2003) further assert that there was an association between fear of crime and newspaper readership, which would appear to confirm the view that media influence is responsible for more fear than is necessary (Cohen and Young, 1973). Women were more worried than men about all violent crime and about walking alone after dark and experienced less violent crime than men (three per cent of women over 16 as opposed to five per cent of men). Young people in the 16-24 age range had been the most frequent victims of crime (15 per of males and seven per cent of females although elderly people were most likely to say that they were afraid of crime.

How these figures might have impacted on patterns of family life and parenting during the last decade, and whether there might be any distinctive characteristic of this aspect of family life in the UK, is almost impossible to judge. The British Crime Survey does not ask specifically about parents' fears for their children's safety so whether parents are more fearful or take different actions than in previous decades is unclear[15]. We have already discussed (Chapter 4) the fact that new technologies (mobile phones and the internet) have added a new area of worry to the list that parents may already have had.

Parents do seem to have particular concerns about adolescents. Research indicates that many expect to have worries over their ability to control their teenagers' behaviour and this appears to apply particularly to sons (though age-old worries about daughters' vulnerability are also still common). This kind of worry is also recognised in the British Crime Survey figures (Simmons and Dodd, 2003) which document that around a third of respondents are fearful of teenagers who hang about on the streets. However, research has also documented the fact that many teenagers have close relationships with their parents, value their advice and also see the family as a source of practical and emotional support (Lewis et al., 2001; Gillies et al., 2001).

Summarising findings from a number of studies, Edwards and Hatch (2003) conclude that teenagers are often portrayed as a risk to society, and that children are perceived to be more at risk than they used to be. Scott et al. (2000) interviewed 52 children (34 under 13 and the rest 13-14) in Edinburgh and East Lothian and 42 of their parents to find out what might comprise their 'landscapes of fear'. They asked children questions designed to elicit information about everyday fears and how they managed these and asked parents about their own childhood experiences as well as their experiences of parenting. They, too, found that teenagers were perceived as a threat, particularly by children. The parents reported feeling that they were living in a world that was changing quickly and that it was less safe for children than it had been. They were particularly concerned about traffic, drugs and 'weirdos and paedophiles'. They felt as well that children were under more pressure than they had been as children, due to economic insecurity and pressures related to consumerism. Scott et al. (2000) also identified that parents had difficulty talking to their children about 'stranger danger' and picked up that children were getting mixed messages on this topic and sometimes seemed confused about what the danger was. Some were construing all strangers as dangerous or misattributing the term strange to other characteristics such as disability.

---

15 That Victorian Britain was a far more unsafe environment for raising children has often been remarked.

This section has been focusing on the question of whether parents over the last decade have felt that the world is becoming a more dangerous place to bring up children. Some social commentators have suggested that both the demise of the 'traditional' family and the disintegration of community networks have contributed to making society less safe. But the real situation seems far more complex than this. Evidence is beginning to emerge from various studies that most families are adapting rather than disintegrating. Family ties are still important to the majority of people but families may be opening up as social systems and drawing support from non-kin members too (and, according to family historians, this is not a new phenomenon). Research being carried out by Roseneil (Roseneil, 2004; Roseneil and Budgeon, 2004) at Leeds suggests that adults across a range of ages, whether living alone or with partners, may be choosing not to charge one close relationship with the responsibility for meeting all their emotional needs. Rather, they appear to be "opening up their homes to people who were not part of their conventionally defined family" (Roseneil, 2004, p. 14) and forming friendship-kinship networks. Perhaps it will be this kind of process that will prove valuable in strengthening the social units that offer children care and protection.

5.5 Is Britain becoming less family-minded as increasing numbers of women choose not to raise children?

Elsewhere in this report, we have commented on the fact that the population re-placement rate is lower now than it was before the introduction of effective birth control. According to Pearce et al. (1999), the UK and the republic of Ireland stand out as countries in which childlessness has substantially increased. Whereas 11 per cent of women born in 1940 remained childless at the age of 40, 14 per cent of women born in 1950 did so, and 17 per cent of those born in 1955. McAllister and Clarke (1998) further report that by age 45, 14 per cent of women in the 1950 birth cohort had remained childless and that ONS projections for 1996 estimated that 20 per cent of women born in 1957, 1962, 1967 and 1972 would still be childless by age 45.

Regardless of the accuracy of these predictions, there does appear to be evidence that a minority of women may elect never to have children, that this minority may (or may not[16]) be growing and that attitudes and practices in relation to having children have, in some ways, changed. McAllister and Clarke (1998) suggest that practices such as men leaving the parental home later in life, women's greater in-volvement in education, training and work, changes in patterns of consumerism, and different modes of relationship formation, including higher incidence of less stable cohabiting relationships, may all be contributing not only to deferral of first births but also to reduced incentives for women to raise children. Clarke and Owen (reported in McAllister and Clarke, 1998, pp.17-18) derived information from General

16 There is really no way of being sure what the situation might have been for women in the past as no relevant records exist

Household Survey data about changes in expectations of remaining childless across birth cohorts and concluded that there was no evidence that the expectation of remaining childless was on the increase. However, McAllister and Clarke speculated that there might be a different relationship between intentions and behaviour in respect of childbirth among younger and older women and concluded that the nature of decision-making was both extremely complex and changed over the lifespan.

The apparent increase in numbers of women who are choosing not to have children has been seen by some social commentators to reflect increasing individualism. This is often assumed to involve a rather narrow focus on self interests as opposed to the greater good of one's social group. Whether this assumption is justified is open to question as is the proposition that the choice not to have children is associated with greater individualism.

McAllister and Clarke (1998) were interested to explore this matter when they carried out their qualitative study of childless people. They conducted interviews with 44 individuals (34 women and 10 men ranging in age from 33 to 49) and explored what the decision not to become a parent might have involved. They reported on the accounts given by 39 whom they described as being 'voluntarily childless'. They identified people who were always 'certain' that they did not want children (12 people; 31 per cent), those who were 'certain now' having in the past been potential parents (10 people; 26 per cent), those who 'accept' childlessness having been potential parents (six women in their 40s; 15 per cent), and those who have made no decision but are 'ambivalent' about being childless and may still become parents in the future (eight women and three men; 28 per cent). The lack of volition in this 'ambivalent' group immediately raises questions about the validity of the term 'voluntary childless' in this context and whether, in fact, a more precise operational definition might be needed in any future research into this topic.

Some of the key findings from this study suggested the need to challenge stereotypes that conceptualise women who choose to be childless as more selfish or more individualistic than mothers. McAllister and Clarke (1998) argued that the choice to be childless was usually very complex and not usually dependent on any one factor, such as career aspirations or materialism. Also, in this sample, the women who remained childless did not appear to hold any less conventional views on partnerships, parenting, or the value of children, though there was a tendency among several to view the responsibilities of parenthood and its financial demands as too much of a risk to personal security. The fact that most of the interviewees were in favour of supporting other people's children through taxes also lent support to the notion that childlessness is not necessarily associated with greater individualism or with 'anti-childness'.

This is one very small study and there is clearly a need for more extensive research in this area, if only to explore the possibility that changing patterns of fertility may, in fact, hold a potential for increasing rather than decreasing the social capital available for care of children. There is a very widely-held assumption among parents, and among campaigning groups or organisations aiming to support parents, that non-parents can have no understanding of what is involved in parenthood. To some degree, this may be true and, for some people, it most certainly will be true. But, among many of the caring professions, there have always been a proportion of childless women, for example, teachers, doctors, nurses, nannies, childcare workers, etc. who devote their lives to other people's children and provide substantial social capital which is available for parents and children to draw upon. Similarly, among the population of parents, there have always been a proportion who, becoming parents almost by default, find themselves out of their depth and out of tune with the demands of family life.

In other words, biological parenthood, for all that is currently known, may be as likely to be associated with individualistic interests as non-parenthood. Is it possible that, by placing such importance on the need for childcare to be situated within biologically-related families, as a society, we might be making less than optimal use of the social capital at our disposal? Perhaps if there were more well-monitored systems in place that enabled those childless people who were interested to help parents with the care of children, children's safety might be increased. Certainly, more research (perhaps along the lines of that currently being conducted by Rose-neil, 2004) would seem to be called for, to investigate whether this kind of strategy may be an option.

5.6 Do parents need more or different forms of support and guidance from sources outside the family?

From the end of the nineteenth century to the present, the market of literature on parenting has burgeoned. Whether this growth reflects the diminishing influence of wisdom traditionally transmitted from parent or older generation to younger generation, the increased sophistication of parenting knowledge, the growing skills of parenting experts, the inapplicability of traditional solutions to the complex family forms that have evolved in more recent years, or other factors, is not known. What is known is that it caters for parents who are often extremely anxious to do their job as well as possible, who often feel the need for reassurance, support and impartial information, and who at times do not find the task of parenting easy.

Although there is some evidence from opinion polls and surveys which suggests that parents in the 1990s felt that parenting is more difficult than it used to be (e.g. NOP, 1999), assessment of the precise nature of these difficulties is a delicate and complicated task. One of the first projects undertaken by the National Family and Parenting Institute[17] (NFPI) was to commission a review of surveys of the needs of parents (Moorman and Ball, 2001). A key finding to emerge from this review was that

---

17 The National Family and Parenting Institute was set up by New Labour as an independent charity working to support parents in bringing up their children, to promote the wellbeing of families and to make society more family friendly.

one of the most commonly mentioned requirements was the need for information that was user-friendly, accessible and culturally sensitive. Examples of the kinds of information sought were: health (27 per cent of all problems mentioned fell into this category), behaviour problems (20 per cent), speech and learning problems (17 per cent). Further needs were identified as the need for help with understanding family relationships and information relevant not just to very young children but to older children, teenagers and young people.

To find out how parents might prefer to receive information the NFPI commissioned a MORI poll (NFPI, 2001) which showed that parents rated different sources in the order shown in table 5.2.

Table 5.2: Preferred source of information
Source: NFPI, 2001

Information source	% endorsement
Family and friends	60
Schools and playgroups	29
GP surgery/Health centre	28
Local parenting groups	28
Leaflets and posters	15
Internet	14
Telephone helplines	9

While this exercise showed something about how parents tended to find information, it did not identify what use they were making of the information, nor which parents benefited from the information available to them. In the next stage, NFPI undertook an exercise which involved mapping family services in order to: provide a comprehensive overview of services throughout England and Wales; identify good practice and where it occurs; pinpoint gaps in services; describe the views of practitioners, managers and commissioners of parenting services about how these are managed and resourced; give recommendations for future development of family support; identify policies and practices which will enhance the provision of family support.

The main recommendation from this mapping exercise was that there should be a co-ordinated plan to deliver family support throughout existing health, education, social and criminal justice services. Delivery was to be accompanied by a publicity campaign to alert families to the existence of support. Support was to be sensitive to the needs of minority groups or groups known not normally to access support services (e.g. fathers).

The specific proposals were for a combination of universal, minimum support to enable families to access services, and a menu of services tailored to local conditions which could meet individual families' needs. The universal support (which should be nationally stipulated) was to be comprised of four elements: the first element involved antenatal support; the second, postnatal support; the third, support across the rest of the childhood spectrum; and the fourth, single information sessions at transitional points throughout children's school careers (table 5.3).

Table 5.3: National Family and Parenting Institute service plan
Source: Henricson, 2002

ANTENATAL SUPPORT
Genuinely universally available antenatal classes Flexible timing Midwife assistants as additional support Review of course content to ensure parents' access to child development and birth information Mentor support for prospective parents where feasible
POSTNATAL SUPPORT
Expanded postnatal services to meet 6 week target More practical and befriending support through midwife assistants, community mothers, volunteers, Home Start
SUPPORT THROUGHOUT CHILDHOOD
A pivotal family services role for health visitors Direct support to families Facilitation of self-help groups Referral point to other agencies
TRANSITION POINTS IN SCHOOL
Single information point sessions in schools at four key stages: Entry to early learning Entry to primary school Entry to secondary school (Year 8/9) Year 14

Implementation of this approach is gaining momentum, as evidenced by the publication of the Green Paper, *Every Child Matters* (HM Treasury, 2003) and the subsequent Children Bill. The Green Paper, strongly influenced by the child protection concerns arising from Lord Laming's enquiry into the death of Victoria Climbie, sets out the Government's long-term vision for improvement of parenting and family support. Essentially, it aims to empower parents and to build their capacity by delivering more effective informational support at all levels, with specific projects designed to provide additional practical and material support. Through universal, primary services, such as schools, health centres, childcare, more information and advice is to be offered (e.g. about children's development and about available help). Additional support is to be offered at the level of secondary or targeted interventions (e.g. where special needs have been identified). At the tertiary level (i.e. where problems, such as persistent truancy or offending, are evident), parents are to be more effectively engaged in addressing the problems posed by their children's behaviour, through the imposition of Parenting Orders where necessary. Though controversial, this latter strategy appears to have achieved some success in supporting parents who may otherwise have felt unable to influence their children's behaviour (Ghate and Ramella, 2002; CCFR, 2002) though more time is needed for full evaluation.

In addition, the Green Paper proposed a number of measures designed to improve communication between children's services. These included: Directors for Children's Services, accountable for local authority education and children's social services, a lead council member for children, integration of all key children's services to form Children's Trusts (which would report to local elected members), and Local Safeguarding Children's Boards to replace Area Child Protection Committees. To co-ordinate policies across Government and support local integration, a new Minister for Children, Young People and Families has now also been created.

5.7 Should the Government intervene more to ensure that the rights and responsibilities of parents are more clearly defined?

During the 1990s, New Labour has introduced many innovative schemes, the majority of which are intended to maximise opportunities for healthy social development. Concern to limit the damage wreaked by an anti-social minority can often divert attention from the need to improve support more universally by focusing on crisis management rather than prevention or longer term policies. It can also produce rather too 'heavy-handed' or intrusive measures which ultimately undermines social stability further by creating a form of "nanny state". To avoid this, MacLeod (2003) stresses the need to define the boundaries between family and state as clearly as possible.

Henricson (2003) wonders what kind of process might be needed in order to clarify the respective roles of parents and government in bringing up children. She asks whether there is a case to be made for the establishment of new processes or practices relating to the rights and responsibilities of families in the UK. Specifically, she discusses the pros and cons of regular policy reviews as well as the possible development of a sort of parent-government contract, which would set out a basic, though not necessarily set-in-stone, agreement on what parents might expect of the government as well as what the government might expect of parents.

Henricson's report examines the contradictions and ambiguities in government policy on parenting and considers whether there may be ways of resolving some of these while also avoiding the trap of rigid, impractical or over-prescriptive rules and regulations. She points to the potential value to parents of having a clearer understanding of their entitlements to financial support, to support in bringing up children and to support for themselves as parents. Henricson recognises that support is needed by parents in a wide number of areas in relation to the social, emotional, intellectual and physical well-being of children and that most parents, at some point, are likely to seek this support outside the family. However, obtaining appropriate support is more difficult for some parents than others and Henricson asks whether it might be possible to address this difficulty and to ensure greater equality of opportunity by developing a code or a contract between parents and government. Such a code might facilitate appropriate uptake of services and make it clearer to parents what services they can expect, by right, to obtain. In this way, parents might be better helped to carry out their responsibilities.

Henricson argues that the development of such a contract is not without precedent: to some extent, the Scottish Children Act sets out parents' rights and responsibilities, and other European countries, too, have developed policy and practice initiatives which the UK could draw upon in developing its own system. Council of Europe recommendations also offer important directions in establishing what might be agreed parental responsibilities, for example, to take care of the person of the child, to maintain personal relationships with the child, to provide the child with education, to maintain the child, to act as the child's legal representative and to administer the child's property.

Evolving an agreed statement of rights and responsibilities is inevitably a complicated task, overshadowed by the dilemma of deciding where the boundary lines might be drawn, between private and public lives, and between parental autonomy and state or government intervention. Henricson acknowledges these problems but sums up the arguments in favour of developing a statement (Appendix 5.1) in terms of greater clarity, rights (for parents and government), transparency, a more proactive approach and benefits to public attitudes on parenting. She does, however, also recognise possible pitfalls which would need to be avoided, such as the danger of over-prescriptiveness versus over-generalisation, the danger of being under-inclusive in respect of the wide diversity among community values among UK parents, and the difficulty of balancing rights and responsibilities. Nevertheless, she recommends that discussion should continue on the question of whether a statement of rights and responsibilities might be developed and points to the need for further research to determine what its most useful legal form might be, to find out whether there are further examples of this sort of contract elsewhere and to ascertain parents' views.

References to Chapter 5

AARP (American Association for Retired Persons) (2001) *The AARP grandparenting survey: The sharing and caring between mature grandparents and their children.* Online at http://research.aarp.org/general/grandpsurv.html

Abramson, L.Y., Seligman, M.E.P. and Teasdale, J.D. (1978) Learned helplessness in humans: Critique and reformulation. *Journal of Abnormal Psychology*, **87(1)**, 49-74.

Ahmed, S., Cheetham, J. and Small, J. (Eds.) (1986) *Social work with black children and their families.* London: British Association of Adoption and Fostering.

Arthur, S., Snape, D. and Dench, G. (October 2002) *The moral economy of grandparenting.* Paper presented at workshop sponsored by the Nuffield Foundation, Worcester College, Oxford.

Ballard, R. (Ed.) (1994) *Desh Pradesh: The South Asian presence in Britain.* London: Hurst.

Baumann, G. (1996) *Contesting culture: Discourses of identity in multi-ethnic London.* Cambridge: Cambridge University Press.

Becher, H. and Husain, F. (2003) *Supporting minority ethnic families. South Asian Hindus and Muslims in Britain: developments in family support.* London: National Family and Parenting Institute.

Bengston, V.L. (2001) Beyond the nuclear family: The increasing importance of multigenerational bonds. Burgess Award lecture. *Journal of Marriage and the Family*, **63**, 1-16.

Bonney, N. and Love, J. (1991) Gender and migration: geographical mobility and the wife's sacrifice. *The Sociological Review*, **39**, 335-348.

Bose, R. (2000) Families in transition. In A. Lau (Ed.), *South Asian children and adolescents in Britain* (47-60). London: Whurr Publishing.

Burger, J.M. (1984) Desire for control, locus of control, and proneness to depression. *Journal of Personality*, **52(1)**, 71-89.

Butt, J. and Box, L. (1998) *Family Centred: A study of the use of family centres by black families.* London: Race Equality Unit.

Chapman, R, Peel, M. and Ward, H. (2002) *Evaluation report for the Centre for Fun and Families (August 1999-March 2002).* Loughborough: CCFR/Centre for Child and Family Research, Department of Social Sciences.

Clarke, L. and Roberts, C. (October 2002) *Grandparents' contribution to family life.* Paper presented at workshop sponsored by the Nuffield Foundation, Worcester College, Oxford.

Cohen, S. (1970) *Folk devils and moral panics.* London: MacGibbon and Kee.

Cohen, S. (1976) *Images of deviance.* Harmondsworth: Penguin.

Cohen, S. and Young, J. (1973) *The manufacture of news: deviance, social problems and the mass media.* London: Constable.

Cooke, T. J. and Bailey, A.J. (1999) The effects of family migration, migration history, and self-selection on married women's labor market achievement. In P. Boyle and K. Halfacree (Eds.), *Migration and gender in the developed world* (102-113). London: Routledge.

Crow, G. and Maclean, C. (2004) Families and local communities. In J.L. Scott, J. Treas and M.E.P. Richards (Eds.), *The Blackwell Companion to the Sociology of the Family* (69-83). Oxford: Blackwell.

Doshanjh, J. and Ghuman, P. (1996) Childrearing in ethnic minorities. Clevedon: Multilingual Matters.

Drew, L.M., Richard, M. and Smith, P.K. (1998) Grandparenting and its relationship to parenting. *Clinical Child Psychology and Psychiatry*, **3(3)**, 465-480.

Dunn, J. and Deater-Deckard, K. (1999) *Children's views of their changing families.* York: York Publishing Services for Joseph Rowntree Foundation.

Edwards, L. and Hatch. B. (2003) *Passing time: A report about young people and communities.* London: Institute for Public Policy Research.

Furstenberg, F.F. and Kaplan, S.B. (2004) Social capital and the family. In J.L. Scott, J. Treas and M.E.P. Richards (Eds.), *The Blackwell Companion to the Sociology of the Family* (218-233). Oxford: Blackwell.

Garber, J. and Hollon, S.D. (1980) Universal versus personal helplessness in depression: Belief in uncontrollability or incompetence? *Journal of Abnormal Psychology*, **89(1)**, 56-66.

Ghate, D. and Ramella, M. (2002) *Positive parenting: The national evaluation of the Youth Justice Board's Parenting Programme.* London: Youth Justice Board for England and Wales.

Giddens, A. (1999b) *BBC Reith Lecture 4: Family.* Available on the LSE website by courtesy of the BBC.

Gillies, V., Ribbens McCarthy, J. and Holland, J. (2001) *Pulling together, pulling apart: The family lives of young people.* London: Family Policy Studies Centre for the Joseph Rowntree Foundation.

Green, A. and Canny, A. (2003) *Geographical mobility: family impacts.* York: Joseph Rowntree Foundation.

Grieco, M. (1987) *Keeping it in the family: Social networks and employment chance.* London: Tavistock.

Grundy, E. (1999) Looking beyond the household: intergenerational perspectives on living kin and contacts with kin in Great Britain. *Population Trends*, **97**, 19-27.

Hall, S. (1991) Old and new identities, old and new ethnicities. In A.D. King (Ed.), *Culture, globalisation and the world system* (41-68). Houndsmills: MacMillan.

Halstead, M. (1994) Between two cultures? Muslim children in a Western liberal society. *Children and Society*, **8(4)**, 312-326.

Harper, S, Smith, T., Lechtman, Z. and Zeilig, H. (October 2002) *Lone mothers, work and grandparent childcare.* Paper presented at workshop sponsored by the Nuffield Foundation, Worcester College, Oxford.

Henricson, C. (2002) *The future of family services in England and Wales: Consultation responses to the mapping report.* London: NFPI/National Family and Parenting Institute,

Henricson, C. (2003) *Government and parenting: Is there a case for a policy review and a parents' code?* York: Joseph Rowntree Foundation/York Publishing Services.

HM Treasury (2003) *Every child matters.* London: HMSO. Available online at: http://www.dfes.gov.uk/everychildmatters/pdfs/EveryChildMatters.pdf

Humphreys, C., Hester, M., Hague, G., Mullender, A. with Abrahams, H. and Lowe, P. (2000) *From good intentions to good practice: mapping services working with families where there is domestic violence.* Bristol: Policy Press.

Kornhaber, A. and Woodward, K. (1981) *Grandparents and grandchildren: The vital connection.* Garden City, New York: Doubleday.

Lane, R. (2003) *Intergenerational relations: Should we be looking towards intergenerational policies?* United Nations programme on ageing, Department of Economic and Social Affairs. http://www.un.org/esa/unyin/helsinki/ch15_intergenerations_lane.doc

Lau, A. (2000) *South Asian children and adolescents in Britain.* London: Whurr Publishing.

Lewis, C., Solomon, Y. and Warin, J (2001) *Family understandings: Closeness, authority and independence.* London: Family Policy Studies Centre for the Joseph Rowntree Foundation.

Lye, D.N. (1996) Adult child-parent relationships. *Annual Review of Sociology*, **22**, 79-102.

MacLeod, M. (2003) Drawing the boundaries between state and family. *The Edge*, **13**, 25-27.

McAllister, F. and Clarke, L. (1998) *Choosing childlessness.* London: Policy Studies Centre.

Miller, I.W. and Norman, W.H. (1978) Learned helplessness in humans: A review and attribution-theory model. *Psychological Bulletin*, **86(1)**, 93-118.

Minkler, M. and Fuller-Thomson, E. (1999) The health of grandparents raising grandchildren: results of a national study. *American Journal of Public Health*, **89(9)**, 1384-1389.

Moorman, A. and Ball, M. (2001) *Understanding parents' needs: A review of parents' surveys.* London: National Family and Parenting Institute.

NOP (1999) *Attitudes towards parenting.* London: NOP Research Group.

Office of National Statistics (1998) Attitudes towards grandparenting. *Social Trends,* **31**, Data set ST31224.

Office of National Statistics (2000) Labour market status of women with young children. *Labour Market Trends*, **108**, 10.

Office of National Statistics (2001) Frequency of adults having contact with their grandchildren. *Social Trends*, **33**, Data set: ST33207.

Office of National Statistics (2004) *Focus on gender.* Online (May 2004) at http://www.statistics. gov.uk/cci/nugget.asp?id=442

Pearce, D., Cantisani, G. and Laihonen, A. (1999) Changes in fertility and family sizes in Europe. *Population Trends*, **95**, 33-40.

Qureshi, T., Berridge, D. and Wenman, H. (2000) *Where to turn? Family support for South Asian communities – A case study.* London: National Children's Bureau for the Joseph Rowntree Foundation.

Riley, M.W. and Riley, J.W. (1993) Connections: Kin and cohort. In V.L. Bengston and W.A. Achenbaum (Eds.), *The changing contract across generations* (169-190). New York: Aldine de Gruyter.

Roseneil, S. (2004) Towards a more friendly society? *The Edge,* **15**, 12-13.

Roseneil, S. and Budgeon, S. (2004) Cultures of intimacy and care beyond 'the family': Personal life and social change in the early 21st century. *Current Sociology*, **52(2)**, 135-159.

Scott, S., Harden, J, Jackson, S. and Backett-Milburn, K. (2000) *The impact of risk and parental risk anxiety on the everyday worlds of children.* ESRC, Online at: http://www.hull.ac.uk/ children5to16programme/briefings/scott.pdf

Seligman, M.E.P. (1975) *Helplessness: On depression, development, and death.* San Francisco: Freeman.

Silverstein, M. and Bengston, V.L. (1997) Intergenerational solidarity and the structure of adult child-parent relationships in American families. *American Journal of Sociology*, **103**, 429-460.

Simmons, J. and Dodd, T. (2003) *Crime in England and Wales, 2002/3.* London: HMSO. Available online at: http://www.homeoffice.gov.uk/rds/pdfs2/hosb703.pdf

Smith, P.K. and Drew, L.M. (2002) Grandparenthood. In M.H. Bornstein (Ed.), *Handbook of parenting, Volume 3: Being and becoming a parent* (141-172). 2nd edition, Mahwah, New Jersey: Lawrence Erlbaum Associates.

Spitze, G. (1984) The effect of family migration on wives' employment: how long does it last? *Social Science Quarterly,* **65**, 21-36.

Vertovec, S. (1999) Conceiving and researching transnationalism. *Ethnic and Racial Studies,* **22(2)**, 447-462.

Concluding comments

In this attempt to examine how family life in the UK has changed in the decade between the first International Year of the Family 1994 and its tenth anniversary in 2004, it seems that we may have just begun to open the door on some of the many ongoing debates and the complex theorising about the nature of family life in the UK. The view through this door has acquainted us with information that is relatively easy to access, as well as having given us a sense of what remains to be discovered.

There are many more aspects of family life that we could have examined, for example, we have touched cursorily on families as consumers but are aware that there is much more information available in this area, concerning ways in which children's spending patterns may have changed, the extent to which parents regulate their children's spending, attitudinal changes in expectations about life-style, social class and ethnic group differences in these behaviours, and so on. There are many other large, important areas of family life in today's Britain that we have not touched upon. Some of these include: children in care and child abuse, poverty and the impact of income inequalities on family lives, youth offending, homeless children, unaccompanied children and refugee families, health, the changing nature of intimate relationships, the role of the school in relation to family, the role of mentors, religion, aunts and uncles, professionals and community support in the lives of families, etc.. But purely pragmatic reasons, time and space, forced us to draw a line somewhere.

So, in many ways, we feel that this report may best be seen as a test run, or as the beginning of an evolving process rather than as a definitive document. To research more thoroughly the question of how families change within one decade, arguably, certain conditions would be desirable: for example, an agreed definition of what is to be covered under the rubric of the term 'family', sound information about the nature of family life before the start of the decade, research tools capable of eliciting the information we sought, acquaintanceship with and access to all the databases holding relevant information, records of all the issues of interest, and appropriate information collected at key points throughout the decade of interest.

In the event, most of these conditions were not met. Instead, we found ourselves uncovering a wealth of information of various shapes and sizes, which gave us a sense that we had possibly discovered only the very tip of an iceberg (or of an incredibly long, thick beanpole!). So we cannot guarantee that the interpretation of the data that we have alighted upon is necessarily one hundred per cent accurate or that we have included all the data relevant to our project that is currently in existence. On the contrary, it seems inevitable that specialist researchers in many of the areas that we have touched upon will have more to add to the rather rudimentary picture that we have drawn.

In trying to piece together this picture of how families might have been changing at this time, we have been mindful of the aims and objectives set out by the United Nations General Assembly in relation to the observance of International Year of the Family 1994 (IIYF, 1999).

The objectives set for IYF 1994 in Resolution 44/82 (United Nations, 1991)[18] were "to stimulate local, national and international actions as part of a sustained long-term effort to:

a)   Increase awareness of family issues among Governments as well as in the private sector. IYF would serve to highlight the importance of families; increase a better understanding of their functions and problems; promote knowledge of the economic, social and demographic processes affecting families and their members; and focus attention upon the rights and responsibilities of all family members

b)   Strengthen the capacity of national institutions to formulate, implement and monitor policies in respect of families

c)   Stimulate efforts to respond to problems affecting, and affected by, the situation of families

d)   Enhance the effectiveness of local, national and regional efforts to carry out specific programmes concerning families, generate new activities and strengthen existing ones

e)   Improve collaboration among national and international non-governmental organisations in support of families

f)   Build upon the results of international activities concerning women, children, youth, the aged, the disabled as well as other major events of concern to the family or its individual members".

---

18 In Resolution 5/124, 1997, the General Assembly reaffirmed these objectives, though omitted the second clause of (a), modified (b) to read "strengthen the capacity of national...", replaced (f) with "Undertake at all levels reviews and assessments of the situation and needs of families, identifying specific issues and problems" which was inserted at (d) so that (d) and (e) became (e) and (f).

We feel that the spirit of this report may be very much in tune with these objectives and that, through it, we may have arrived at a point where we have a better sense of what might be needed if we are to continue more effectively to track family change in the future.

In the following section, we outline the areas in which we feel action might be valuable in this endeavour. However, we are keen that this report should be taken as a starting-point for further discussions. and not as a set of final conclusions. In this regard, we would very much welcome readers' comments and additions.

Recommendations

I **CREATION OF** *Family Trends*
   (to complement *Population Trends* and *Social Trends*)

- We have identified some variables that have not yet been captured by ongoing National or International Surveys, e.g. questions on parents' feeling about children's safety in British Crime Survey, information about parental status in Labour Force Surveys.
- We need to identify further variables and explore possibilities for including new questions in future surveys, with a particular view to being able to make both national and international comparisons.
- It may be possible to extract more information about cultural variations in the formation and structure of families from census and birth cohort data (though minority ethnic groups tend to be under-represented in UK birth cohort studies and this applies even to the current ALSPAC[19] study): we need to explore further the extent of information being collected.
- More fine-grained analysis of ethnicity variables would be desirable, including examination of differences between white UK residents by social class and geographical location: the white population is not homogeneous and false dichotomies may being introduced by analyses that treat it as though it is.

II **BRITISH SOCIAL ATTITUDES (BSA) SURVEYS**
- A review and possible upgrade of the British Social Attitudes surveys may be useful; this is a valuable source of information but its current relatively small scale often limits its generalisability and reliability.
- It would be valuable to obtain information about attitudes by monitoring larger, more representative samples; increased sample sizes might permit examination of population variance, i.e. effect sizes become very small with current sample sizes, so that analyses by subgroups soon yield unreliable results.

---

19 Avon Longitudinal Study of Parents and Children: 14,541 pregnant women with babies due between 1 April, 1991 and 31 December 1992; around 13,953 children and their parents are being followed up; this study is part of the European Longitudinal Study of Parents and Children

- There would appear to be a need for re-examination of some items and their validity.
- In the context of long-term plans for re-administration of BSA measures, it would be useful to discover whether data relevant to *Family Trends* is likely to be collected.
- We plan to visit the existing data-bases to see whether more information relevant to *Family Trends* can be extracted.

III QUALITATIVE OR SMALLER-SCALE QUANTITATIVE PROJECTS

- We have identified a need for qualitative or smaller-scale quantitative projects to discover more about smaller communities.
- More information about attitudes towards family life and values among minority ethnic communities might usefully be explored using qualitative, or quantitative, approaches; in these, a key objective might be to identify differences in attitudes and practice, and possible areas of disagreement or diverging views (e.g. in relation to issues such as physical punishment, sex outside marriage, family size, child rearing practices, etc.) so that difference can be recognised and respected.
- In view of the inequalities associated with household income and work, it would be valuable to explore further whether there might be specific difficulties, unique attitudes or work experiences which might be influencing Pakistani and Bangledeshi men's and women's access to work (e.g. experiences of racism, difficulties obtaining work, retaining it, or balancing care of children, etc.).
- We would be particularly interested in exploring the role of fathers in Minority Ethnic families, for example, their views on preferred social conditions for raising children, the extent to which they are involved in their children's education, whether they are physically present, and what role other family members might perceive them as having, etc.
- Qualitative approaches might be particularly effective in eliciting information about the experiences and support of unaccompanied children as well as of refugee families in the UK.
- Children and adults in Minority Ethnic and other Minority groups, whether 'visible' or 'non-visible' (e.g. gay or bi-sexual parents), too often have experiences of racism or discrimination; this can influence outcomes, e.g. in respect of education and employment. More information about the nature of these experiences, how they are managed within different families and communities, and how they might be better prevented could be explored through qualitative methods.
- Qualitative approaches may also be valuable in eliciting information about what might be needed if parents are to be able to maximise their use of positive socialisation methods; this may be particularly relevant to adolescent parents and other younger parents, especially fathers.
- We have identified the issue of parents' perceptions of and responses to risks to children as being important to investigate further, to find out more about how strategies adopted by parents may protect, fail to

protect or even over-protect children, and to ascertain the nature of advice, support or educational input needed in this area; we consider that a mixture of qualitative and quantitative methods would be most appropriate to carry out this investigation.

IV WORK/LIFE/CHILDCARE BALANCE

- The need for more research is indicated, to look at the potential for rationalising hours of work; this might be accomplished through a systematic review of secondary studies or by accessing available data sets (e.g. ALSPAC, birth cohort) to discover who works long hours and why; additional primary research may also be valuable to explore issues such as, whether women's greater involvement in the workforce is placing family relationships under strain, e.g. whether, in two-parent families where mothers have become the main or sole breadwinner, gender roles are re-negotiated.

- Both working and non-working mothers appear to need more support; it may be valuable to explore how coping strategies employed by mothers (and their partners) in different ethnic communities, in different income brackets and in different geographical locations might be shaped by support from both within and outside the family; such information might be useful in identifying both the most useful mode of delivery for services as well as the most efficacious points of intervention.[20]

V FATHERS

- We have identified a need for more information about differences in fathers' attitudes to childcare, domestic work, and work outside the home in other European countries; to discover how the situation of parents in the UK differs from that of parents in more or less 'family-friendly' cultures.

- There is also a dearth of information about cultural differences in UK resident fathers (see III above).

- It may be useful to investigate further why fathers work such long hours, the feasibility of shorter hours, disincentives to working flexibly; to discover whether an alternative work cultures could be developed.

- A need has been identified for fathers to be integrated more fully into settings where mothers are usually targeted (i.e. health, childcare, family service settings), which is particularly important for lone and for Minority Ethnic fathers; this may require more attitudinal research to explore potential barriers to greater involvement, and scrutiny of action research projects (such as some Sure Start initiatives) to identify the most effective strategies.

---

20 It is possible that some information relevant to this is available within the data in process of being collected during evaluation of Sure Start programmes.

VI DAY CARE

- There appears to be a need for evaluation of the effects of recent developments in regulation and provision of day care, to ascertain both how parents feel about the regulation processes and to see whether they are effective.
- A consultation process with parents may be timely, to evaluate perceived satisfaction with recent changes in provision and regulation of day care facilities.[21]
- It would be particularly valuable to evaluate the effectiveness of the recent decision to extend regulation to include nannies and au pairs, to ascertain whether there is any difference in the quality of care provided by registered and non-registered carers in different settings, to assess the effectiveness of inspections in monitoring standards, to obtain more information about parents' satisfaction with day care provisions, and to gauge the need for extra support by parents and home-based carers.

---

21 Some of this information may already be available within the ALSPAC study and within the longitudinal British 'Families, Children and Childcare' study (Leach and Barnes, not yet published)

Appendix 2.1

Financial support for children and their parents, 1975-2003
(*Source: Rubery et al., 2004*)

Date	Changes introduced
1976	Introduction of One Parent Benefit (then called Child Interim Benefit). Introduction of Invalidity Care Allowance. Introduction of Mobility Allowance.
1977	Abolition of Family Allowance and introduction of Child Benefit (paid for first child, unlike family allowance). Most non-means-tested benefits stop being weighted towards first child from 1978.
1977-79	Child Tax Allowances phased out; Child Benefit (usually paid to mother, unlike Child Tax Allowance) increases commensurately.
1984	Means test on partner's income introduced for child additions to most non-means-tested benefits. Child additions to Unemployment Benefit and Sickness Benefit abolished for claimants under pension age. Non-contributory Invalidity Pension replaced by Severe Disability allowance.
1987-91	Child Benefit frozen at £7.25 per week. Maternity Grant replaced by Sure Start Maternity grant.
1988	Family Income Supplement replaced by Family Credit (paid to the mother and requiring couples to work fewer hours); supplementary benefit by Income Support (higher for lone parents and eldest children); and Standard/Certificated Housing Benefit replaced by Housing Benefit (lower for younger children)
1990	Individual system of income tax introduced
1991	Higher rate of Child Benefit introduced for eldest child. Many non-means-tested benefits become weighted against the first child from 1992
1991-92	Substantial increase in the rates of Child Benefit, Family Credit and the Child Allowances and Family Premiums in Income Support

1992	Hours requirement in Family Credit relaxed (*see note 1 below*). Attendance Allowance and Mobility Allowance replaced by Disability Living Allowance.
1995	Sickness and Invalidity Benefits replaced by Incapacity Benefit
1996	Income-based Jobseekers' Allowance introduced.
1997	Child Maintenance Bonus introduced (*see note 2 below*)
1998	One Parent Benefit (and its corollaries in income-related benefits) abolished for new claimants
1998-2000	Child Allowances in the major means-tested benefits equalised for all children under 16
1999	Large increase in Child Benefit for the eldest child and in Child Allowances and Family Premiums in Income Support
1999	Family Credit replaced by Working Families' Tax Credit (*see note 3 below*)
2000-01	Children's Tax Credit replaces less generous Married Couple's Allowances and Additional Personal Allowance
2000-02	Maternity grant increases five-fold
2003-04	Introduction of Child Tax Credit and Working Tax Credit to replace Working Families' Tax Credit, Children's Tax Credit and child-related elements of Income Support and income-based Jobseeker's Allowance. Child additions removed from most non-means-tested benefits. Child Maintenance Premium introduced. (*see note 4 below*)

Notes

1. The threshold for claiming Family Credit was reduced in 1992 from 24 to 16 hours, allowing more financial assistance for part-time workers in families on low incomes and possibly encouraging more mothers to take up part-time work.
2. Child Maintenance Bonus is a one-off payment of up to £1,000 for people who receive child maintenance and leave benefit to start work.
3. The Government introduced in work tax credits in October 1999, replacing Family Credit with the more generous Working Families Tax Credit (WFTC) which included assistance with the cost of 70 per cent of childcare costs through the Childcare Tax Credit. This change to financial assistance for low income families may have impacted on the proportion of lone parents subsequently able to work part-time.
4. Child Maintenance Premium is a child support scheme introduced for new cases (and some existing cases) from 3 March 2003. If a claim for Child Support Maintenance was calculated after 3 March 2003 under the new rules, the first £10 of any maintenance paid can be kept.

Appendix 2.2

Major policy changes relating to work conditions, 1994-2004

New Deal for Lone Parents (NDLP)
New Deal for Lone Parents is one of a raft of New Deal programmes. New Deal aims to increase social inclusion by facilitating access to employment in targeted client groups. New Deal for Young People (NDYP) and New Deal for the Long-Term Unemployed (NDLTU) are aimed at unemployed jobseekers. NDLP was the first programme to be introduced, in 1997, and is targeted at lone parents on income support whose youngest child is above school age. It became a full national programme in 1998 of which the first evaluation reports became available in 1999. Information about these reports is available on the Department of Work and Pensions website.

European Time Directive
In October 1998, a European Time Directive came into force laying down a maximum of 48 working hours a week and the right to three weeks' paid annual leave (which rose to four weeks in November 1999). More pertinent perhaps, for working mothers and their expressed preference for working part-time, was the Working Part-Time Directive which came into force by July 2000. This directive ensures that part-time workers should not receive any less favourable treatment than full-time employees with regards to pay, maternity and paternity leave, holidays, access to pension schemes and eligibility for public holidays.

National Childcare Strategy
In 1998, the Department for Education and Employment (now the Department for Education and Skills, DfES) launched the National Childcare Strategy (NCS), a framework and consultation on childcare in Britain. The NCS was developed to address a number of problems that had been identified in the provision of childcare: the geographical variations in quality of childcare; between the types of providers and depending on the age of the child, there were no set definitions for standards other than basic registration for health and safety checks; high cost of childcare with families spending up to a third of income on paying for childcare leading many to opt for informal care as prohibitive childcare costs were simply not an option; too few places for the number of children, and lack of information for parents on available childcare.

Sure Start

The Sure Start programme was announced in 1998, with its initial remit of providing increased childcare and early education places alongside health and family support for children aged up to four years from disadvantaged areas. All programmes involved consultation and collaboration with parents in the local area to develop and support initiatives that addressed identified local needs. The Sure Start programme was extended in 2002, to include all children up to the age of 14 and up to 16 for children with disabilities.

Employment Relations Act 1999

The Employment Relations Act 1999 made provision for working parents to take a reasonable length of time off to deal with unexpected or sudden emergencies involving dependents and leave of absence to make any longer-term arrangements. The Employments Relations Act 1999 also made provision for parents to take unpaid parental leave. The right applied to parents (and persons who have obtained formal parental responsibility for a child under the Children Act 1989 or its Scottish equivalent) and lasts until the child's fifth birthday. Parents are able to start taking parental leave as soon as the child is born or placed for adoption, or as soon as they have completed the required one year's service with their employer. In response to pressure from parenting groups and parents, the Government introduced changes to the right to parental leave in January 2002. Previously only children born, or placed for adoption on, or after, 15 December 1999 were eligible for parental leave. Subsequent to the changes made in 2002, parents of children born or adopted between 15 December 1994 and 14 December 1999 were also included and became eligible for employees' rights until March 2005. These changes benefited parents of disabled children under 18 years, and parents of children under five years on 15 December 1999 (the date the right was first introduced).

Employment Act 2002

In November 2001 the Government announced new legal standards to help parents work flexibly. The package came in response to the Work and Parents Taskforce review on how best to implement the legislative right for parents of young children to request flexible working hours. The provision for flexible working for parents was set in the Employment Act 2002, and came into effect in April 2003. The new legislation gives working parents with children under six years, or disabled children under 18 years, the legal right to get their employer to consider requests for flexible working to help them balance their careers with childcare. The new rights apply equally both to mothers and fathers.

The Employment Act 2002 also concerned maternity pay and leave. Under provision in the Act, ordinary maternity leave increased to 26 weeks; additional maternity leave increased to 26 weeks from the end of ordinary maternity leave, with the maximum entitlement being 52 weeks. Statutory Maternity Pay also increased from

April 2004 to a flat rate of £102.80 a week following the initial six weeks of 90 per cent of average earnings. Additional maternity leave remains unpaid. Fathers also gained the right to two weeks' paid paternity leave from April 2003.

Spending Review 2002
The Review set out a £1.5 billion combined budget for childcare, early years and Sure Start by 2005-2006 and a doubling of spending in real terms on childcare by 2005-2006. The funding was intended to: create at least 250,000 new childcare places by 2005-2006, in addition to the earlier target of new places for 1.6 million children by 2004; establish new children's centres to provide childcare, family support and health services in one centre, reflecting the early lessons of Sure Start, to benefit up to 650,000 children in disadvantaged areas by 2006; integrate responsibility for childcare, early years education and Sure Start within a new interdepartmental unit so that new services are coordinated to best meet the needs of children, families and communities.

Childcare Review
In July 2003 the Chancellor, Gordon Brown, announced details on the three key reviews to feed into the next Spending Review. These reviews included the Childcare Review which was to consider whether the long-term projection for childcare and early years education was sufficient to meet the Government's aims for employment and educational attainment. The Review was intended to examine how quickly the sector could expand and what more would need to be done in particular areas such as childcare for school age children and the role of extended schools.

Appendix 4.1

Legislation against physical punishment

1.1: Countries in which physical punishment has been banned
Source: Boyson and Thorpe, 2002

Country	Explicit abolition	Date	Wording
Sweden	Children and Parents Code (Civil Law)	1979	Children are entitled to care, security and a good upbringing. Children are to be treated with respect for their person and individuality and may not be subjected to corporal punishment or any other humiliating treatment (1983 version).
Finland	Child Custody and Rights of Access Act (Family Law)	1983	A child shall be brought up in the spirit of understanding, security and love. He shall not be subdued, corporally punished or otherwise humiliated. His growth towards independence, responsibility and adulthood shall be encouraged, supported and assisted.
Denmark	Majority Act	1985	Parental custody implies the obligation to protect the child against physical and psychological violence and against other harmful treatment.
Denmark (*cont*)	Parental Custody and Care Act	1997	A child has the right to care and security. He or she shall be treated with respect as an individual and may not be subjected to corporal punishment or other degrading treatment.
Norway	Parent and Child Act (Family Law)	1987	The child shall not be exposed to physical violence or to treatment which can threaten his physical or mental health.
Austria	Youth Welfare Act (Civil Law)	1989	[In the implementation of parents' orders to the child] the use of force and the infliction of physical or mental suffering are unlawful.
Country	Explicit abolition	Date	Wording
Cyprus	Prevention of Violence in the Family and Protection of Victims Law	1994	[Prohibits] any unlawful act or controlling behaviour which results in direct actual physical, sexual or psychological injury to any member of the family (*physical punishment is included under the aegis of domestic violence*).
Latvia	On Children's Rights Protection	1998	1. A child has rights to his private life, secrecy of apartments and correspondence, personal inviolability and freedom 2. Cruel treatment of a child, physical punishment and offences against the child's honour and respect are not allowed.
Croatia	The Family Act	1998	Parents and other family members must not subject the child to degrading treatment, mental or physical punishment and abuse.
Germany	German Civil Law	2000	Children have a right to be brought up without the use of force. Physical punishment, the causing of psychological harm and other degrading measures are forbidden.
Israel	Supreme Court judgement	2000	Parents are now forbidden to make use of corporal punishments or methods that demean and humiliate the child.

Appendix 4.2

Physical punishment in UK law
(adapted from Boyson and Thorpe, 2002)

Date	Reform
1860	Chief Justice Cockburn's ruling on 'reasonable chastisement' (R v. Hopley).
1889	Prevention of Cruelty to and Protection of Children Act confirms parents' and guardians' rights to administer punishment.
1933	Children and Young Persons' Act confirms common law right of parents to use physical punishment on children.
1937	Children and Young Persons' (Scotland) Act confirms common law defence for Scotland.
1968	Children and Young Persons' Act (Northern Ireland) confirms common law defence for Northern Ireland.
1986	Education Act 1986, Section 47, No. 2, 'Abolition of Corporal Punishment - end of corporal punishment in state-supported education in England and Wales.
1987	Education Act 1986, Section 48, 'Abolition of Corporal Punishment - end of corporal punishment in state-supported education in Scotland and Northern Ireland.
1989	Children Act: prohibits physical punishment in local authority, voluntary and private children's homes (does not apply to private day care).
1991	Regulations on foster care oblige local authorities and voluntary organisations to get written agreement from foster carers that they will not use any physical punishment on children placed with them.
1998	School Standards and Framework Act, extended abolition of physical punishment to cover all schools and nursery education, and effectively criminalised 'reasonable' corporal punishment by teachers by removing the defence in criminal and civil proceedings.
1998	Implementation of Human Rights Act: European Court of Human Rights rules in favour of boy who took action against step-father's use of garden cane (A v UK) - UK held responsible for boy's mistreatment because it had failed to protect child under Article 3.
2000	Young Offender Institution Rules do not list physical punishment under the section dealing with permissible punishments.
2001	National Standards for the 'regulation' of all day care make one of the inspection criteria that 'physical punishments, including shaking, [should not be] used'. The Standards specifically permit childminders to smack children in their care with the written permission of parents (the National Childminding Association has campaigned to disallow this since the inception of the Children Act).
2002	Wales became the first country in the UK to use regulations to prohibit physical punishment in all forms of day care, including childminding.
2003	The Day Care and Child Minding (National Standards) (England) Regulations 2003 (SI 2003 No. 1996) came into force on 1 September 2003. Smacking abolished in *all* forms of Day Care in England. - "A registered person shall not give corporal punishment to a child for whom he acts as a child minder or provides day care and, so far as is reasonably practicable, shall ensure that corporal punishment is not given to any such child by – (a) any person looking after children on the premises; (b) any person in charge, or (any person living or working on the premises).
2003	19 November: Corporal Punishment of Children (Abolition) Bill presented to Parliament and received support from Members and Peers.

Appendix 4.3

Additional information about teenage birthrate data

Trends in teenage pregnancy in Scotland
Source: ISD, March 2004

The chart below shows the rate of teenage pregnancy in each year from 1991 to 2002 for each of two age groups: 13-15 and 16-19 years.

Teenage conceptions (Scotland)

Among 13-15 year olds the rate remained almost unchanged between 1991 and 1995 ranging between 8.4 and 8.8 per thousand women. Following a rise in 1996, the rate fell in each subsequent year to a provisional 7.4 per thousand women in 2002, the lowest in the period reported. Among 16-19 year olds the rate was highest in 1991 at 78.2 per thousand women, declining to 68.4 by 1995. Following a rise to 72.8 in 1998 the rate has subsequently fallen to a provisional 68.1 per thousand women in 2002, again the lowest in the period reported.

Among 13-15 year olds, the delivery and abortion rates were similar for all years. In 2002, the delivery rate was 3.1 per thousand women and the abortion rate was 4.2 per thousand women. Among 16-19 year olds, the abortion rate is considerably lower than the delivery rate in all years, remaining stable at around 26 to 29 per thousand. In the periods reported the 2002 rate is the lowest ever recorded for deliveries (40.0 per thousand women).

The proportion of teenage pregnancies resulting in a delivery or an abortive outcome has changed over the years, particularly among 16-19 year olds. For example, among 16-19 year olds, the percentage of pregnancies resulting in an abortion or miscarriage rose from 35.2 per cent in 1991 to 41.2 per cent in 2002. Among the 13-15 year olds the percentage of 57.5 per cent for 2002, is the highest ever recorded during the periods reported. The total number is, however, very similar to that of previous years but the number of deliveries has fallen noticeably.

For comparison with England and Wales (EW) we have calculated our aborted rate excluding miscarriages (16 - 19) and the results for 2000 (the latest EW available) are shown here.

	Scotland	England and Wales
Delivery	43.4	45.1
Aborted (excludes miscarriages)	23.1	27.7

Teenage pregnancy in England and Wales (number of conceptions by age)

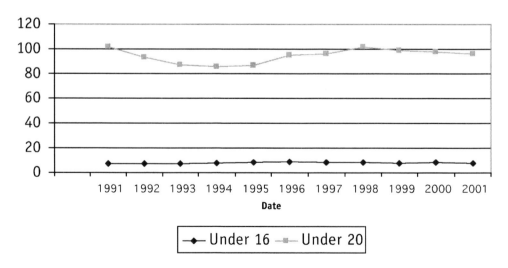

Note

Although some raw data is available online at the Office of National Statistics website, it is difficult to elicit accurate information about rates of conception, abortion and childbirth in each UK country at different time points for the reasons listed below:

- A variety of strategies is used to report information about women's ages: instead of reporting each year of age separately, different reports use different clusters (e.g. 13-15, 17-19; or under 16, under 20; or 15-17, 18-19, etc.). Such aggregated data is rarely dis-aggregatable without going back to source (and not always even then) which makes rapid comparisons difficult if not impossible - throughout most of the 1990s, this problem appears to have complicated comparisons between the different countries in the UK.

- Some reports only give the total number of conceptions, rather than details of births, miscarriages and abortions.

- While some reports give information in terms of rates per thousand women, others give numbers or percentages, either with or without details of the population sample size: more uniformity in this area would greatly facilitate data interpretation.

- Some reports provide year by year information but this usually consists of summaries of selected details. Again, different reports give different details making comparisons difficult.

- Very few reports give details of ethnicity and, since it is known that cultural variations exist in respect of reproductive activity, this makes any general conclusions difficult to interpret.

- Many reports define teenage pregnancy as under 20. Given that the age of consent is lower than this and that, in some cultures perhaps more readily than others, it may be usual to begin child-bearing between the ages of 17 to 19, it may be more useful to investigate outcomes for older teenagers separately.

Appendix 4.4

British Social Attitudes Survey: attitudes to teenage pregnancy (%)

From: Clarke and Thomson, 2001/2

	Agree strongly	Agree	Neither	Disagree	Disagree strongly
Teenage pregnancy isn't really that much of a problem in Britain today	1	4	11	56	26
People in Britain are far too tolerant of teenage pregnancies	13	41	25	17	2
Television and advertising put teenagers under too much pressure to have sex before they are ready	16	46	18	17	2
If a teenage couple aged 16 or older are in a stable relationship, there's nothing wrong with them having a child	2	18	20	46	12
A teenager can be just as good a parent as someone who is older	3	36	24	29	6
Bringing up a child is simply too hard for most teenagers to do alone	20	63	10	5	1
Bringing up a child is simply too hard for a woman of any age to do alone	6	36	24	30	3
One of the main causes of teenage pregnancy is the lack of morals among young people	13	43	19	21	3
Teenage girls living in run down areas are more likely than others to become teenage mothers	11	51	17	16	2
Teenage girls who want to get on in life don't usually become teenage mothers	17	54	15	10	1
All too often Britain's welfare system rewards teenage mothers	12	43	25	14	2
Teenage girls who have children often do so to jump the housing queue	10	36	26	22	3
There would be fewer teenage pregnancies if sex education at school gave more advice about sex, relationships and contraception	14	40	19	21	4
Giving teenagers lessons at school about sex and contraception encourages them to have sex too early	4	18	26	44	6
There would be fewer teenage pregnancies if more parents talked to their children about sex, relationships and contraception	18	57	14	9	*
Contraception should be more easily available to teenagers, even if they are under 18	13	51	12	18	4

* No data reported

Appendix 5.1

Reasons for and against a parent/state statement of rights and responsibilities

Source: Henricson, 2003

ARGUMENTS IN FAVOUR OF A STATEMENT OF RIGHTS AND RESPONSIBILITIES BETWEEN PARENTS AND THE STATE

CLARITY

There is a deficit of clear messages and commonly recognised obligations and entitlements attributable to parenthood.

RIGHTS

A statement would provide the opportunity to set out parental rights to support from the state and the parameters of the parent-state partnership in child rearing. Open to scrutiny, a statement would provide a framework for as fair a balance as possible to be struck between parents' obligations and entitlements.

TRANSPARENCY

Parents have a human right to know the sorts of issues that will be considered in prompting intervention with their social parenting responsibilities.

PROACTIVE APPROACH

A statement could offer positively framed messages around expectations of parents.

PUBLIC ATTITUDES

A statement has the potential to influence attitudes to parenting, enhancing its social significance and creating an ethos where parents have a more fully recognisable role.

DIFFICULTIES INVOLVED IN DEVELOPING A STATEMENT OF RIGHTS AND RESPONSIBILITIES BETWEEN PARENTS AND THE STATE

OVER-GENERALISATION or OVER-PRESCRIPTIVENESS

The construction of the statement would need to avoid the pitfall of over-generalisation in order not to be meaningless on the one hand. On the other hand, it would need to avoid over-detailed stipulations or unnecessary statutory prescription about, for example, personal relationships and their cultural determinants.

COMMUNITY VALUES

The limitations of agreed community values about child rearing would need to be recognised, with a focus on the commonly endorsed essentials of civilised upbringing.

BALANCING RIGHTS AND RESPONSIBILITIES

In establishing a set of responsibilities, equity demands some balancing rights, but there is a reluctance to acknowledge this, particularly in relation to rights vis-à-vis the child.

Author Index